Understanding School Leadership

British Educational Leadership, Management & Administration Society

Published in Association with the British Educational Leadership, Management and Administration Society

This series of books published for BELMAS aims to be directly relevant to the concerns and professional development needs of emergent leaders and experienced leaders in schools. The series editors are Professor Harry Tomlinson and Dr Hugh Busher, School of Education, University of Leicester.

Titles include:

Educational Leadership: Personal Growth for Professional Development (2004)
By Harry Tomlinson

Developing Educational Leadership: Using Evidence for Policy and Practice (2003)
By Lesley Anderson and Nigel Bennett

Performance Management in Education: Improving Practice (2002)
By Jenny Reeves, Pauline Smith, Harry Tomlinson and Christine Ford

Strategic Management for School Development: Leading Your School's Improvement Strategy (2002)
By Brian Fidler

Subject Leadership and School Improvement (2000)
By Hugh Busher and Alma Harris with Christine Wise

Living Headship: Voices, Values and Vision (1999)
Edited by Harry Tomlinson

School Culture (1999)
Edited by Jon Prosser

School Improvement After Inspection? School and LEA Responses (1998)
Edited by Peter Earley

Policy, Leadership and Professional Knowledge in Education (1998)
Edited by Michael Strain, Bill Dennison, Janet Ouston and Valerie Hall

Managing Continuous Professional Development in Schools (1997)
Edited by Harry Tomlinson

Choices for Self-managing Schools: Autonomy and Accountability (1997)
Edited by Brian Fidler

Understanding School Leadership

Peter Earley and Dick Weindling

P·C·P
Paul Chapman
Publishing

First published 2004

 Paul Chapman Publishing
A SAGE Publications Company
1 Oliver's Yard
55 City Road
London EC1Y 1SP

SAGE Publications Inc
2455 Teller Road
Thousand Oaks, California 91320

SAGE Publications India Pvt Ltd
B-42, Panchsheel Enclave
Post Box 4109
New Delhi 110 017

Library of Congress Control Number: 2004102382

A catalogue record for this book is available
from the British Library

ISBN 0 7619 4370 6
ISBN 0 7619 4371 4 (pbk)

Typeset by C&M Digitals (P) Ltd., Chennai, India
Printed in India at Gopsons Papers Ltd., Noida

Contents

List of Figures

List of Tables

Series Editor's Preface

BELMAS is particularly pleased to present this book by Peter Earley and Dick Weindling. It is one of the most important books on school leadership because it incorporates so much research evidence from the work of the two authors themselves, and such a perceptive and intelligent understanding of the research of others. The authors have worked together and independently on major research projects starting with their NFER project over 20 years ago, their first major and landmark research project on the early years of headship. This book has provided them with an opportunity to reflect on and analyse the experience of that particular cohort of heads at different stages on their journey throughout the last twenty years. They were even able to find some of them still in their first headship post in 2003. The authors recognise that the head's role is not limited to being the leader, because headship also incorporates management, but also that leadership has been distributed for at least these twenty years.

Peter Earley and Dick Weindling have followed very different but complementary career and research paths and consequently their combined strength for an undertaking such as this is a powerful partnership. This book provides an opportunity for two of the senior researchers in the field over the last 20 years to reflect on their own significant contribution to research and, with evidence from the work of others wisely selected, to provide a lucid presentation of purposeful research. The high quality of their research as a basis for practice and understanding is clearly evidenced here.

Inevitably the initial focus was and is on headship because, for much of this period, leadership was assumed to be manifested through headship. However there is a danger now that the importance of the school leader in the leadership of the school may be underestimated. The stages of headship, the evidence of the socialisation and career trajectories of heads and the models which are developed from their research and that of others, are considered alongside the National College for School Leadership model which has three stages for headship, the third of which is a particular role supporting other heads. Longer serving heads appear to plateau beyond about 8 years and to be subsequently either enchanted or disenchanted! This issue has not yet been sufficiently addressed in research on experienced heads. The characteristics of outstanding values-driven school leaders are presented through high quality focused research, and an extended case study. The courageous chapter on unethical and less effective leadership focuses on working with newly qualified teachers but has broader implications. The imaginative chapter on the use of metaphors presents new and idiosyncratic research evidence, which asserts a distinctive challenge to received wisdom.

The second part of the book on 'Distributed Leadership for School Improvement' draws again on major research projects that the authors have been responsible for or associated with for the chapters on leadership teams, middle leaders and governors as leaders. This latter is particularly welcome since Peter Earley is arguably the leading researcher on governing bodies, and they are rarely given such prominence in studies of school leadership. The quality of the authors' judgements in the selection of other researchers to complement their own experience in this part also, and the thoughtful use of Ofsted evidence, guarantees that this is a book which will be essential for those who are studying school leadership. The argument is rounded with an exploration of the significance of leadership within the school improvement and school effectiveness traditions and more recent work on the development of leaders.

What Peter Earley and Dick Weindling have achieved is a book which provides a profound historical perspective which is often lost elsewhere in an excessive focus on the present and the supposed future. Here there is such clear and high quality research evidence underpinning their presentation of school leadership that it has to be taken seriously not only by those seeking understanding but also by policy makers. BELMAS is delighted to be associated with such an important project successfully completed.

Harry Tomlinson, Visiting Professor,
Leeds Metropolitan University

Dedication

This book is dedicated to our friend and colleague, Lawrie Baker, who sadly died soon after we submitted the manuscript to the publishers. Lawrie worked with us on the headship study when he was seconded to NFER in the late 1980s and on the DfES 'baseline' project in the early 2000s. He will be sorely missed.

Acknowledgements

We would like to thank all those who helped and contributed in some way to the writing of this book, particularly the heads involved in the NFER study. Many teachers and school leaders have been involved in our many research projects over the years and we would like to thank them all for their contributions. We would also like to offer our appreciation to our co-researchers and colleagues – Lawrie Baker, Sara Bubb, Michael Creese, Jennifer Evans, Anne Gold, David Halpin, Keith Pocklington and Geoff Southworth – for allowing us to draw on some of their work. Finally, special thanks must go to Sara Bubb who took on the challenge of reading our early drafts and editing our work – a challenge which we think she met very well!

In 2002 we undertook a research project for the DfES as reported in 'Establishing the Current State of School Leadership in England', Research Brief and Report No. 336, Nottingham: DfES. Some of the material in this book, such as the data analyses and case studies in Chapters 2, 5 and 6, draws on this research and is published with permission of the DfES. Chapter 11 reproduces some material originally published in 'Research Matters', No. 20 on school governing bodies and we would like to thank the School Improvement Network of the Institute of Education, University of London, for permission to reproduce this.

We would also like to thank Ofsted for permission to use Figure 1.1, *Leadership, management and governance – inspectors' questions* and Figure 1.2, *Main findings regarding leadership and management.*

Biographical Details

Peter Earley, formerly of the National Foundation for Educational Research (NFER), is Reader in Education Management at the Institute of Education, University of London, head of the management and leadership development section and an Associate Director of the International School Effectiveness and Improvement Centre. He co-edits the practitioner journal *Professional Development Today* and is an accredited adviser to governing bodies on head-teacher appraisal, a process he is currently researching.

Dick Weindling previously worked in industry and commerce, before entering education and becoming Head of Educational Management at the NFER, where he directed (working with Peter Earley) a unique national study of new secondary heads which followed them for over ten years. He is co-director of Create Consultants and is working again with Peter Earley (and others) on the evaluation of the leadership strategy of the London Challenge. Both authors have conducted several research projects for the National College for School Leadership.

Introduction

It was in late 1982 when one of us (Peter Earley – PE), after a five-year stint of working in Australia, joined the National Foundation for Educational Research (NFER), to work with the director of a research project (Dick Weindling – DW) on the first years of headship. This three-year project was funded by the local education authorities' (LEAs') membership programme and was concerned to document the demands made on headteachers in their first years in post. The research study – *Secondary Headship: the First Years* (Weindling and Earley, 1987) – was the beginning of a partnership between the authors which continued for a number of years and resulted in a series of studies on school leadership, management and governance. One important outcome of that partnership was an ongoing study which followed the fortunes of the group of new heads who were researched in depth between 1982 and 1985. The cohort of heads – that is, all those appointed to their first secondary headship in the academic year 1982–83 – were studied in detail over their first two years in post. A questionnaire was sent to the new heads in 1984 with a follow-up survey taking place five years later in 1989 (Earley et al., 1990). A further survey of the heads took place in 1994, about ten years after the cohort had commenced headship (Earley et al., 1994/95). Finally, in 2003, we tried to locate the heads and to see 'where are they now' over 20 years after taking up their first headships.

This unique longitudinal study informs a significant part of this book, but we also draw on a wide range of our other work on leadership, management and governance over this considerable time span. One of us (DW) left the NFER in the late 1980s to become, after a spell at a university, a freelance consultant undertaking research and evaluation, whilst the other (PE) remained at the Foundation for about ten years in total before joining the Institute of Education, University of London. Together we have researched and published extensively in the field of school leadership, management and governance, and have conducted numerous projects, not only whilst at NFER but also for external sponsors such as government departments (e.g. Department for Education and Skills, Department of Employment), government agencies (NCSL, Ofsted), charitable trusts (e.g. Nuffield Foundation, Esmee Fairbairn) and professional associations (e.g. National Association of Head Teachers, Association of Teachers and Lecturers, National Union of

Table 1   Research projects, 1982–2004

1982–1996	1996–2004
• NFER headship project 1982–85 (Weindling and Earley, 1987)	• ESRC review of 15 projects (Wallace and Weindling, 1996)
• NFER middle management project (Earley and Fletcher-Campbell, 1989)	• DfEE study of governing bodies (Scanlon et al., 1999; Creese and Earley, 1999)
• Follow-up in 1989 (Earley et al., 1990)	• DfES study of school leadership (Earley et al., 2002)
• School management competences project (Earley, 1992)	• LEA good practice guide for NCSL (Earley and Evans, 2002b)
• DfEE study of effective management in schools (Bolam et al., 1993)	• Project on heads of large primary schools (Southworth and Weindling, 2002)
• DfEE evaluation of heads' mentoring (Bolam et al., 1995; Pocklington and Weindling, 1996)	• Independent school leaders (Earley and Evans, 2002a)
• NFER school governors project (Earley, 1994)	• Follow-up 3 – attempt to contact 1982–83 cohort.
• Follow-up 2 in 1994 (Earley et al., 1994/95)	• Leadership development review for NCSL (Weindling, 2004)
• School inspection and 'failing' schools (Earley, 1996; 1997a; 1997b; Ferguson et al., 2000)	• The selection of heads – pilot study for NCSL (Weindling and Pocklington, 2004)
	• Induction practices (Bubb and Earley, 2004)
	• External advisers to governing bodies (Earley, 2004a)

Teachers, Headmasters and Headmistress Conference). Table 1.1 lists the main research projects we draw upon.

It is this wealth of empirical research and study over the last 20 years or so that forms the foundation of this book. It is therefore different from the many books published on school leadership in the last few years; indeed, we like to think it is unique.

The book is made up of two parts. In the first part we shed light on the changing role and nature of headship, both primary and secondary, whilst the second part is entitled 'Distributed Leadership for School Improvement'. The focus in Part 1 is intentionally on headship. Although we subscribe to a view of leadership that is shared in broad terms, including with the school's governing body, without an effective head a school is unlikely to be successful.

We begin in Chapter 1 by outlining the nature and theory of leadership and management, and we note the changing discourse in education – from management to leadership. We also discuss recent approaches to leadership – from the individual leader to distributed and learning-centred leadership. We raise a number of questions, arguing that we need to be careful that we do not lose the management baby with the leadership bathwater!

The second chapter considers professional and organisational socialisation and, using the NFER longitudinal study, we put forward our own stage theory or model of headship socialisation. We link this to the National

College for School Leadership's five stages of headship (NCSL, 2001) and other models of headship transition.

The next chapter also draws upon our longitudinal study to ask who becomes a headteacher and why? We draw on the more recent Department for Education and Skills (DfES) study conducted in 2001 (Earley et al., 2002) to make comparisons over the years. What are heads' typical career trajectories and what do they want to do in the future? The vexed issue of length of tenure and performance is raised, along with the question of whether leaders have a shelf-life.

The changing appeal of the job and what motivates heads are considered in Chapter 4. Indeed, has that appeal been lost as governing bodies are finding it increasingly difficult to appoint school leaders? How the role has changed is considered further by drawing extensively on the group of heads (the NFER cohort) who have worked through the radical educational reforms of the 1980s and 1990s. We draw on other research we have been involved with to gain insights into the reality of headship and what turns people on and what turns them off!

The next two chapters in Part 1 examine further the task of headship and attempt to give some specific examples of highly effective practitioners – what is it they do in leading successful schools? This includes some research findings about 'outstanding' leaders and values-driven leadership (Chapter 5) and a case study of leadership in action in a primary school (Chapter 6).

Chapter 7 offers a rather different perspective, in that it focuses on less effective and unethical leadership. Using the example of the contravention of induction regulations for new teachers, we consider the notion of 'rogue' schools and ethically responsible school leadership, arguing the need for more rigorous systems of professional responsibility and public accountability. The final chapter in Part 1 uses metaphors and images of leadership to provide further insights into the role of the head.

The second part of the book on distributed leadership for school improvement is made up of six chapters. It takes us beyond the study of headteachers to school leaders more generally. The notion of distributed or shared leadership is being promoted by the NCSL and the first three chapters consider key players in the success of any school – senior management or leadership teams, governing bodies and middle managers – or middle leaders as the College is now calling them.

The chapter on leadership teams draws upon three studies that we have been involved in over the last 20 years to document changes and developments. Teamwork at senior level is crucial and it is only recently that this importance has been reflected in training programmes for whole-school teams (e.g. NCSL's programme entitled 'Working Together for Success').

Middle managers or middle leaders, it is often suggested, are the key to school success or the 'heart of the school' and their roles and responsibilities as subject leaders, pastoral heads and curriculum co-ordinators are considered in Chapter 10. Particular reference is given to their strategic role and their work in enhancing the quality of teaching and learning.

Governing bodies, the subject of Chapters 11 and 12, are considered in terms of their leadership role, particularly in relation to what is broadly called strategic direction. How do governing bodies 'add value' to the work of the school, develop a strategic role and become an asset, particularly to heads and leadership teams? Also, what do we know about their 'single most important job' – that of appointing the headteacher? They also have a key role to play in school improvement, including providing the climate for improvement through a combination of pressure and support and acting as critical friends. This is explored in Chapter 12.

The penultimate chapter focuses on what is known about school effectiveness and strategies for improvement. It documents heads' views about change and considers what is known about 'failing' schools and those in challenging circumstances and the crucial role that school leaders can play.

The book concludes with an examination of how leaders and the organisations in which they work can be developed for school improvement. School leaders' training and development needs are considered and the importance of heads as 'lead learners' and leaders of learning communities stressed. A key part of a learning community is the professional and personal development of all adults – heads, teachers and support staff. A culture of continuing professional development is crucial to the success of schools. Modern notions of leadership, including distributed leadership, whilst welcomed, are shown to rely heavily on leadership, alongside effective management, being successfully demonstrated at the apex of the organisation.

We conclude with a review of the future role of headteachers against a context of recruitment and retention problems, and stress and burnout. Our overall conclusion is a positive one however. We show that headship continues to remain an exciting prospect and that most heads continue to enjoy the work. Despite the changes to the role, they still consider it to be 'the best job in education'.

PART 1

THE CHANGING ROLE AND NATURE OF HEADSHIP

1

A Changing Discourse: From Management to Leadership

Notions of leadership and management
Theories of leadership
A changing discourse

This chapter considers the role of school leaders and especially headteachers, within the context of what we know about effective leadership and management. It begins with a brief section on the nature of leadership before offering an overview of theories of leadership and the main concepts associated with educational management and leadership. The concepts of leadership, management and administration are differentiated and leadership theories briefly reviewed from the 'great man' theories of the early twentieth century through to modern conceptions of leadership – transformational, distributed and learning-centred. Finally, we explore the changing discourse – from management and management competences to leadership and leadership development, culminating in the setting up of the National College for School Leadership.

NOTIONS OF LEADERSHIP AND MANAGEMENT

Numerous research studies and reports from school inspectors and others, claim that leadership, especially headship, is a crucial factor in school effectiveness and the key to organisational success and improvement. Our own work on secondary heads in the late 1980s (Weindling and Earley, 1987) reiterated what many studies were suggesting – that the quality of those at the organisational apex or how headship was enacted – was crucially important to school success. Ours was not a study of the relationship between leadership and school effectiveness however. Those studies that have specifically considered this matter (e.g. Hallinger and Heck, 1998; 1999; 2003) argue that the effect of leaders, including headteachers, is largely *indirect*; what heads do and say, how they demonstrate leadership, does affect pupil learning outcomes but it is largely through the actions of others, most obviously teachers, that the effects of school leadership are mediated. Achieving results through others is the essence of leadership and it is the 'avenues of leader influence' that matter most (Hallinger and Heck, 2003, pp. 220–6).

3

Leadership as a concept has always been widely written about – probably more so than any other single topic in educational management and administration – and its importance has long been recognised. Leadership itself however remains an elusive concept as Leithwood et al. note:

> Leadership as a concept and a set of practices has been the subject of an enormous quantity of popular and academic literature ... Arguably, a great deal has been learned about leadership over the last century. But this has not depended on any clear, agreed definition of the concept, as essential as this would seem at first glance.
>
> (Leithwood et al., 1999, p. 5)

One of the first things that the National College for School Leadership did when it was set up in England in November 2000 was to commission a series of reviews of the school leadership literature. One of these, by Bush and Glover (2003), quoted Larry Cuban who over 15 years ago stated that there were 'more than 350 definitions of leadership but no clear and unequivocal understanding as to what distinguishes leaders from non-leaders' (1988, p. 190, cited in Bush and Glover, 2003, p. 4). Since that time of course there have been many other studies of leadership – several hundred per year! – and Mullen et al. (2002) talk about a 'veritable cascade' of publications on leadership and associated concepts. In their useful overview of the literature, Bush and Glover explore various definitions of school leadership (ibid., pp. 4–8) before offering their own working definition. They state that:

> Leadership is a process of influence leading to the achievement of desired purposes. Successful leaders develop a vision for their schools based on personal and professional values. They articulate this vision at every opportunity and influence their staff and other stakeholders to share the vision. The philosophy, structures and activities of the school are geared towards the achievement of this shared vision.
>
> (ibid., p. 8)

As the result of a century or more of learning about leadership we have some shared insights into the nature of leadership and how it differs from management and administration. But for some, leadership is like beauty – it is in the eyes of the beholder – although most people 'recognise it when they see it!'

Any analysis of leadership would, initially, need to acknowledge two central factors: the relationship between leadership, power and authority (with authority defined as legitimate power or, following Bush and Glover, influence); and that leadership is about groups, and the interaction of people in groups. There are according to Fidler (1997) two key features associated with leadership:

- a sense of purpose and confidence that is engendered in followers
- the followers are influenced towards goal or task achievement.

Indeed, the emphasis is as much on the followers or followership (the led) and the task, rather than on the individual as leader. Similarly, as we show later, recent writing on leadership has emphasised that there is a need for leadership to be demonstrated at all levels in an organisation and not just at the top.

Over the years there has been considerable discussion in the literature about the similarities and differences between the notions of leadership, management and administration. The terms tend to have differing definitions; for example the meaning of administration in North America and Australasia is quite different from that in the UK where it tends to be associated with 'lower level' and more operational matters than leadership or management. Leadership tends to be more formative, proactive and problem-solving, dealing with such things as values, vision and mission, whereas the concerns of management are more to do with the execution, planning, organising and deploying of resources, or 'making things happen'. Management is focused more on providing order and consistency to organisations, while leadership is focused on producing change and movement (Kotter, 1990, cited in Fidler and Atton, 2004).

The differences between the concepts have been considered in detail by Bush and Glover (2003), and by Ofsted (2003a) in the latest inspection framework for schools in England. The former note that:

Leadership is a process of influence leading to the achievement of desired purposes. It involves inspiring and supporting others towards the achievement of a vision for the school that is based on clear personal and professional values. Management is the implementation of school policies and the efficient and effective maintenance of the school's current activities.

(Bush and Glover, 2003, p. 10)

The central inspection agency in England (Ofsted, 2003a) has suggested some key differences (see Figure 1.1). Interestingly, Ofsted makes a clear distinction between leadership, management and governance – the three central themes of this book. The inspection framework, used in all state schools since September 2003, notes that:

Leadership and management at all levels in the school should be judged by their effect on the quality and standards of the school. Leadership should provide the drive and direction for raising achievement, while management should make best use of the resources and processes to make this happen. Management includes effective evaluation, planning, performance management and staff development. Inspectors should consider the extent to which leadership is embedded throughout the school and not vested solely in the senior staff. They should explore how well the leadership team creates a climate for learning and whether the school is an effective learning organisation.

(ibid., p. x)

How well is the school led and managed?

☐ The *governance* of the school

Assessing the extent to which the governing body:
■ *helps shape the vision and direction of the school;*
■ *ensures that the school fulfils its statutory duties, including promoting inclusive policies in relation to special educational needs, race equality, disability and sex;*
■ *has a good understanding of the strengths and weaknesses of the school;*
■ *challenges and supports the senior management team.*

☐ The quality of *leadership* of the school, particularly by the headteacher, senior team and other staff with responsibilities

Assessing the extent to which:
■ *leadership shows clear vision, a sense of purpose and high aspirations for the school, with a relentless focus on pupils' achievement;*
■ *strategic planning reflects and promotes the school's ambitions and goals;*
■ *leaders inspire, motivate and influence staff and pupils;*
■ *leaders create effective teams;*
■ *there is knowledgeable and innovative leadership of teaching and the curriculum;*
■ *leaders are committed to running an equitable and inclusive school, in which each individual matters;*
■ *leaders provide good role models for other staff and pupils.*

☐ The effectiveness of *management*

Assessing the extent to which:
■ *the school undertakes rigorous self-evaluation and uses the findings effectively;*
■ *the school monitors performance data, reviews patterns and takes appropriate action;*
■ *performance management of staff, including support staff, is thorough and effective in bringing about improvement;*
■ *a commitment to staff development is reflected in effective induction and professional development strategies and, where possible, the school's contribution to initial teacher training;*
■ *the recruitment, retention, deployment and workload of staff are well managed, and support staff are well deployed to make teachers' work more effective;*
■ *approaches to financial and resource management help the school to achieve its educational priorities;*
■ *the principles of best value are central to the school's management and use of resources.*

Figure 1.1   Leadership, management and governance – inspectors' questions (Ofsted, 2003a)

Most writers who make the distinction between 'leadership' and 'management' recognise that the two concepts overlap and that both are necessary for organisational success. Both are about motivating people and giving a sense of purpose to the school and their role in achieving it. The terms 'transformational' leadership and 'transactional' leadership are also sometimes used to differentiate the two. Such distinctions are helpful conceptually but effective leaders need to draw upon a wide repertoire of both management and leadership skills. Organisational success depends on both effective leadership and management as well as effective governance. The link between governance, leadership and management, and standards and quality is made more directly

- The proportion of schools in which leadership and management are good or better has increased significantly since 1996/97. The proportion of schools with excellent or very good leadership and management has more than doubled over the same period. There is, however, a small minority of schools in which leadership and management are still unsatisfactory or poor
- Aspects of leadership in schools are generally better than aspects of management
- There is more very good leadership and management in secondary schools than in primary schools
- The monitoring, evaluation and development of teaching and the school's strategy for appraisal and performance management are aspects of management which are still in need of improvement in many schools
- There is a strong link between the quality of leadership and management of the headteacher and key staff in a school and the quality of teaching
- Strong leadership and good management are very important in bringing about improvement in schools, particularly in schools which are implementing special programmes to address low achievement and social inclusion, including those facing challenging circumstances
- Strong leadership and good management are very important in ensuring a broad and balanced curriculum in primary schools and good subject teaching in secondary schools
- The way in which the characteristics of strong leadership and good management are applied in different circumstances is of fundamental importance.

Figure 1.2   Main findings regarding leadership and management (Ofsted, 2003b)

than in earlier versions of the Ofsted framework for inspecting schools (Ofsted, 1999a; 2003a).

The Education Reform Act 1988 reallocated the balance of responsibilities and authority for managing schools from LEAs to the headteacher and governors of individual schools. This shifted a much greater responsibility for decision-making to school level. In recent years, the proportion of funding delegated to schools' own control has increased (to around 90 percent) and this has added to the powers of headteachers and governing bodies to manage their schools.

Schools have been inspected since 1993 so what do we know about the quality of their leadership, management and governance? Ofsted has recently published an account of this (Ofsted, 2003b) and it is worth looking at their main findings (those that relate to governance are considered in Chapter 12). These are shown in Figure 1.2. A key finding – which may indeed be one of the significant consequences of Ofsted inspections themselves – was that the proportion of schools with 'excellent' or 'very good' leadership and management has more than doubled over the last five years.

Evidence from Ofsted inspections suggests that schools do better on some of the key aspects of leadership than on those of management. The most effective aspects of the work of both primary and secondary headteachers are ensuring a clear educational direction, and reflecting the school's aims and values in its work. Both these aspects suggest headteachers 'leading from the front', setting the school's agenda and direction, and promoting shared values in pursuit of the school's aims. Headteachers are less effective in carrying out some of their managerial responsibilities, such as establishing effective governing bodies, monitoring teaching, and developing appraisal and performance management systems.

The above is of particular interest to us because, as we argue later, there is a need to ensure that the current concern, indeed preoccupation, with 'leadership' does not marginalise the importance of management and management development. Bush and Glover are of a similar mind: 'Given the now widely accepted distinction between leadership, an influence process based on values and a clearly articulated vision leading to change, and management, the effective implementation of decisions based mainly on notions of maintenance, it is vital that *both dimensions of this duality are given equal prominence'* (2003, p. 10, our emphasis). They remind us of Bolman and Deals's important comment that:

> Leading and managing are distinct, but both are important. Organisations, which are over managed but under led eventually lose any sense of spirit or purpose. Poorly managed organisations with strong charismatic leaders may soar temporarily only to crash shortly thereafter. The challenge of modern organisations requires the objective perspective of the manager as well as the brilliant flashes of vision and commitment wise leadership provides.
>
> (Bolman and Deal, 1997, pp. xiii–xiv)

Both aspects are necessary for successful schools and we agree with Bush and Glover who argue that 'in the current policy climate, schools require both visionary leadership and effective management' (2003, p. 10). But is there a danger that the latter is being sidelined in the drive to develop the leaders of our schools? The reality, of course, is that leaders and managers are almost indistinguishable and both are needed for successful schools. In fact Pedlar et al. (2003), writing in a business context, have recently noted that management *is* leadership: the ability to mobilise collective action to face a challenge. Leadership is a response to challenge which puts the emphasis on the here and now, a task and a context. For Pedlar et al., leadership therefore has little meaning in the abstract.

THEORIES OF LEADERSHIP

Many theories have been advanced over the years to explain how leaders lead, whether in schools or elsewhere. Bush and Glover build on the work of Leithwood et al. (1999) to develop a typology of leadership consisting of eight broad theories (Bush and Glover, 2003, pp. 11–22). These are:

- instructional leadership
- transformational leadership
- moral leadership
- participative leadership
- managerial leadership
- post-modern leadership

- interpersonal leadership
- contingent leadership.

This is a useful typology but leadership can, of course, be conceptualised or theorised in many other ways. We would like to suggest that leadership theory can be broadly categorised, chronologically, under five headings. What is interesting about these five theories is that it could be said that we have come full circle with what might broadly be termed personal 'trait' theories that reappeared in the late 1990s and early 2000s. These five theories are:

- trait theory (leadership as an attribute of personality)
- style theory (leadership as management style)
- contingency theory (leadership as the conjunction of the person and the situation)
- power/influence theory (a function of power and how it is exercised)
- personal trait theory (effective leadership as superior individual performance).

To this list we wish to add a sixth – *learning-centred leadership* – which is beginning to gain ascendancy as it is promulgated by the NCSL. Brief consideration is given below to each of the first four theories, whilst modern 'personal trait' theory is examined in more detail and learning-centred leadership is explored further in the last section.

Trait theories

'Trait' theories (or 'great man' theories), popular in the 1920s, were concerned to study the attributes and characteristics of successful leaders, particularly military leaders, in order to describe what was different about them. Despite a lot of research pointing to a number of characteristics, there was little consistency in the findings. Traits most consistently found included intelligence, self-confidence, high energy levels and dominance.

Style theory

'Style' theories became popular from the 1930s onwards initially through the work of Lippitt and White in the USA, who studied autocratic, democratic and laissez-faire leadership styles, and their effects on participants at summer camps. This approach led to the development of number of self-completion questionnaires that attempted to ascertain types of leader. Blake and Mouton's managerial grid, developed in the 1960s, was one of the better known of these and examined the extent to which a leader's style gave emphasis to 'people' or to 'task' (Blake and Mouton, 1964). Was the leader's concern for relationships (were they people orientated), or to achieve results (task orientated)? These two-dimensional models were further developed – for example, McGregor's (1960) 'Theory X' and 'Theory Y' (about the leader's belief about the motivation of the led) – and included continua of leadership styles of which Tannenbaum and Schmidt's (1973) 'tell', 'sell', 'consult' and 'share' (or 'boss-centred' or subordinate-centred' leadership) was probably the best known. More recently, Adair's (1986) notion of 'action-centred' leadership gave importance to achieving the correct balance between achieving the *task*, building and maintaining the *team*, and developing the *individual*. The language used by various leadership theorists was slightly different but the underpinning ideas essentially the same.

Contingency theory

By the 1970s and early 1980s the notion that the context within which leadership was enacted was beginning to come to the fore and Fiedler's (1967) 'contingency' theory and Blanchard and Hersey's notion of 'situational leadership' gained prominence. Contingency theory perceived leadership as the conjunction of person and the situation, and gave consideration to the power of the leader, the structure of the task and the leader-led relationship. Hersey and Blanchard (1977) developed a complex model of four leadership styles – delegating, supporting, coaching and directing – which depended on such factors as the level of support needed and the development level of team members. The development level of individuals was said to depend on competence and commitment. Situational leadership therefore meant the leader (at any level in the organisation) choosing the right style of leadership behaviour to suit both the development level of the team member and the job or task.

Power and influence

Power/influence theories of leadership see leadership as a function of power and how that power is exercised (e.g. Pfeffer, 1992). Key questions for such theorists would include who exerts influence, what are the sources of that influence and what are the purposes and outcomes of influence. Leithwood and colleagues (1999) have used the notion of power and influence to categorise leadership theories into a number of types – instructional, transformational, moral, participative, managerial and contingent.

Personal trait theory

The question needs to be asked whether modern theories of leadership, especially those which give emphasis to notions of competence and capability, are returning to the earlier 'trait' theories, albeit perhaps in more sophisticated guises. Have we turned full circle with the emphasis on effective leadership as 'superior' individual performance and the competence approach stressing the qualities of the person and the skills they possess? More recent notions of leadership styles and effective performance give prominence to such factors.

One of us (DW) was involved in an influential study into effective leadership and management commissioned by the Department for Education and Employment (DfEE) in the early 1990s (Bolam et al., 1993). The research focused on those schools whose staff felt they were well managed and led. Through the use of questionnaire surveys of the 57 schools and detailed case studies it highlighted many factors making for effectiveness (see Chapter 9). In particular it noted that effective leaders were characterised by particular managerial and personal qualities. For example, *ineffective* leaders were said to demonstrate the following:

Managerial qualities

- Being insufficiently decisive.
- Failing to delegate sufficiently or leaving staff too much to their own concerns.
- Failing to unite the staff, and to build a sense of a community whose members were all pulling together.
- Failing to communicate effectively.
- Lacking proficiency in managing fellow professionals.
- Failing to display interest in and concern for staff, or to praise and celebrate their achievements.
- Being disorganised and insufficiently thorough, especially as regards administration.

Personal qualities

- Lacking dynamism and failing to inspire.
- Being insufficiently forceful.
- Failing to be at ease with others.
- Inability to accept any form of questioning or perceived criticism.

Very similar findings emerged from our earlier studies of headship (Weindling and Earley, 1987, p. 70) and middle managers (Earley and Fletcher-Campbell, 1989, p. 52). Both these research projects investigated teachers' and others' perceptions of effectiveness. How leaders enact leadership or leadership styles are important as they impact on how people feel and are motivated to perform at higher levels. It is known that effective leaders use a range of styles according to the demands of the situation (contingent or situational leadership). Research by the management consultancy firm Hay-McBer (better known in England as the Hay Group), who were responsible for developing the 'Leadership Programme for Serving Heads' in England, suggested six leadership styles. These are:

- coercive (main objective: immediate compliance)
- authoritative (providing long-term direction and vision for staff)
- affiliative (creating harmony among staff and between leaders and staff)
- democratic (building commitment among staff and generating new ideas)
- pacesetting (accomplishing tasks to high standards of excellence)
- coaching (main objective: long term professional development of staff).

Other research in business and industry has shown that highly effective leaders are characterised by such things as an awareness of the environment, they are positive and optimistic and possess such traits as the desire to be best, a willingness to take risks and to create a 'no blame' culture. They also surround themselves with good people, continually ask for feedback and are self-evaluative. Effective leaders are said to like people, they relate well to them and enjoy seeing them grow (in Bennis's terms 'releasing intellectual capital' [1999]). They are interested in new ideas and challenges. But it is lonely at the top of any organisation and there is a need for external support of some kind. Effective leaders are said to operate as facilitators, advisers, teachers, supporters and coaches.

In recent years the notion of 'emotional intelligence' has been seen as critically important to effective leadership and 'superior performance'. According to Daniel Goleman (1996; 1998; Goleman et al., 2002), the leading exponent of the concept, the higher an individual rises in an organisation the more important emotional intelligence (EQ) becomes. He claims there are five domains of EQ:

- self-awareness (ability to recognise one's emotions, strengths/weaknesses, a sense of self-worth/confidence)
- self-regulation (ability to control your emotions rather than allowing them to control you)
- motivation (strength of will needed to meet goals, drive to improve, initiative, etc.)
- empathy
- social skills.

The first three domains relate to an individual's emotions, while empathy and social skills refer to other people's emotions: the ability to recognise them and to nurture relationships or inspire others.

As far as job performance is concerned Goleman (1998) claims that EQ is (at least) twice as important as IQ or technical skills. He states that three 'motivational competences' typify outstanding performance of individuals. These are:

- achievement drive (striving to improve or meet a standard of excellence)
- commitment (embracing the vision and goals)
- initiative and optimism (mobilising people to seize opportunities and allowing them to take setbacks and obstacles in their stride).

Hay-McBer or the Hay Group (of which Goleman is a partner) have studied individual leaders, whom they call 'star' performers and compared them with average performers. They claim the former are in possession of EQ competences. It is also believed that leaders can obtain 30 percent extra from their people if they are able to 'light their blue touch paper'. This 'discretionary effort' is said to be strongly affected by the climate that is personally felt and that up to 70 percent of that climate is created by the team leader, by the way they behave and conduct their affairs. Advocates of emotional intelligence claim that if leaders – and not only those at the top of the organisation, but all those with a leadership role – can ignite that 'touch paper' then it is possible to obtain that extra performance from team members. It is stated that for leaders (at all levels) EQ is 90 percent of what separates 'star' performers from others.

In the educational world there is a growing body of research on highly effective practitioners. For example, a small-scale study of highly effective headteachers in England found that they were characterised by the following:

1 The ability to work simultaneously on a variety of issues and problems.
2 Has clear, shared values and vision.
3 Passion for pupils' development and achievement.
4 Understands the need for and practices well developed interpersonal skills.
5 Sets high expectations.
6 Uses monitoring and evaluation for improvement.
7 Prepared to take risks.
8 High levels of knowledge, understanding and professional confidence.
9 Appropriate use of structures and systems.
10 Efficient use of time.
11 Political awareness and skills.
12 Integrated approach to strategic and operational issues.
13 Whole school perspective and approach.
14 Positive commitment to staff development (Lawlor and Sills, 1999).

The methodology used by Hay-McBer (critical incident analysis and behavioural event interviews) has also been deployed to identify highly effective classroom teachers (Hay-McBer, 2000).

A CHANGING DISCOURSE – FROM MANAGEMENT TO THE LEADERSHIP OF LEARNING

An analysis of the recent history of the training and development of heads and other senior school staff would suggest that 'leadership' as a concept is currently very much in the ascendancy. This is true not only of England. As Fullan notes 'virtually every state department in advanced countries passed new policies for developing and certifying educational leaders' (2003a, p. 16). However, a decade or so ago the dominant training and development discourse in England was not about leadership per se, as much as it was about developing and improving the 'management' of schools. Indeed, the government of the time set up a task force – the *School Management Task Force* – specifically to address such matters (DES, 1990). This was a time when the full force of the 1988 Education Reform Act was being felt and when local management of schools (LMS) was coming into its own. Many heads were having to come to terms with a 'whole new world' and our own ongoing study of headship documented this changing scenario in full (Earley et al., 1994/95; Weindling, 1998).

At about the same time, national occupational standards for managers (not leaders) of organisations were developed by the Management Charter Initiative with a version for educational managers (Earley, 1992). Leadership (when it was discussed) was often seen as a subset of management; there was no equivalent set of leadership skills and tasks, rather the demonstration of leadership was contained within a framework of management competences (Earley, 1993). The evolving national standards for headteachers (TTA, 1998a) could also be said to be informed largely by this management-dominated even managerial discourse. They can interestingly be compared with the second version, put out for consultation in 2004, which gives greater prominence to 'leadership' (NCSL, 2003c).

The move away from 'management' and towards seeing 'leadership' as the key factor underpinning school success was fully realised when in November 2000 the National College for School Leadership was established with the explicit aim of transforming leadership in English schools. The late 1990s also saw the growth of a number of regional leadership centres, and a national college for other sectors within education has also been established. The establishment of leadership colleges and leadership centres has seen an accompanying growth of discussion and debate about the nature of leadership, its constitution and enactment. Senior management teams also were now increasingly referred to as the 'leadership group' (DfEE, 2000d) and middle managers were now seen as middle leaders (NCSL, 2003b; also see Chapters 9 and 10).

The emerging model or theory of leadership that underpins current discourse, as expounded by NCSL and others, is one of transformational and instructional leadership (e.g. see NCSL, 2001) or, even more recently, 'learning-centred leadership' (Southworth, 2003). These forms of leadership focus less on the leader – leadership is not perceived as simply a trait of an individual – and more on the sharing of leadership throughout the organisation. It is an inclusive leadership and one that is *distributed* throughout the school. In addition, and most significantly, 'learning-centred leadership' also has close connections to learning and pedagogy and andragogy. It is about learning – pupil, adult (teachers, staff and governors), organisational learning and leadership networks – and teaching. The notion of learning-centred leadership has developed from both transformational and instructional leadership.

Transformational leadership, one of the types of leadership mentioned earlier, conceptualises school leadership along a number of dimensions, and gives emphasis to building vision, establishing commitment to agreed goals, providing intellectual stimulation, offering individualised support, and explicating and encouraging high expectations for staff (Bass, 1999; Campbell et al., 2003; Gold et al., 2003; Hallinger, 2003a; Leithwood et al., 1999). However, there is no evidence to suggest that, *on its own*, this form of leadership brings about anything but modest improved consequences for pupil outcomes, and for this reason the transformational approach to school leadership has been complemented by the instructional leadership model (Earley et al., 2002; Hallinger, 2003a). This model typically assumes that the critical focus for attention by school leaders should be the behaviours of staff as they engage in activities directly affecting the quality of learning and teaching in the pursuit of enhanced pupil outcomes.

Instructional leaders are concerned to promote and develop their schools as learning organisations or professional learning communities in order to help bring about the school's learning goals for its pupils (see Hopkins, 2001; NCSL, 2001; 2002). Transformational leadership focuses on developing the organisation's capacity to innovate but as Hallinger (2003a) has noted, the similarities between the two leadership models are more significant than the differences. Indeed, Marks and Printy (2003) use the term 'integrated leadership' – both transformational and instructional – in eliciting the instructional leadership of teachers for improving school performance. Responsibility is shared and the head is no longer the sole instructional leader but the 'leader of instructional leaders' (Glickman, 1989, cited in Marks and Printy, 2003). Both Hallinger (2003a) and Marks and Printy (2003) see headteachers who share leadership responsibilities with others as less subject to burnout than principal 'heroes' who attempt the challenges and complexities of leadership alone.

Therefore the modern conception of leadership in schools focuses strongly on 'learning' and does not reside within any one individual. Indeed, it is seen as an essential component of the organisation and it is part of the head's role to develop leadership capacity – and learning – within the school (Harris and Lambert, 2003). Leadership is dispersed throughout the whole organisation and it is not the leader but leadership that is the key factor. Today's leadership needs to be decentralised and distributed in every part of the organisation so those on the periphery who are first to spot challenges can act instantly on them (Pedlar et al., 2003). Nevertheless, the leadership demonstrated by the chief executive or head, at the apex of the organisation, is obviously crucially important. Part of that leadership is to distribute or disperse responsibility and to empower others to give of their best and, in schools, to keep learning at the centre of their activities. As Egan (1993, p. 80), writing in a business context, notes 'if your organisation has only one leader then it is almost certainly short of leadership'. Leaders are people who, as Senge comments, 'lead through developing new skills, capabilities and understandings. And they come from many places within the organisation' (Senge, 1990, p. 15). More recently Goleman et al., have put it as follows:

There are many leaders, not just one. Leadership is distributed. It resides not solely in the individual at the top, but in every person at every level who, in one way or another, acts as a leader to a group of followers – wherever in the organisation that person is, whether shop steward, team head or CEO.

(Goleman et al., 2002, pp. xiii–xiv)

The NCSL's think tank similarly saw leadership as a function that needs to be distributed throughout the school community. Its view of leadership is quite clear, it is 'not hierarchical, but federal and involves clarity of direction, structures and support' (NCSL, 2001, p. 11).

Notions of dispersed or distributed leadership raise interesting questions about its character, the degree of dispersal and the relative importance of leadership at different levels. For example, is the leadership demonstrated by the headteacher of equal value to that demonstrated by subject leaders or classroom teachers? The NCSL's think tank report is quite clear about this: 'instructional leadership is not inextricably linked to status or experience. It is distributed and potentially available to all' (2001, p. 11) and that: 'Successful school leadership is not invested in hierarchical status but experience is valued and structures are established to encourage all to be drawn in and regarded for their contribution ... Collaborative work has been found to increase the involvement, engagement and affiliation across all staff ' (ibid.).

Notions of dispersed or distributed leadership are considered further in Part 2 and a useful review of the literature is provided by Bennett et al. (2003). However, it is clear that unless attention is paid to the effectiveness of those leading at the top of the organisation – in our case headteachers – then notions of dispersed leadership become meaningless. A headteacher recipient of a knighthood in the New Year's honours list put it well when he said: 'I work with a lot of talented teachers, but the role of the head is an essential precondition. In any organisation, people can only work within the climate that is set. That's what leadership and management are about. I don't think you get good schools without good heads' (Sir Dexter Hutt, cited in *Times Educational Supplement*, 2 January 2004, p. 10). Thus, headship – the main focus of this book – remains crucially important, as do both leadership and management. The next chapter looks at the transition to headship and the different stages which heads go through.

2

Stages of Headship

Stages heads went through in the NFER project (1982–94)
Professional and organisational socialisation
Stage theories of socialisation
Transition to headship: Stages of socialisation

In this chapter we explore the common stages within headship. Although each school is different and the particular circumstances in each make it unique, there are common patterns, knowledge of which can be used to improve the preparation and support for heads. We summarise what the heads we studied in the NFER research went through over ten years. We look at a range of models of leadership transition in both business and education, and produce a stage theory of headship ourselves that can be used both as a research tool and to assist the development of heads and prospective heads.

STAGES HEADS WENT THROUGH IN THE NFER PROJECT (1982–94)

New heads do not start with a clean slate, as some heads mistakenly believe. The shadow of 'headteachers past' hangs over and influences them for longer than they expect. The previous head had often retired, having been in post for a lengthy period, often 15 to 20 years. They had 'shaped the school in their image' and while this might be apparent in the form of structure, it was much harder to see the school culture they had forged. New heads were often surprised when they confronted existing routines, to be told, 'that's the way we have always done it'. The main problems reported by the new heads who started in 1982–83 were:

- difficulties caused by the style and practice of the previous head
- the school buildings
- communication and consultation with staff
- creating a better public image of the school
- coping with a weak member of the senior management team (SMT)
- dealing with incompetent staff
- low staff morale.

17

The heads differed in their approaches to change. Some chose to make early changes, others to move cautiously, while some were delayed and hindered by a poor or ineffective SMT. Almost all the changes made in the first year were organisational. Curricular changes began in the second year and continued into the third year and beyond. A few of the changes to the pastoral system occurred in the first year, but these were mainly introduced in years two and three of their tenure.

The organisational changes made soon after the new head's arrival were frequently concerned with communication and consultation. Another group of early changes was concerned with promoting a positive image for the school, something of particular concern to the new heads, especially where the community held the school in low esteem or student numbers were falling.

Of the many changes introduced in the first years, it was noticeable that only a handful did not originate with the new heads themselves. Once the decision to adopt a change had been made, day-to-day responsibility was usually delegated either to a deputy head or a head of department.

The external changes produced by the Educational Reform Act and other legislation had only just begun when we conducted the second phase of the research in 1988. The following five years saw the heads attempting to cope with substantial changes imposed from outside.

In order to explore how the problems changed over time a set of core questions were used in the first and last surveys. Table 2.1 shows heads' perceptions in 1984 and 1993 on the core questions where a direct comparison is possible.

Most problems were perceived to lessen over time, for example: getting staff to accept new ideas; creating a good public image of the school; dealing with poor staff morale; improving communication and consultation; managing staff development and INSET; establishing discipline; dealing with finance; and issues concerning support staff. However, a few problems seemed to have increased, for example: managing time and priorities; and working with the governors, while dealing with incompetent staff appeared to have continued over time. Working with LEA officers and advisers remained a very minor problem for most heads.

These findings are likely to be due to the interaction of several complex factors. With time, heads and staff get to know each other's strengths and weaknesses; the heads have made some key staff appointments; they have gained a deeper understanding of the school and have introduced most of their intended changes. But the world outside also changes. During the ten-year period a large number of national changes occurred, such as the changing role of governors, local management of schools (LMS), grant maintained schools, the National Curriculum, league tables, and Ofsted inspections.

Changing culture

We asked the heads after ten years in post what advice they would give to a new head. We found that they put most emphasis on the importance of

Table 2.1 Comparison of problems perceived by secondary heads in 1984 and 1993 (percentages)

	Percentages					
	V. serious or serious		Moderate or minor		Not a problem	
	1984	1993	1984	1993	1984	1993
Getting staff to accept new ideas	47	20	47	68	6	12
Creating a good public image	42	21	43	60	15	19
Dealing with a weak member of SMT	38	27	36	39	26	34
Dealing with incompetent staff	37	31	32	63	31	6
Dealing with poor staff morale	36	16	51	58	13	26
Improve consultation/ communication	35	18	46	66	9	16
Managing staff dev. and INSET	30	5	60	60	10	35
Establish good standards of discipline	27	6	51	65	22	29
Managing time and priorities	21	40	54	50	25	10
Dealing with LMS and finance	19	10	58	57	23	33
Issues concerning non-teaching staff	19	11	57	52	24	35
Working with LEA officers	7	7	42	27	51	66
Working with the governors	6	11	42	50	52	39
Working with LEA inspectors	5	3	32	28	61	69

n = 228 (1984)
n = 100 (1993)

interpersonal skills and relationships, political power and teamwork – all factors imbedded in the school context. While formal study during preparation programmes tends to emphasise technical skills, the advice these heads offered after ten years on the job emphasised the skills and processes that Gabarro (1987) argued distinguished between those managers who were successful and those who were not:

1 Assessing the organisation and diagnosing its problems.
2 Building a management team focused on a set of shared expectations.
3 Bringing about timely changes that address organisational problems.

In contrast, weak managers tend to function as 'Lone Rangers': they involved others to a much lesser degree in the work of assessing and diagnosing problems within the organisation, resulting in a narrow focus and incomplete diagnosis. The NFER heads' advice illustrates these points:

● Assess *school* needs.
● Build an effective senior management team but make sure it is not separated from the body of the staff.

- Delegated team management is essential for a successful school, allow all staff to be involved in the development of the school.
- Remember that the staff are your most important resource.
- Ensure a good working relationship with the chair of governors as quickly as possible. Err on the side of over-informing your governors.
- Cultivate your governors ... you need their support and trust if you are to be free to manage.
- Have a vision for the school; share it with colleagues and students. Believe in others as well as yourself and consult widely.
- Have your vision, yes, but carry your staff, your governors, your parents and your children with you. Keep in touch all the time.
- Accept that change will be constant, some of it turbulent.
- Make good use of your honeymoon period, but do not arrive with too many preconceived ideas or make too many changes too quickly. Do not import too much from your last school.
- Be clear about your values. Trust your own judgement.
- Establish clear principles and priorities and communicate them.
- Be prepared to lead from the front.

The learning process that makes this flexibility possible requires adjustments and adaptations to the expectations of a school on the part of a new school leader. These adjustments make co-operative effort possible and construct an orientation towards common needs and goals. Through the adjustment process, people come to internalise the values, norms and beliefs of others in the same school, and to see things as others see them. As school leaders adapt and adopt the generally accepted explanations for events, they are 'socialised' but not enslaved.

PROFESSIONAL AND ORGANISATIONAL SOCIALISATION

The research on effective schools shows the importance of school culture (see Chapter 13). The main task for the head is to create a shared vision and provide the necessary leadership to shape the culture of the school. Schein (1987, p. 2) writes:

> Organisational cultures are created by leaders, and one of the most decisive functions of leadership may well be the creation, the management, and if and when it becomes necessary, the destruction of culture. Culture and leadership, when one examines them closely, are two sides of the same coin, and neither can really be understood by itself. In fact, there is a possibility underdeveloped in the leadership research that the only thing of real importance that leaders do is to create and manage culture and that the unique talent of leaders is their ability to work with culture.

Changing the culture of the school cannot be done easily or quickly, the NFER research shows that the 'class of '82' had continued this difficult task.

They seemed intuitively to know that 'School improvement is steady work, and there is no quick fix'.

Dan Duke (1987, p. 261) points out the developmental nature of becoming a school leader and the importance of socialisation:

> School leaders do not emerge from training programs fully prepared and completely effective. Their development is a more involved and incremental process, beginning as early as their own schooling and extending through their first years on the job as leaders. Becoming a school leader is an ongoing process of socialisation.

A useful approach to understanding leadership and headship development derives from Merton's (1963) socialisation theory. The stress here is on the two-way interaction between the new leader and the school situation (with each trying to change and influence the other). In this view of socialisation there are two main overlapping phases:

- *professional socialisation,* which involves learning what it is to be a head-teacher, prior to taking up the role, from personal experience of schooling and teaching and from formal courses
- *organisational socialisation,* which involves learning the knowledge, values and behaviours required to perform a specific role within a particular organisation after appointment.

When school leaders enter a school as new members, they experience a form of organisational socialisation. This teaches a person the knowledge, values and behaviours required of them in a particular role within a particular organisation. These values and norms may be very different to those the person learned as part of their professional socialisation.

Professional socialisation generally begins in the pre-appointment phase of a school leader's career and continues into early post-appointment growth and development. Pre-appointment professional socialisation includes:

- management courses for certification (mandatory, such as the National Professional Qualification for Headteachers [NPQH], and voluntary)
- first-hand experiences of leadership and management tasks
- modelling and social learning (learning by observing both good and bad models, help form a notion of what is good and poor leadership, and deliberate mentoring by some existing school leaders who see importance in their role in preparing future leaders).

Organisational socialisation begins upon appointment and is specific to the education context. This simple definition belies the complexities. For example, an insider (someone appointed internally from within the school) brings past experiences and knowledge to this process, even though socialisation to the headship in each school is fundamentally unique (Hart, 1993).

We contend that post-appointment processes, dominated by organisational socialisation, create the interactions that legitimate and validate a new school leader within a school, preparing the way for her or him to exert influence. Gabarro (1987) called this 'the taking charge' process. This crucial period consequently warrants the careful attention of those committed to improving the quality and effects of school leaders.

The school leader tries to take charge and bring about school improvement. At the same time the school is changing the school leader. Even writers who focus on the cultural aspects of leadership sometimes emphasise ways in which the leader socialises the staff – but not the reverse (Schein, 1992). The NFER study shows that effective new leaders enter with a notion of what they want their school to be like. When they get to the school and begin to see where the school does or does not lend itself to the elements of their rough blueprint, they must go through the surprise and sense-making process laid out by Smircich (1983) and adjust their expectations. Smircich described a process through which new members of an organisation deal with the differences between their pre-arrival beliefs and expectations and actual experiences upon entering the organisation. Surprise is the most common response, and negative surprises tend to outnumber positive surprises. As the new member makes sense of these surprises, they come to understand and eventually become integrated within the group.

In summary, no matter how good the preparation programmes and prior experience, a major transition occurs when a school leader takes on a new formal leadership role that requires tailor-made responses to that particular situation. Consequently, fixation on pre- or post-appointment training, formal and informal processes, and the curricula of programmes leaves new school leaders wanting. More attention to the induction or taking-charge stage is needed, because it always is problematic and requires careful analysis and action *in situ*.

STAGE THEORIES OF SOCIALISATION

A large body of work exists, drawn mainly from the non-educational sector, which proposes stage theories to explain the transition phases experienced by leaders. These theories commonly identify three main periods of organisational socialisation. Hart (1993) provides the most detailed synthesis and critical analysis of the field, and the following is adapted from her work.

Stage 1: Encounter, anticipation or confrontation

The initial arrival stage requires considerable learning on the part of new heads as they encounter the people and the organisation. Cognitive approaches focus on rational interpretations and the understandings that new heads construct; what Louis (1980) called the *sense-making* process in an unfamiliar situation.

Stage 2: Adjustment, accommodation, clarity

This involves the task of attempting to fit in. New leaders must reach accommodation with the work role, the people with whom they interact and the school culture. They look for role clarity in this new setting and may face resistance from established group members.

Stage 3: Stabilisation

In this stage, stable patterns emerge but this is only visible in data from longitudinal studies. Nicholson and West (1988), using a cyclic model, treat the stages of stabilisation and preparation (for the next change) together, because they found that stabilisation did not occur for some managers. They had moved on to their next post before stabilisation.

A number of models have been developed to describe the various stages of school leadership development. The National College for School Leadership (NCSL, 2001) has produced a 'leadership development framework' which considers five stages of school leadership from teacher to head:

- Emergent leadership – when a teacher is beginning to take on management and leadership responsibilities and perhaps forms an aspiration to become a headteacher.
- Established leadership – comprising assistant and deputy heads who are experienced leaders but who do not intend to pursue headship.
- Entry to headship – including a teacher's preparation for and induction into the senior post in a school.
- Advanced leadership – the stage at which school leaders mature in their role, look to widen their experience, to refresh themselves and to update their skills.
- Consultant leadership – when an able and experienced leader is ready to put something back into the profession by taking on training, mentoring, inspection or other responsibilities.

This framework is being used as an organising structure for the various NCSL activities and programmes.

A few empirical studies have looked at the period of deputy headship as preparation for headship. Ribbins (1997), for example, interviewed 34 heads and found that, while some enjoyed their experience as deputies as an appropriate preparation for headship, relatively few remembered it enthusiastically or their former heads with unqualified warmth. Although most felt that their heads had not positively prepared them for headship, they believed that they had learned from the negative experiences, often vowing never to act like that themselves.

Leithwood et al.

Findings from four studies involving both aspiring and practising principals in Canada are reported by Leithwood and colleagues (1992). They charted the various socialisation experiences which occur prior to appointment or after appointment as a principal, and which are seen as useful or not. The researchers found these ranged from carefully planned, formal training programmes, through less formal but still planned experiences (e.g. working with a mentor) to quite informal, unplanned on-the-job experiences.

Leithwood et al., concluded that most people thought they had experienced a moderately helpful socialisation and any differences were strongly related to the local education districts. Women and men experienced very similar socialisation patterns, although men appeared to receive earlier encouragement to consider the principal role. Formal preparation programmes appeared to vary widely in their perceived value.

Parkay and Hall

Parkay and Hall (1992) conducted a project in the USA modelled on the NFER research. They surveyed 113 new high school principals and carried out case studies of 12 throughout their first year in post. A return visit was made after three years. The authors derived a five-stage developmental model to describe the career patterns of new principals:

1 Survival.
2 Control.
3 Stability.
4 Educational leadership.
5 Professional actualisation.

Four basic assumptions underlie the model:

- Principals begin at different stages and not all start at Stage 1.
- Principals develop through the stages at different rates.
- No single factor determines a principal's stage of development. Personal characteristics, the school context and the previous principal all play a part.
- Principals may operate at more than one stage simultaneously, i.e. the stage is their predominant orientation.

Day and Bakioglu

In this country, Day and Bakioglu (1996) surveyed 196 headteachers and interviewed a sample of 34, and derived a four-phase, developmental model:

1 Initiation: idealism, uncertainty and adjustment. This lasted about three years and involved two key processes: learning on the job and accommodating to the existing framework and structure of the school.
2 Development: consolidation and extension. Heads with four to eight years' experience were still enthusiastic, saw this as more satisfactory and rewarding

with fewer difficulties than the other phases, built new management teams as inherited senior staff left and delegated more.

3 Autonomy. Here heads continued to be self-confident, felt they had management expertise but had less energy, a nostalgia for the past and saw externally imposed national initiatives as causing lack of enthusiasm. 'Autonomy' was positive in that they felt in control of the school, but negative because this was threatened by external change and pressure to work with governors.

4 Disenchantment. A decline in confidence, enthusiasm and fatigue were the characteristics here. Heads started to ease off and their health (physical and mental) deteriorated as they approached retirement. The Education Reform Act had had a major impact on many of them.

Ribbins

Ribbins (1998) adapted Day and Bakioglu's phases and a stage model developed by Gronn (1993; 1999) to produce a model of typical pathways for school leaders:

- Formation – the early socialisation influences from agencies such as the family, school and other reference groups which shape the personality of a future head.
- Accession – career advancement and preparation for headship.
- Incumbency – the total period of headship, from appointment to leaving, subdivided into Day and Bakioglu's four phases, to which Ribbins adds 'enchantment' as an alternative to disenchantment for some long-serving heads.
- Moving on – leaving headship which may involve divestiture for the disenchanted or reinvention for the enchanted.

Woods

An NCSL research associate, Woods (2002), interviewed eight long-serving primary heads (all had been in post at least 15 years), to explore further the idea of enchantment. These heads were found to be proud of their schools: 'Their pride was in the achievements of their children, their awe at the skill and craft of their teachers and the tremendous support they had received from parents and governors' (ibid., p. 8). The heads were close to the children and had a passion for teaching and learning. They were skilled at building teams and developing staff. While acknowledging problems they viewed change optimistically. Woods concludes that this group of 'enchanted' heads had been able to sustain their commitment and enthusiasm over a long period.

Reeves et al.

A stage model was also developed by Reeves et al. (1998) from interviews with 29 headteachers (five in Denmark and 24 from England and Scotland).

The analysis showed a fairly consistent developmental pattern, which the researchers divided into eight stages, each of which seemed to mark a qualitative change in the school leaders' experience and orientation to practice.

Stage 1   The warm up   (pre-entry)
Stage 2   Entry   (0–6 months)
Stage 3   Digging the foundations   (6 months–1 year)

During the first three stages the heads were trying to come to terms with the school and the school was trying to get the measure of the new leader.

Stage 4   Taking action   (9 months–2 years)
Stage 5   Getting above floor level (18 months–3 years)
Stage 6   The crunch   (2–5 years)

For these stages the head is taking action and making changes. These are initially small changes, followed by more substantial ones often aligned to the leader's beliefs and values.

Stage 7   Reaching the summit   (4–10 years)
Stage 8   Time for a change   (5–10 + years)

At this point the leader and the school have reached a mutually agreeable way of working. Having empowered others to take a more active leadership role within the school, the head turned increasingly to the outside world. This was often followed by some loss of interest and a desire for pastures new. The authors point out the similarity of their results to those of our original NFER study (Weindling and Earley, 1987).

Gabarro

Gabarro (1987) conducted research on 17 senior management successions in business and industry, pointing out that while there has been research on management succession, very little work has examined the activities and problems facing a new manager after they take up their post. He calls this process 'taking charge', which is:

> the process by which a manager establishes mastery and influence in a new assignment. By mastery, I mean acquiring a grounded understanding of the organisation, its tasks, people, environment, and problems. By influence, I mean having an impact on the organisation, its structure, practices, and performance. The process begins when a manager starts a new assignment and ends when he or she has mastered it in sufficient depth to be managing the organisation as efficiently as the resources, constraints, and the manager's own ability allow.

(ibid., p. 6)

He characterised it as a series of five predictable, chronological stages of learning and action. The timings covering a three-year period are approximate:

- Taking hold (the first 6 months). This period involves intense learning as the manager develops a cognitive map of the organisation using processes of orientation, evaluation (an assessment of staff, understanding where the problems lie) and establishing priorities. 'Corrective' actions are taken to address emerging problems and 'turnaround' actions to deal with urgent problems.
- Immersion (6 to 12 months). This very important period of deeper learning and diagnosis involves relatively little organisational change activity. Managers develop a much better understanding of the basic issues and underlying problems. They often question more sharply if they have the right people in place as they understand their strengths and weaknesses.
- Reshaping (12 to 21 months). This is a time of major change, organisational reconfiguration and implementation. The transition to reshaping often involves the use of task groups and external consultants.
- Consolidation (21 to 27 months). Earlier changes are consolidated. Learning and diagnosis tend to be evaluative. The manager and key colleagues assess the consequences and unanticipated problems of earlier changes and take corrective actions.
- Refinement (27 to 36 months). A period of fine-tuning with relatively little major additional learning.

Gabarro found that the organisational changes managers made as they worked through these stages characteristically occurred in three waves: the first wave occurs during the taking-hold stage; the second, and typically largest, during the reshaping stage; and the last and smallest during the consolidation stage. These stage and wave patterns are found in successful transitions regardless of the kind of succession (insider versus outsider; turnaround versus non-turnaround cases), the industry of the organisation involved, or the manager's prior functional background or speciality.

TRANSITION TO HEADSHIP: STAGES OF SOCIALISATION

A problem with much of the previous research on organisations be they schools or businesses is the lack of a sufficiently long time frame to see all the phases or stages of development: hence the value of the NFER ten-year study.

Gabarro's work shows interesting parallels with the NFER study where the new heads attempt to 'take charge'. But it is well known that public sector workers, such as the NFER heads, are more constrained than business managers in their ability to hire and fire, and the fixed nature of the school year and timetable delay major curricular changes. Nevertheless, the waves of changes described by Gabarro have great similarity to the way that the NFER heads introduced change. Another common finding was that internally appointed heads/managers tended to make fewer changes and to move more slowly than external appointees.

Day and Bakioglu's final phase of disenchantment produces a new perspective, while Ribbins (1997) and Woods (2002) offer the alternative of enchantment for some long-serving heads. The NFER data show that some heads are enchanted and others disenchanted by their experience of headship. (The relationship between length of service and performance is considered further in the next chapter.)

The NFER results and the work of other authors have been used to produce our model, which maps out the stages of transition through headship. The timings are approximate.

Stage 0 – Preparation prior to headship

Throughout their career people develop a conception of headship during their professional socialisation which is learned through both formal and informal processes. As the NFER and other studies (e.g. Ribbins, 1997) show, they learn from both good and bad headteacher role models.

The NFER heads said they learned about headship throughout their career but they particularly stressed the value of the following experiences prior to appointment as heads:

- the need for a wide variety of experience, especially as a deputy head
- the value of a period as acting head
- the importance of delegation by the head
- the rotation of deputies' responsibilities
- the need to work with heads who saw deputy headship as a preparation for headship.

Some heads spoke highly of management courses that they had attended as deputies, but most agreed that off-the-job training and development complemented experiences gained as a deputy working with 'a good practitioner'. The gulf from deputy to head was, nevertheless, seen as enormous: 'no course or reading matter can really prepare you for the job'. (Chapter 14 considers preparation and training for headship.)

Stage 1 – Entry and encounter (first months)

The first few days and weeks are a critical period when the new head's notions of headship meet the reality of a particular school. It is a time of 'surprise' and the importance of sense-making is highlighted as organisational socialisation begins and the new head attempts to develop a cognitive map of the complexities of the situation, the people, the problems and the school culture.

Stage 2 – Taking hold (3 to 12 months)

The newcomer strives to 'take hold' in Gabarro's terms, and the new heads begin to challenge the 'taken for granted' nature of the school. The NFER heads introduced a number of organisational changes. They develop a deeper understanding and their diagnosis of key issues during this stage was used to decide priorities.

This is also part of the 'honeymoon period', when staff are more lenient and open to change. In the NFER study we found that all new heads had such a period, though some did not realise it! The length of time varied, from about a term to possibly a year. It was often ended suddenly by negative staff reaction to an action of the new head, e.g. an internal appointment whom the majority of the staff considered the wrong person for the job (see Weindling and Earley, 1987, ch. 5).

Stage 3 – Reshaping (second year)

After a year in post most heads felt more confident and were beginning to feel that they could take off their 'L' plates! They had experienced a complete annual cycle of school events and learned about the strengths and weaknesses of the staff. Conversely, the staff had also learned about the new head's strengths and weaknesses, and their mutual expectations had become more realistic. The seeds planted in the previous stage now produced the implementation of major changes to reshape the school. This was the period of major change.

Stage 4 – Refinement (years 3 to 4)

After two years many of the structural changes were in place. But during this stage further curriculum changes were introduced and a number of refinements made. Previous innovations were fine-tuned and heads felt they were 'hitting their stride'.

Stage 5 – Consolidation (years 5 to 7)

After about five years a period of consolidation seems to have occurred after the heads had introduced most of their planned changes. However, in the NFER study this was affected by the introduction of a plethora of legislative and external change. These, as Gabarro similarly found, required attention as their impact may affect the school during any of the stages.

Stage 6 – Plateau (years 8 and onwards)

The NFER heads suggested that about seven years in one school was sufficient to see through a cohort of pupils and to have initiated most of the changes they wanted. This period corresponds with Day and Bakioglu's phase of disenchantment or Ribbins's enchantment. The NFER data showed that about a third of the headteacher cohort felt they had reached a plateau after ten years but that this was far less likely if they had moved to a second headship. Those in their second headship would move back to Stage 1. Motivating heads who stay in one school until the end of their career can be a problem (see next chapter). However, many of the NFER heads said they still enjoyed their work and, despite the changes to the role, still considered it to be the 'best job in education'.

The model is in the form of an ideal type and some caveats are necessary. Clearly the time periods attached to each stage must be treated as approximations. For example, if the school is in 'special measures' following an Ofsted inspection, the head has an external mandate to change and will move forward much more quickly. Also, different heads move at different speeds.

Whereas the NFER heads (1982–94) were able to introduce many changes internally, today's headteacher has to manage major multiple initiatives which originate externally, while at the same time, attempting to integrate themselves and shape the culture of the school. It seems likely that primary heads can move through the stages more rapidly than secondary heads owing to the smaller size and the less hierarchical structures of primary schools. They are also more likely to move schools rather than stay in the same post for many years. Unfortunately, the NFER study had too few woman heads – about one in eight – to make a comparison between male and female secondary heads. This means that it is not possible to say how gender differences might have affected the various stages of headship. Similarly, although gender issues and headship have been explored by Evetts (1994), Hall (1996) and Coleman (2002), who suggest that the career paths of women heads and the way they approached management differ from those of men, none of the three researchers develop a stage theory of headship.

But what do we know about heads, who becomes a head and how long do they stay? Do they have a shelf-life and how can they remain 'enchanted'? These matters are considered in the next chapter.

3

Who Becomes a Head and How Long Do They Stay?

The road to headship
Future plans
Length of tenure and performance

Of course, not all teachers enter education with a view to becoming a headteacher. Indeed, it is just as well they do not, as with over 400,000 teachers and only about 23,000 state schools in England there would be a lot of disappointed people! We know from our own research that of those who do become heads, there are some who achieve this via a clear and predetermined career plan ('I want to be a secondary head by the time I'm 40') and others who simply drift into headship ('I just felt ready for a change' or 'the job became available'). Serendipity and being in the right place at the right time were often important factors. The 2001 study of school leadership (Earley et al., 2002) found that 40 percent of current deputies had no plans to take on a headship although the percentage was much lower for those undertaking the qualification for headship (NPQH). So what do we know about the sort of teachers who become heads, in terms of their age, gender and other background characteristics, and what are their typical career paths and future plans? How long do they tend to stay in post and how do they maintain their effectiveness? These questions form the focus of this chapter.

THE ROAD TO HEADSHIP

There is little information available on heads' career paths. However, issues emerge when we compare what we found in our ten-year-long study of people who started their secondary headship in 1982–83 (Weindling and Earley, 1987) with the study of primary and secondary heads in 2001 (Earley et al., 2002). An overview of the path to headship of the two groups of headteachers is given in Tables 3.1 and 3.2.

Some interesting similarities between the two groups are found. The NFER cohort of secondary heads appointed to their first posts in 1982–83 were surveyed along with a sample of heads with three to five years' experience – referred

Table 3.1 Profile of secondary heads in the 1980s

New heads in 1982			Heads with 5 yrs' experience in 1982	
% of cohort	Average (yrs)		Average (yrs)	% of sample
100	42.1	Age on appointment	40.9	100
100	19.1	Years in teaching	17.2	100
25	0.8	Years as acting head	1.0	15
97	6.5	Years as deputy head/ senior master/mistress	5.0	88
26	3.2	Years as senior teacher	3.1	18
44	4.4	Years as head of house and/or head of year	4.0	47
86	6.4	Years as head of department	6.0	86
(n = 188)			(n = 228)	

Source: Weindling and Earley (1987)

Table 3.2 Heads in 2001: average number of years in senior posts

Post held	Average no. of yrs	% of sample		
		All	Primary	Secondary
Headteacher in another school	6.3	27	30	22
Acting headteacher	1.0	29	36	21
Deputy headteacher/deputy principal	5.4	86	81	93
Assistant head/senior teacher	4.0	11	3	22
SMT/leadership team member	2.9	27	37	19
Senior role in education outside of school sector	2.6	5	5	10
Senior role outside of education	–	0.5	0	2
(n = 758)				

Source: Earley et al. (2002)

to in the study as 'old' heads. Data from this survey are included to enable us to gain a better understanding of how the path to secondary headship has changed over the last few decades. In fact where comparisons can be directly made, the data show a broadly similar pattern to that of the route to headship 20 years ago.

In 2001, the positions that were held immediately before becoming a head were broadly similar to the 1980s (Table 3.3) with over three-quarters (77%) having held the post of deputy head immediately before becoming a head-teacher, and about one in eight being acting heads, although not necessarily at the same school. Far more primary heads (17%) than their secondary school counterparts (4%) had been acting heads immediately before taking up a headship.

Table 3.3 Post held immediately before becoming a head (percentages)

	1982 new heads (n = 188)	1982 experienced heads (n = 228)	2001 heads (n = 758)	2001 pri (n = 492)	2001 sec (n = 218)
Acting head	11	6	12	17	4
Deputy head	86	81	77	69	91
Senior teachers/ Assistant HT	1	7	2	–	–
Other (e.g. LEA officer, adviser, middle manager)	2	6	5	4	1

The possibility of becoming a headteacher without a considerable period as a deputy head is very small – it is rare in secondary schools and unusual amongst primary school heads. The proportion of people who had served as assistant head/senior teacher was similar in the 1980s to 2001 – 22 percent compared with 26 percent in secondary schools. Only 3 percent of primary heads in 2001 had been assistant heads as there are smaller numbers of such posts in primary schools.

About a quarter of heads in 2001 had served as headteachers in other schools. People on their second or third headship were more likely to be in the primary (30%) than secondary (22%) sector. A few had worked outside the school sector (more secondary than primary) and literally a handful outside of education.

The proportion of heads that were appointed internally to their posts has changed considerably over the last 20 years. In the early 1980s just fewer than one in ten heads were internally promoted but this figure had increased to 22 percent by 2001. The role played by the governing body in the appointment process is worth further investigation not only to explore governors' views of the merits or otherwise of internal candidates, but also to test out some anecdotal evidence about how appointment panels tended to opt for 'safe' white, middle-class, male candidates. (Chapter 11 explores the role of governing bodies in more detail, including their role in the appointment process.)

Secondary heads were appointed at about 42 years of age in the early 1980s – but the age groupings of heads in 2001 can be seen in Table 3.4. The appointment to one's first primary headship is usually at a much earlier age than it is to secondary headship. About three in ten heads of primary schools (29%), compared to one in 25 of secondaries (4%), were 40 or younger. At the other end of the age spectrum, nearly 15 percent of secondary heads, but only nine percent of primary, were over 55.

As far as gender and age was concerned, the female (primary and secondary) headteachers in the 2001 DfES study tended to be slightly younger than the males. Exactly one-half of male heads were over 50, compared with 40 percent of female heads. The most common age range for male and female heads was

Table 3.4   Age of headteachers in 2001 (percentages)

Age group	30 and under	31–5	36–40	41–45	46–50	51–55	56–60	Over 60
All heads	0.3	1.3	7.4	18.2	27.5	34.1	9.7	1.6
Primary	0.4	1.6	8.8	18.2	26.0	35.2	8.2	1.4
Secondary	0.0	0.5	3.7	16.5	30.3	34.4	12.4	2.3

(n = 758)

Table 3.5   Headteachers: time in post (percentages)

Time in post	Less than 1 year	1–5 years	6–10 years	11–15 years	16–20 years	More than 20 years
All heads	5.3	46.1	24.4	17.9	5.3	1.1

51–55, but there were significantly more female than male heads in the 46–50 age bracket (almost one-third of females compared to one-quarter of males were in this age bracket).

Only one in eight secondary heads in the 1980s were women. In 2001 the proportion of male to female headteachers was identical to the whole population – 47.5 percent were male and 52.5 percent were female. However, school phase was significant: 65 percent of the primary heads were female and 35 percent were male, compared with the 59:41 ratio for primary school teachers nationally. For secondary heads, the ratio was 33:67 female to male compared to 29:71 ratio for secondary teachers nationally. So the percentage of female secondary heads has increased considerably since the 1980s – from just fewer than one in eight in the early 1980s to about three out of ten in the early 2000s.

The heads in the 2001 survey had been in their present post for an average of 6.6 years, although again the range was wide from less than one year to 29 years, with the median or mid-point figure being five years. One-half had been in post for less than six years (see Table 3.5).

FUTURE PLANS

Headteachers in both the 1980s and 2001 studies were asked about their future work or career preferences. As can be seen from Table 3.6, the heads' preferred options were to remain at their present school (about 60% of all the three samples) or to seek retirement (37% of 2001 heads). Three out of ten of the 2001 heads included 'moving to another school' as a possible future work preference, which was a much lower proportion than the 1980s heads and one in five included amongst their options becoming a consultant or trainer. Exactly the same percentage of heads (13%) were considering leaving the education sector altogether.

Table 3.6 Future work preferences of serving headteachers (percentages)

Preference	1980s heads	2001 all	2001 primary	2001 secondary
Remain at present school	57 (60)	60	60	59
Retirement/early retirement*	–	37	35	38
Move to a different school	51 (42)	29	30	29
Become a Consultant/Trainer		20	18	24
Leave the education system for employment elsewhere	13 (19)	13	15	10
Take up an LEA post	17 (15)	10	10	6
Become an HMI/Inspector	13 (6)	9	7.5	10
Become a University lecturer	6 (6)	4	4	3
Other*	12 (16)	6	5.5	5.5

Notes. (Percentages do not add up to 100 as more than one response could be made)
(Figures in brackets for the new heads are from the 1988 follow-up survey)
*The 1980s study did not include this preference but 'Other' could include early retirement.

Of those considering moves, primary school heads were more likely to be considering leaving education altogether. Secondary school heads were more likely to consider consultancy work or becoming an HMI or inspector. Interestingly, the attraction of LEA work as a career option for secondary heads seems to have decreased over the years. No headteachers had worked outside education although 13 percent of the sample noted 'leave the education system for employment elsewhere' as a possible future work preference.

As might be expected, the older respondents were more likely to express a future preference to seek retirement or early retirement; however, nearly a third (30%) of those heads citing this preference were 50 or younger. In addition, 63 percent of those considering leaving education altogether were 50 or younger.

Table 3.7 shows the future headship preferences. Women were more likely than men to consider a second headship in challenging schools such as 'failing' or 'inner city' schools. Men were more likely than women to express a preference for a 'successful' school. The majority of heads who ranked their preferences for particular types of school, avoided schools in challenging circumstances. However, many expressed a preference for taking on a 'coasting' school, which, in itself, is a challenge and would provide an opportunity for a new head to make his or her mark. As one noted: 'I would enjoy shaking a coasting school into success – a challenge. But I'm less attracted to one already at the peak of success.'

LENGTH OF TENURE AND PERFORMANCE

Most headteachers – or rather secondary ones – do not move on to subsequent headships. The majority, once appointed, remain in the school for the rest of their careers. Of the people who were heads in 1982–83, nine out of ten were still there after five years and seven out of ten were still there after ten years.

Table 3.7 Future posts and school preferences of serving headteachers (percentages)

	Most likely		Least likely	
A 'failing' school	17	28	22	33
A 'successful' school	20	42	25	13
A 'coasting' school	23	43	17	16
An inner city school	17	23	19	41
A 'fresh start' school	11	21	25	42
A school situated in the 'leafy' suburbs	11	35	29	25
A school in the countryside	23	33	22	21
A school in an EAZ	7	33	29	32
A specialist school	12	25	24	38
A Beacon school	10	26	28	35
A school receiving Excellence in Cities grant	8	24	30	38

(n = 350)

At the time of the second survey (1989) the NFER heads were asked about their predecessors. It is not known how many of the NFER heads' predecessors had previously held other headships, but less than one in five (18%) went on to a second (or subsequent) secondary headship, whilst five percent took up other posts, usually related to education. The majority of the previous heads (71%) had taken some form of retirement with about one in six heads leaving their posts because of ill health (Earley et al., 1990, p. 6).

By the time of the third survey in 1994, 70 percent of the NFER heads were still in the same post as when they took up their first headship in 1982–83. This figure represents about one-third of the 1982–83 cohort of just over 200 secondary heads. Only one in 50 planned to move to another post. The vast majority of respondents (90%) said that there was a strong likelihood that they would remain in their present post in five years' time ('I'll still be here'). Many noted they were now 'far too old to move' and that modern headship was so demanding that headship candidates over a certain age were not looked upon favourably.

In the initial research of the 1982–83 cohort several heads, whilst recognising the value of career mobility and job movement for both themselves and their institutions, remarked that after five years or so it would be difficult to secure a second headship as appointment panels would most likely consider them too old for such a challenge. It is, therefore, interesting to note that, of the NFER heads' predecessors who were appointed to other headships, about one-half had been in post for seven to ten years, whilst the remainder had served as heads for between three and six years. All therefore had been in post for ten years or less – career movement to another headship after ten years was not common. Seventeen percent had been in post for 20+ years and 57 percent for ten years or more. The norm was, therefore, that the new post-holder followed a previous head who had been at the school for a considerable period of time until they reached the end of their careers.

Table 3.8 Current status of NFER heads in 2003

Retired	60
Still in post	5
Died	4
LEA/HEI/self-employed	4
Professional association	2
Unobtainable	6
Don't know	19

(n = 100)

Attempts were made to re-establish contact with the NFER heads who had responded to the 1994 survey in 2003, nearly 20 years after the first survey. It was extremely difficult to obtain information from schools about the where-abouts or present status of the heads. We found, as might be expected, that only a handful (n = 5) were still in their first headship post. The vast majority had retired although a small number had become consultants or taken up other jobs in education (see Table 3.8). What the data reveal, however, is that secondary heads do not in the main move on to second or subsequent head-ships. The majority, once appointed, remain in the school for the rest of their careers.

It could be argued that the above statistics from the longitudinal study along with those regarding career preferences (Table 3.6) create a static and rather disheartening picture in terms of current heads using their experience and expertise across a number of schools during their working lives. This sug-gests that attention needs to be given to finding ways in which the experience and expertise of serving heads may be used more creatively and flexibly. This is currently being addressed and is linked to the NCSL's notion of the fifth stage of headship – the consultant head (see Chapter 2).

Do leaders have a shelf-life?

Should headteachers be appointed, like many of their counterparts in business and commerce, on short-term contracts (say of five years' duration), as is the case in other parts of the world such as New Zealand? Do school leaders have a 'shelf-life', or is it more likely to be the case that the constantly changing educational environment in which they now work means that few get the chance to 'plateau out'? This was an issue we explored with the NFER cohort of heads (Earley et al., 1990). Did they feel there was an optimum period in post – say a five- to seven-year cycle – as has been suggested by some, after which leaders were not so effective?

In 1982 we asked newly appointed heads to comment on what they regarded as a reasonable period of time to be in post in any one school. Although there was not complete agreement, by far the most common response was to suggest an optimum period of between four and ten years. Yet 70 percent were still in the same school after ten years.

They were concerned that age was a factor that significantly influenced the likelihood of gaining a second headship. Heads who were approximately 50 years of age remarked how they were 'too old', although it was noted that there was no necessary relationship between age and performance. Of more importance was the willingness and ability to take on a fresh challenge. Headship was not seen as a job for those whose enthusiasm and energy had waned or weakened.

They also remarked that at a time of major educational reform it was not necessary to move posts in order to acquire new challenges and, in the current situation, schools required stability. Most could see the advantages that a limited term contract could bring, both for themselves and their schools, provided that proper guidance was available and that alternative career avenues (e.g. LEA officers and advisers) were viable options. Salary differences between sectors and the constraints of pension arrangements were also mentioned. The following extracts from the interviews with the NFER case study heads are illustrative of the range of views expressed (Earley et al., 1990, pp. 9–12):

> My gut reaction is that it's a good idea, it's in the interests of the service. On the other hand they (the LEA) have such difficulty getting heads that if they limited tenure I don't know what would happen ... If there were no security of tenure people would be severely put off.

> In terms of planning one's career it would be reasonably useful as an idea to have a limited contract ... I usually find myself looking for fresh challenges after six or seven years. I think that's about the right time to see a whole cohort through and then a short time for evaluation.

> I hope the days of 10 to 15 year headships are numbered. There is a point of staleness. It is only when you move into the next one that your energy comes back. The majority of heads are pretty good, but there should be an escape clause for those who are not so good.

> I don't think ten years is too long, given the role of the head, provided you can renew other areas of the school and you don't run out of steam, that you have energy still.

> I've always said if a school is not going forward it is actually going backwards. So a change is crucial and if you've been in post 12 or 13 years it is difficult to maintain the momentum.

Limited tenure?

Over the years there have been continued calls from educationists and others to introduce short-term renewable contracts for headteachers. In 1988, for example, David Hargreaves suggested that heads be appointed for three years in the first instance and then perhaps for subsequent periods of five years (*Independent*, 1 November 1988). In fact, 1989 saw the first limited period headship advertised. The post, a junior school headship in a Conservative-controlled metropolitan district in the West Midlands, had to be re-advertised and it is not known how many applications were received. The teacher unions advised their members to boycott the post and the successful candidate was given dispensation to apply by his professional association, as he was the school's acting head. The contract was for a five-year period and attracted a salary approximately ten percent higher than that normally received for the size of the school (*Times Educational Supplement*, 6 October 1989). Interestingly, this development has not been taken forward.

However, does it really matter how long heads serve? The response to this question largely depends on whether or not there is a relationship between length of tenure and levels of performance. There has been very little research into this key question, although a study of effectiveness in 50 primary schools in London, undertaken by Peter Mortimore and colleagues in the early 1980s (Mortimore et al., 1988), suggested that heads in mid-term (i.e. three to seven years) tended to have the most positive impact on their schools. A correlation was found between effectiveness and primary heads' length of service, although no details were given in the book. One of the authors, Pam Sammons, has recently written:

> We found long serving heads were associated with less effective schools – of course this does not mean all schools with long serving heads were less effective, it was a trend across our sample. Long serving heads were those with 11 or more years in the same post. We also found new heads were generally less effective (first 3 years). Mid term heads were associated with most effective schools (3–7 years in current post).
>
> With long serving headteachers the task is different and the implication for LEAs is that they need to find ways of supporting those heads and if possible of rekindling their energy and enthusiasm. In this situation in many school boards in the US or Canada, heads would simply be transferred from one school to another. In England, where heads have tenure within their schools, this is not possible. One way of helping would be for LEAs to provide sabbaticals of a term, or even a year, to [such] headteachers. Whilst out of their schools they could visit other schools, follow academic courses, or use the time to reflect on their aims and the changes that have taken place in education and in society, since they first became a head. When they returned to their school it is hoped they would have developed new ideas and enthusiasm. (Personal communication, March 2003)

In addition, the 'School Matters' study commented on the potential role of headteachers' centres and support networks linking new and experienced heads, ex-heads and advisers, and the need for suitable training in management and leadership, which as Sammons (2003) notes, are 'ideas which in the 1990s "took off" with the London Leadership Centre and the National College and special qualifications for heads (NPQH) and so on'.

Workplace performance is, of course, a notoriously difficult area to research but we wanted to gather views about how the heads themselves perceived this. We therefore asked the heads if, at this point in their career (i.e. in 1994, ten or more years after their initial headship) and with regard to their own performance, they felt: (a) they were continuing with the same enthusiasm as when they first became heads, (b) they had reached a plateau, and (c) they were able to face the challenges that lie ahead for the school. Just over 60 percent stated that they were working as enthusiastically as when they first started as heads, whilst about three out of ten commented that they were not. The same proportion (30%) noted that they had reached a plateau – 'had given of their best'.

Some made reference to such factors as age or the need to pace oneself: 'age is taking its toll on energy'; 'the enthusiasm is still there but not always the energy'; 'I'm aware I don't have the same energy as I had ten years ago'; 'I'm slower than I used to be'; 'fatigue does impair performance'. Others remarked how their motivation and enthusiasm had been negatively affected by years of constant change, initiative fatigue and 'poorly planned and faulty legislation'. One said, 'I am fed up with what I see as constant threatening political pressures, such as league tables and inspection'.

The strength of the senior management team was also seen as crucial: 'with a good SMT I'm sure we'll survive'. Governors were also seen to be useful here in providing different perspectives and acting as constructively critical friends (see Chapter 12).

A number of heads made reference to how their enthusiasm had been rekindled and 'plateauing out' avoided by the wealth of legislative change (e.g. 'being grant maintained prevents plateau'; 'It would be impossible to remain on a plateau in the present educational climate'). Similarly, the role of headship was constantly changing (e.g. 'the job has radically changed therefore enthusiasm continuing') and, for some, the school presented fresh challenges. However, the changes in the role of headship were not always welcomed. Several heads reported that their enthusiasm and performance 'waxes and wanes', 'varies from day to day' or was dependent on so many different factors. One head remarked: 'maybe my performance is OK but I feel my own enthusiasm has gone; the job is now a chore not a challenge'.

Professional refreshment

Very few had had the opportunity to work outside headship. One head had worked in an LEA's advisory service before moving back into headship and spoke of how stimulating this break from headship had been, providing as it did both personal and professional refreshment (Earley et al., 1994/95). An interesting small-scale study on this theme was recently published by a head-teacher research associate at the NCSL (Woods, 2002). His was a study of primary heads and, following Ribbins (1997) he referred to them as 'enchanted' – as opposed to disenchanted (see Chapter 2).

The choices of future work preferences made by the heads in our various studies raise further interesting questions. For example, one-fifth of head-teachers in 2001 mentioned becoming a consultant or trainer and about one-tenth mentioned becoming an inspector or HMI. To what extent is the current system sufficiently flexible to allow, indeed encourage, school leaders to become involved in these activities, particularly on a part-time basis? We know, for example, that by 2003 over 400 heads had been trained as 'consultant leaders' to engage in a range of NCSL 'level 5' activities, such as NPQH tutoring or coaching and mentoring. But it is not known what proportion of those undertaking activities such as Ofsted inspectors, threshold verifiers and performance management consultants are serving headteachers. The only area where we have accurate data concerns external advising to governing bodies, where about 40 percent of all advisers are currently serving heads and 29 percent were previously headteachers (Earley, 2004a).

There is already some evidence (e.g. Ofsted, 1999b) that such 'extra-curricular' activities can be powerful learning opportunities that bring benefits to both the individuals performing them and their host institutions. Providing assistance to those schools in special measures can also be an important source of professional development and growth (Ofsted, 1998). Participation in such a range of activities – what NCSL refers to as the fifth stage of headship: consultant leadership – not only promotes a broader perspective on the part of the individual, but also, most importantly, allows for developmental opportunities to be embraced back at school for those having to take on new responsibilities. Again, the role of governing bodies in encouraging or inhibiting school leaders from participating in this diverse and growing range of opportunities as 'consultants' is crucial here.

Sabbaticals and secondments in rejuvenating school leaders can also be helpful (e.g. see Clayton, 2001) as can a range of other activities, such as overseas visits and study tours (see NCSL website for the international opportunities currently available to school leaders).

Unfortunately we did not collect data on reasons for leaving education or for taking early retirement, so we do not know the proportion of our NFER heads who took early retirement and for what reasons. This is an important but unexplored area and was the subject of a small-scale project by an NCSL research associate. Alan Flintham (2003) in a report entitled *When Reservoirs Run Dry: Why Some Heads Leave Headship Early* divided departing heads into three types: 'striders', who move on in a planned way to a new challenge; 'strollers', who retreat but in a controlled way; and 'stumblers', who leave headship defeated, perhaps with ill-health retirement. He found the responses of heads differed and suggests that what is needed are mechanisms by which heads can share their experiences – 'to have someone to talk to'. Flintham argues that this should be a formal entitlement and be 'funded and legitimatised reflection opportunities, part of the leadership entitlement package available to all heads'. It appears that the loneliness and isolation of headship that we identified in the initial NFER study remains a key issue (Weindling and Earley, 1987, esp. ch. 8).

But what about the appeal of headship more generally – what is it about the job that makes people want to take it on? It is to this that we turn in the next chapter.

4

The Changing Appeal and Reality of Headship

The appeal of headship
Motivational factors
Demotivators
A changing role
Delegation
Teaching commitments

Why do people choose to become heads, to take on what is generally considered to be one of the toughest jobs in education? It was mentioned in the previous chapter that for some heads headship is thrust upon them, yet for others it is part of a carefully devised plan 'to reach the top'. So what is it that motivates people to want to become a head and, once in post, what keeps them going? This chapter begins by considering these questions before looking at the role of headship and how that role has changed and is likely to continue to change in the near future. What do heads think about their new role? In discussing this it draws extensively upon our data sets, the NFER longitudinal study – a unique cohort of heads who have lived through the major education reforms of the 1980s and 1990s – and the 2002 DfES project on the state of school leadership.

THE APPEAL OF HEADSHIP

Headship in 2001 was still an attractive option: 60 percent of the sample of deputy heads were considering the possibility of becoming a headteacher (Earley et al., 2002). But why?

When asked to provide reasons for wanting to become a headteacher, typical responses from NPQH candidates included the following:

To create a school community where everyone is respected and valued and where the pupils have the opportunity to excel in a variety of areas

I feel passionate about the role of a school and being a headteacher would allow me to implement and take forward my vision.

To become fully involved in community regeneration through accessing resources, sharing vision, offering enthusiasm and commitment and developing multi-agency links. To inspire and strive for high achievement for all stakeholders.

These aspiring heads clearly perceived headship in terms of 'making a difference', 'having an influence' or 'implementing their own vision'.

Others spoke of the importance of vision and teamwork. As one noted: 'My first task was to share my vision with all the staff and ask them did they feel they could work with this vision? Could they come with me?' Several of them also wrote about leadership and children, and the importance of 'keeping the child at the centre': 'My head and I constantly talk about what is really important for our school, our children and the future of the school.'

The above statements and the values that underpin them were very similar to what headteachers were telling us in the early 1980s. They too wanted to make a difference to the lives of young people; they too had a vision for their schools and wished to share that with their colleagues.

Middle managers interviewed in 2001 frequently made reference to headteachers who paid attention to 'strategic direction' and 'vision' and 'facilitating and leading teams'. They also appreciated headteachers who 'lead with a clear vision of development across the school'. In discussing the nature of leadership, middle managers also placed emphasis upon consultation: that they were consulted by those who lead them and that they in turn consult those they led. They valued team-building and advising and supporting colleagues as a major part of their leadership task. Similar sentiments were expressed about what staff looked for in their headteachers both in terms of desirable characteristics and traits (Weindling and Earley, 1987, p. 70). The Effective Management in Schools study (Bolam et al., 1993), in which one of us was involved (DW), also provides useful insights into what others deem to be 'good' leadership and management.

But what is it that motivates heads to give of their best and what do they find demotivating?

MOTIVATIONAL FACTORS

What is interesting is that the factors that motivate and demotivate – or in Linda Evan's (1999) terms 'what makes teachers (heads) tick' and 'what makes them cross' – also do not seem to have changed much over the years. Some of the motivating factors which inspire teachers to want to lead a school are implicit in the above quotes and comments. Becoming a school leader gives the opportunity for those who feel passionate about the job to 'implement their own vision', to 'make a difference', 'to give themselves a challenge'.

Perhaps unsurprisingly, the key aspects of leadership which heads found most motivating, in all our research studies, centred chiefly on people management – interacting with staff and pupils. Both were crucially important motivators for heads.

I love the job. I love children. I never stop being fascinated by them, entertained by them, amused by them, irritated by them. Never stops ever. That never changes. Everything else changes around you.

The joy you get from internal pressures because you're in control of that. And see children grow.

The really important pressures are the ones I feel in myself. Things that I want to do and be and enable other people to be. So that when I go they've got the rock that I feel now I can hang on to, that won't let me down whatever the outside pressures are.

A further important motivator was school success. For a number, this was closely linked to harmonious relations with pupils and staff. Heads referred to the school ethos, the growth and progress of the school, and academic results. One head expressed his satisfaction in leading 'a highly successful school with predominantly excellent working relationships' and another experienced 'a feeling of progress, achievement and worth' (Baker et al., 1995). Heads were also motivated by expressions of appreciation by pupils, staff, parents, visitors and the local community. What still made the job worthwhile was, in the words of one head, 'working with pupils, parents and staff, in a dynamic, warm and very supportive environment'.

Planning was also mentioned – by almost four out of every ten of the 2001 headteachers – and decision-making or challenge mentioned by just under one-third. About one in six said liaising with parents and the community was a motivating factor. The satisfaction of working with supportive and enthusiastic parents was mentioned by about the same proportion of heads in 1994.

For many, headship was still the best job in education, albeit exhausting, and offered many rewards. The following quotes from our 1994 survey give an indication of the strength of these views.

Headship as a task or career is potentially as rewarding as ever. It is varied, it is long-term, it involves people, it requires creative ability and vision, Those of us who chose the job because we sought that kind of fulfillment and felt we had those skills, are precisely the people who will feel frustrated, de-skilled and demotivated by the changes imposed by the present Government.

Taking into account the stresses, the strains, the interference, the paucity of budget, the increased competitiveness, Key Stage 3 testing, league tables, the Secretary of State and Ministers, I still love the job and have never got bored.

Headship remains the best job in the educational world – for me! One has a relatively open agenda, enormously varied days, the fascination (and instant delight) of seeing young people grow up, the privilege of working with highly skilled and professional staff and (still) a lot of control over your own patch.

(Baker et al., 1995, p. 39)

Chairs of governing bodies considered that financial remuneration motivated teachers to apply for leadership positions. This is interesting as teachers and deputies hardly ever mentioned money as a central motivating factor.

DEMOTIVATORS

For the 40 percent of deputies who in 2001 had no plans to become a headteacher, the main reasons for rejecting this option were that it involved 'too much stress' and that they preferred to remain a class teacher to maintain contact with children. For the heads the most demotivating aspect of headship mentioned was 'bureaucracy and paperwork', which were seen as overbearing and not always necessary. In 1994 it was 'the effect of government action on education'. Reference was made to government interference, bureaucracy and imposed decisions. Constant change was also seen in a negative light by about one-half of heads in 1994 and one-quarter in 2001.

Other key demotivators mentioned by both sets of headteachers were: budget and resources issues; the low status and negative media image of the profession; more generalised comments about stress and the demands of the job; and, problems with staff recruitment.

In 2001 change and innovation were seen as manageable by some head-teachers because they used new initiatives as a means of fulfilling the aims and objectives they had already set for themselves. Thus, they took control of change and had the confidence to say 'no' if they felt that a particular initiative was not timely or relevant to the needs of their school. Such schools usually had no significant staff recruitment problems, because their good leadership had seemingly set up a 'virtuous circle', resulting in relatively low staff turnover. They managed to get access to adequate resources, either through an LEA which had recognised the needs of their pupils, or through sponsorship and involvement in initiatives which brought in resources, such as an Education Action Zone (EAZ) or having Beacon school or specialist college status. These schools had a positive image of themselves as high performing and communicated this to the outside world both locally and nationally.

A CHANGING ROLE

But what do heads do and how has the role changed over the 20 years or so that we have been studying headship?

It will be of little surprise to know that the vast majority of the people who started headship in 1982 considered that their role had changed significantly since they took up their post. So much happened in that period (see Figure 4.1 for a list of some of the most important changes that have taken place since the Education Reform Act of 1988). The most important change that the heads referred to was the shift of emphasis from being the leading professional to being the chief executive, the business manager, the financial director. Interestingly, with more schools employing bursars or business managers, heads are now, in 2004, returning to the role of lead professional that they felt they were in the 1980s – 'leading the learning'.

In 1988 after five years in post, many heads expressed apprehension about local management of schools (LMS) and the prospect of having to deal with

- A National Curriculum for all pupils aged 5–16
- Assessment of all children at ages 7, 11, 14 and 16
- Publication of National Curriculum assessment, public examination results and truancy rates in the form of school 'league tables'
- A national system of regular external school inspection entailing publication of inspection reports by the Office for Standards in Education (Ofsted)
- An increased proportion of parents and local community representatives on governing bodies
- Headteachers and governors taking responsibility for financial management and the appointment and dismissal of staff under the local management of schools (LMS) initiative
- More open enrolment of pupils to promote greater parental choice
- The ability for schools to opt out of local education authority (LEA) control and become grant maintained (GM), funded directly by central government. 1,100 of the 25,000 schools became GM
- A code of practice governing provision for pupils with special educational needs
- New arrangements for supporting pupils from minority ethnic groups
- Promotion of specialisation through the creation of city technology colleges (CTCs)
- The expectation that each school will have an annually updated school development plan (SDP) and targets for student achievement
- A budget for staff development with an annual entitlement of five training days available for in-service training
- Appraisal of all teaching staff, including headteachers
- A national system for assessment and training for aspiring headteachers, and a requirement that future headteachers will have to obtain a national qualification before appointment
- The requirement that LEAs develop local schemes within central government reforms such as LMS and appraisal and support schools with implementation of all reforms.

Figure 4.1 Changes related to central government reforms that affected heads 1988–1994

the budget and premises. By 1994, however, the majority of the heads had come to terms with their new role as managers, and a number welcomed the opportunity to be 'captain of the ship'. Nevertheless, it was recognised that, with the new management role, there was a consequent increase in administration and paperwork. This resulted in heads having less time for teaching and for day-to-day contact with pupils and staff. Many heads regretted this.

Whereas in 1988, heads observed that they were moving more and more towards a managerial role and away from being the leading professional, in the 1994 survey three out of five respondents maintained that they had now become the managers of their schools. They had, as one head commented, 'even more to do with money, buildings, insurance, VAT and business generally'. Another person described himself as, 'I'm still the head to whom everyone looks for the final answer but I'm also financial director, marketing executive, architectural consultant, governor, trainer, and an expert on drains!'

Local management was now a fact of life and, although a few heads still felt they lacked the necessary skills, the majority no longer expressed apprehension or fear but, rather, welcomed the opportunity. Local management of schools gave them the opportunity and the freedom to make their own decisions. Nevertheless, although heads accepted full responsibility with accountability for their own affairs – the delegated budget, the curriculum, personnel, resources and the school site – they were concerned that they were, in fact, managing someone else's agenda. Multiple innovations driven by the government and centralist initiatives were, in their view, stifling innovation and initiative within the school. Heads registered their concern at government intervention and interference, the most serious of which was in the imposition of a centrally controlled curriculum. One respondent spoke of, 'less creativity in the generation of the curriculum, more institutional management'. Another commented: 'The school used to manage the curriculum, and others the finance. Now, the government tells us what to teach and we manage the money.' With management came an increase in administration and paperwork, much of which heads considered unnecessary and which had 'little to do with learning'. Another pressure from central government was open enrolment, which forced some schools to engage in more assertive marketing and created an atmosphere of competition between local schools. The publication of league tables exacerbated the situation.

Most heads said that the main factors in the changing role of headship were external. Internal factors were seen as having less effect, in contrast to the mid-1980s when industrial action by teachers caused so much disruption and stress.

The most important internal factor affecting the nature of headship by the mid-1990s was the new relationship with governing bodies. Whether this can be regarded as an internal factor is questionable however, since the enhanced profile and increased responsibilities of governors were initiated externally by government legislation. Headteachers found that they were now spending a great deal more time on governing body business. There were more meetings, committees and working groups, all of which had to be serviced. Heads referred to the need for managing the governing body, meeting its demands, keeping it informed and trained. One head regarded himself as a managing director responsible to governors: 'I have to provide a quality service to governors, which involves preparation beforehand, skill during, and action afterwards. It is very time-consuming.' Others maintained that the governing body needed to be managed effectively and this required 'a real balancing act between consultancy and executive action'. For some heads, it was questionable whether the governing body had the time, expertise or experience to carry out their legal responsibilities.

The Economic and Social Research Council (ESRC) review of 15 major research projects from 1991 to 1996, conducted by Wallace and Weindling (1996), confirmed and added to the findings from the NFER longitudinal study. It concluded that:

1 *Headteachers still play the pivotal role in leadership and management* – their authority for day-to-day running of the school means that they shoulder unique responsibility for orchestrating changes in response to reforms and harnessing the support of colleagues and governors to this end.

2 *There have been changes in almost every management task area* – whether they entail the requirement to carry out new tasks (like managing a budget and appraising staff) or to make changes in familiar ones (such as managing the curriculum and catering for pupils with special educational needs).

3 *A new and varied range of people are centrally involved in managing schools, with consequent changes in their working relationships* – reforms altering the balance of authority between school staff, governors and LEA officials have made it imperative to forge new ways of working through a variety of partnerships (within schools, as with SMTs, between school staff and governors, among neighbouring schools, as in cluster arrangements, or between the various agencies associated with exclusion of pupils from schools).

4 *There is greater mutual dependence between those responsible for and affected by management, requiring a substantial degree of participation* – the various partners must not only make an input but must also develop the ability to collaborate in making and implementing decisions.

5 *There is a positive role for LEAs in school leadership and management* – from providing training and other services to schools, through participation of LEA teams in Ofsted inspections, to offering support for management tasks such as development planning and school improvement.

6 *School leaders face a widening range of ethical dilemmas* – whether relating to educational values (e.g. under what circumstances to exclude pupils), political values (e.g. how far to seek a competitive edge by attracting pupils from neighbouring schools), or managerial values (e.g. how closely to involve governors in oversight of teaching and learning in the school).

DELEGATION

The increased workload involved in the overall management of the school, including managing the governing body, had meant a significant change in the way a number of heads approached the distribution of responsibilities. Heads felt the need for more delegation and greater teamwork. For some, this was not only now a necessity but also a deliberate change of leadership and management style. By 1994, with ten or more years of experience behind them, heads were more confident and relaxed about releasing some of their tasks to others. References were made to 'leading a team in a less hierarchical setting' and being 'much more of an enabler with, hopefully, a more open style'. Heads were less involved with the day-to-day management and more with 'leadership' – long-term and strategic planning – recognising that often they 'spent too much time doing jobs that should be done by middle managers and support staff'. But there was a problem, as one head explained: 'Delegating more is not necessarily a bad thing but I am delegating to those who themselves have too little time.'

There were areas of responsibility that heads would not delegate. Nearly half of the heads said they did not delegate matters relating to the budget. This did not mean that they expected to be involved in the day-to-day details of keeping the accounts, which many heads delegated to their deputies or a bursar, but rather that they saw themselves as responsible, together with the governing body, for taking strategic financial decisions and for budgetary policies.

Many heads considered the appointment of staff to be a responsibility they were unwilling to delegate to anybody else. Nevertheless, the majority accepted that making appointments was a responsibility they shared with governors and, more often than not, with members of the SMT. The appointment of staff is, in fact, often a crucial test of the extent of the confidence that exists between the head and the governing body. Most said they would not delegate attendance at governors' meetings. They believed their position was unique, not only in regard to the full governing body but also in relation to the chair of governors. Liaison between the head and the chair of governors forged a vital link in the harmonious relationships that form one of the prerequisites of an effective school. Some heads also wished to retain a personal link with the governing body committees, although, with the increasing meetings this involved, others were happy to delegate membership of some committees to deputy heads.

One in five heads felt they needed to retain responsibility for both staff and pupil discipline. They only expected to be involved in the most difficult issues and, in this sense, were the final arbiters in matters of exclusions and staff grievances, albeit that the governing body had certain powers to exercise in these matters.

For a number of heads, public relations and marketing the school had become of such importance in the competitive climate that they wished to take personal charge of this facet of school managerial responsibility. Other responsibilities mentioned by a few respondents as ones they were unwilling to delegate included the curriculum, curriculum development, and the academic structure of the school. Some heads continued to take personal responsibility for compiling the timetable, perhaps because of the oft-quoted view that 'whoever does the timetable runs the school'.

One in ten heads were unwilling to delegate responsibility for the school development plan, the school's aims and objectives and strategic planning. A similar number, however, were not unwilling to delegate any of their responsibilities, recognising that all decisions came back ultimately to the SMT for approval and that the final responsibility, 'the buck', always rested with the head.

Concern was expressed by heads about the volume and speed of change, the pressure of competition and the lack of time for teaching, talking to colleagues and 'getting round the school'. Nevertheless, heads were enjoying greater freedom for making decisions and easier, closer staff relationships. For many, the job was bigger but more exciting.

They foresaw an increasing emphasis on evaluation and quality assurance. The Office for Standards in Education was seen as playing an important role in the future, with the preparation for inspection being very influential in decision-making. One respondent took the rather gloomy view that, with Ofsted inspections, 'we shall be increasingly expected to conform to a particular management style and be buried under mountains of policy statements'.

The general impression in 1994 was that heads saw their future role as leading the school through a continuing period of great change in which the most important task was to maintain stability and 'keep the boat afloat'. One person saw the future as 'challenging, exciting and enjoyable' whilst another suggested, 'I shall be *primus inter pares*, leading the team of fellow-believers seeking a vision, demanding excellence and caring for all in their efforts to achieve it, ever willing to make and admit mistakes'. But there were some who believed that the head's role had reached its maximum of development: 'any more and it would explode'. A few heads had the pessimistic view that they were heading towards 'the management of chaos' and that, in the end, it would be 'heads and teachers who will have to try to create some semblance of sanity'. Reforms will crumble and heads will have to 'pick up the pieces'. A great deal would depend, it was thought, on what the (Conservative) government decided to do. If, for example, 'the government succeeds in its current agenda of total control and definition of the curriculum', the role will be either to manage as best as possible the narrow curriculum or to put back together the destroyed components of the previous education system. Some heads hoped that the previous system would return, that 'the pendulum will begin to swing back', and that heads will be more involved in teaching and learning and will once again 'exercise pedagogic leadership'.

How true this remark has turned out to be with the NCSL's recent emphasis on the pedagogic, on 'learning-centred leadership'. Notions of distributed leadership and learning-centred leadership currently being promoted by the NCSL, were therefore already beginning to surface as the future direction of headship. Entrepreneurial heads were also mentioned as a continuing trend and one that was becoming more important.

TEACHING COMMITMENTS

The term 'headteacher' has always implied that heads are involved in teaching – leading by example and showing that they can still 'cut the mustard'. The way that the role has changed over the years has meant that teaching is less likely to be a central component of the role. In light of the changing role of headship the question of whether heads should teach was specifically explored in our research. In 1988, the majority of the secondary headteachers (69%) had regular teaching commitments and also provided cover for absent colleagues.

Table 4.1   Secondary heads' teaching commitments (percentages)

	1988 survey (n = 123) %	1994 survey (n = 100) %
No teaching undertaken	3	14
Regular teaching commitment	21	25
Cover or substitution	7	13
Both regular commitment and cover	69	47

Only a very small number (3%) said they did not teach at all. In the 1994 survey, as shown in Table 4.1, the number of heads with a regular teaching commitment whilst also covering for absent colleagues, has fallen to just under one-half – and the number with no teaching commitment was much greater (14%).

Respondents were asked to comment on how important they thought it was for a headteacher to teach 'in the present context'. Considering the widely held belief that 'in the present context' most heads have had to leave the classroom, it is perhaps surprising to find that 85 percent of the headteachers in the 1994 survey were still doing some teaching. It needs to be borne in mind, however, that this survey was of *secondary* headteachers. The effect of the increasing number of other commitments on primary school heads may well be more significant in relation to their teaching.

The heads in our 2001 research – which, it will be recalled, included both primary and secondary heads – were also asked about the amount of time they spent in classroom activities, including teaching. The vast majority of heads (96%) involved in the survey still spent some time each week in the classroom. One in ten spent more than 50 percent of their time in the classroom, but for most (80%) it was a smaller part of their working week – up to 25 percent of their time. The kinds of activities undertaken by heads were: regular time-tabled teaching (cited by 60%), covering for absence (66%), covering for unfilled vacancies (8%), observation (85%) and coaching other teachers (33%). The differences between the phases – primary and secondary – can be seen in Table 4.2 which shows, suprisingly, a large proportion (nearly three-quarters) of secondary heads having a regular teaching commitment. Thus, in 2001, the majority of heads were still very much involved in the teaching and learning which goes on in their schools.

How much teaching was being undertaken by headteachers from 1982 is difficult to assess, but the indications are that the teaching commitment for many was reducing year by year. One head, for example, had reduced his teaching load from 18 periods to eight, out of a possible 45 per week, and others said that they would be teaching far less in the next year or would be giving up teaching altogether. On the other hand, there was a head who taught a 40 percent timetable, made himself available for cover, and did duties every day because he believed that 'that is where the school is'.

Table 4.2   Classroom activities undertaken by heads in 2001 (percentages)

	All (%)	Primary (%)	Secondary (%)
Regular time-tabled teaching commitment	60	57	73
Cover for absent colleagues	66	67	68
Cover for unfilled vacancies	8	5.5	12
Observing lessons	85	88	77
Coaching colleagues	33	24	31
n =	758	492	218

Source: Earley et al. (2002)

Nearly half of the heads who still taught said that the main reason was to retain credibility with staff and parents. They referred to the need to share the same problems, especially to show that they had some experience of teaching the National Curriculum and appreciated the concerns of staff about it. Heads wanted to show support and set an example. For some, it was a question of projecting the right image, of continuing to be 'the leading professional', teaching being part of their management style. Teaching, according to one respondent, was contact with 'the main business of the school which informs all other decisions'.

A number of headteachers continued to teach because they found it personally satisfying, desirable, a 'bonus'. One respondent regarded teaching as 'very good therapy on bad days' and another found it an 'oasis of calmness and peace'. A number of heads, however, recognised that their teaching could be seen as an expensive luxury or 'a piece of escapism'.

As far as contact with pupils was concerned, heads who did not teach a great deal believed that such contact was as effectively, or even more effectively, achieved by talking and listening to the pupils, by after-school activities and by being involved in the pastoral care system. Some heads who did not teach agreed that teaching was important but that it was no longer possible because of other commitments, in particular the number of occasions they needed to be out of school, and that if they were timetabled to teach pupils' education would be disrupted. This was one of the reasons for some heads (13% in 1994) undertaking only 'cover' as a teaching commitment. Substituting for absent colleagues gave heads the advantage of a wider perspective on the teaching and learning within the school. As one explained: 'I do cover as it allows me to keep an eye on grass-roots standards across all departments'.

Heads who did not teach believed that to do so was inefficient, not essential (especially in a large school), and 'not what heads are paid for'. Heads had to 'manage the whole plant' and were judged not by how well they taught, but by how well they managed the school. One head accepted that the teaching of the staff was better than his own, and therefore it was better for the pupils if he did not teach. Others felt deskilled as they had not been able to keep up with developments in the classroom and curriculum.

For the majority of heads, there was a recognition that management had to be their first priority and that the increasing commitments of LMS and, in some instances, grant maintained status, had made a substantial teaching commitment impractical. Nevertheless, they felt it was essential that they 'kept their feet on the ground' and retained contact with 'the core activity of the school'.

The decision whether to teach depended very much on the head's core values. It may be necessary to do some teaching if one's ability or credibility has to be proved but, as one head asked, should it not be assumed that heads had already established their credibility as successful teachers to have gained the positions held? Others remarked that headship in the late 1980s and 1990s did not necessarily include teaching. Staff recognised that it was often more appropriate to employ teachers; heads were paid to lead and manage schools and not necessarily to teach children. As one head commented: 'The head's contribution to the overall development and well-being of the school is better made in contact with the teaching staff, parents, the community and pupils around the school, rather than with a small number of pupils in a classroom' (Earley et al., 1990, p. 23). Heads were seen as having other means of relating to children and of operating as the leading professional. A regular teaching commitment was not necessarily important if heads had a high profile in the school and, it was suggested, this could be achieved by such activities as school patrols, cover and extra curricular activities.

Gray (1986), in an interesting polemic entitled 'Why heads should not teach', touches upon many of the issues raised in this debate. He argues that the deepest problem for heads is their own dilemma over whether they are managers or teachers, and that while most probably became school leaders because they wished to make schools better places, they found managing was, in fact, a less influential task than teaching. As one head remarked: 'It's the only time that one has control!' Gray argues that some heads seek satisfaction in classrooms to compensate for the dissatisfactions of management but 'feeling inadequate as a manager is not changed by engaging in a different activity'.

Gray is also critical of the 'credibility factor' and argues that since heads are essentially managers – or, more recently, leaders – there is no need to prove themselves as teachers. Most staff members, he suggests, will judge a head primarily by their competence as a head – they are more likely to accept someone being a poor teacher but a good head than they are the converse. 'Being a good teacher is not the qualification for being a head; being a good manager is.' Finally, he suggests that heads should indeed see themselves as teachers but not in relationship to the pupils, rather to their colleagues. 'Heads who prefer to teach students rather than work with colleagues are reneging on their managerial duties'. He suggests that heads often lack the skills of the adult educator or professional developer. This is the real challenge of teaching for heads and perhaps the challenge that is the hardest to face.

The next two chapters consider further the nature of modern headship and throw more light on the enactment of headship by examining the words and deeds of highly effective heads from both the primary and secondary sectors.

5

Outstanding Leaders

Characteristics of 'outstanding' headteachers
Leadership in action
Values-driven leadership

There is a growing body of research in the educational world on 'stars' or highly effective or outstanding practitioners. Lawlor and Sills (1999) found that such heads were characterised by a number of features or qualities, including clear, shared values and vision, a passion for pupils' development and achievement; well-developed interpersonal skills; a positive commitment to staff development, high expectations; risk-taking, political astuteness and high levels of knowledge and professional confidence. The primary head introduced in the next chapter could be said to possess all of these qualities and more!

This chapter draws on case studies of four primary, four secondary and two special schools undertaken as part of the 2001 DfES-funded study into leadership (Earley et al., 2002, pp. 90–138). It attempts to bring out the central features of highly effective or outstanding headteachers and we do so using the general term of values-driven leadership or 'principled principals' (see Gold et al., 2003). We chose the case studies on the basis of recent Ofsted inspection reports in which the schools' leadership and management were highly rated. Their excellence was confirmed by telephone calls to local education authority advisers. Six of the headteachers were male and four female. Some had been in post for ten years, whilst others were relatively new to the job. Through speaking to the headteacher, the chair of governors, members of the senior management (or leadership) team, middle managers, classroom teachers, pupils and the LEA adviser, we looked at how in each case the headteacher led their school communities and promoted, encouraged and distributed leadership.

This chapter examines the main characteristics of the outstanding leaders that emerged from the case study data. We also consider specific examples of 'leadership in action', and finally, using evidence from the case studies we show how 'values-driven leadership' (Gold et al., 2003) is central to ways of operating within schools.

1 Problem-solvers and solution driven leaders.
2 High visibility.
3 Development of a senior management or leadership team which was seen as strong and effective by the rest of staff.
4 A culture of clear and high expectations of performance.
5 Middle managers and subject leaders were seen as experts by heads as well as by the rest of the school staff.
6 A strong emphasis on continuous professional development.
7 Change mediated, negotiated effectively and adapted to fit the school's values and ethos.
8 Strong and involved governing bodies, or at least chairs of governors.
9 School leaders were effective 'resource investigators'.
10 Attitudes to ICT varied, although most were now using it for administrative and other purposes.
11 Central involvement in instructional leadership in their schools.

Figure 5.1   Eleven characteristics of 'outstanding' leaders and their schools (Earley et al., 2002, pp. 83–6)

CHARACTERISTICS OF 'OUTSTANDING' HEADTEACHERS

The DfES research identified 11 characteristics of headteachers and their schools (see Figure 5.1). They are presented non-hierarchically: no one characteristic is more significant than any other; rather a combination of the attributes and actions of these leaders seems to make them outstanding.

1   Several headteachers saw themselves or were seen as problem-solvers or as leaders who were solution driven. Sometimes they solved these problems themselves but, usually, they encouraged the rest of the staff to work towards solutions that suited the school community.
2   It was noticeable that there were comments about the high visibility of more than half the headteachers, although one was deliberately self-effacing.
3   Almost without exception, the heads had worked consciously towards the development of a senior management or leadership team which was seen as strong and effective by the rest of staff. Our case studies were of teams that were seen as strong, but consulting, respectful and listening. They managed to be separate enough to lead the school, but accessible enough to know how the school community wanted to be led.
4   The headteachers, staff and students made references to a culture of clear and high expectations of performance. 'No-blame cultures' and ongoing dialogues about the school's aims and processes were common. These leaders had the courage to tackle staff and pupils who were under-performing and the vision to offer support for improvement. The focus on high standards of achievement, both academically and socially, was obvious in the schools, with staff giving constant reminders of what was expected, and celebrating the achievements of all.

5   Middle managers and subject leaders were seen as experts by headteachers as well as by the rest of the school staff. Those middle managers who had been apprehensive and lacking in confidence upon appointment were well supported and the senior managers' reliance on them to manage their curriculum area gave them confidence, and shaped the rest of the staff's perception of them as experts in their area.

6   There was a noticeably strong emphasis on continuous professional development (CPD). In many schools, the headteachers brought courses to the notice of their staff members. But usually they interpreted CPD as much wider than courses, making sure that within the school, there were reflective conversations, 'learning on the hoof', and intentional role models and mentors. These leaders were prepared to take risks and to create a safe environment for others to do so. They were concerned to establish a 'professional learning community' (NCSL, 2001).

7   Most of the headteachers described mediating change, negotiating it effectively, and adapting it to fit the school's values and ethos. Despite their different levels of acceptance of change, all the headteachers were clear that they responded to the changes they thought were important and necessary, fitting them into their own priorities for the school. They varied from those who went to look for new challenges and for new ways of extending the role of the school, to those who were selective about chosen changes, and made sure that they enhanced what the school was trying to do.

8   The schools had strong and involved governing bodies, or at least chairs of governors. It seems that the most productive leadership partnerships were between headteachers and chairs of governors who were knowledgeable and had time for the school. Many of the chairs of governors were either ex-educators or people in allied or similar work who spent up to a day a week on school business. Several governing bodies were described as having 'led' or 'steered' the school through previously challenging changes.

9   Many of the school leaders functioned as superb examples of 'resource investigators' (Belbin, 1993). They investigated new initiatives and made use of the resulting funding; they found appropriate research to support their work, and they gathered evidence to help decide how to react to new initiatives. They saw resources (including information) as key to school development, and they either secured them themselves or encouraged other members of the school community to do so.

10 There were widely differing attitudes to ICT in these schools, although most were now using it for administrative purposes. Some schools consciously used it to look for research findings, others to help teachers manage paperwork, or to track student learning and performance.

11 The majority of the leaders in the case study schools were centrally involved in the instructional leadership in their schools, although in differing ways. Those who were less centrally and formally involved perceived their role as supporting the middle managers, working informally to

address a particular teaching and learning issue, or having professional conversations about the learning of individual pupils. Those who were more centrally involved (working in the smaller schools) did a substantial amount of teaching themselves, or took the responsibility for monitoring teachers' planning.

LEADERSHIP IN ACTION[1]

Several themes about leadership emerged about the leadership of the school in general (including members of the governing body, key parents and middle managers within the school) and some of them directly about the school heads themselves. The heads were mediating government policy through their own value systems, and interviewees spoke of the schools' strong value systems and the extent to which vision and values were shared and articulated by all who were involved in them. Interviewees in several of the schools used the name of their school as a descriptor for the way they operated (e.g. 'Kestonites'). The staff – both teachers and support staff – had absorbed the supportive and egalitarian ethos of the school, or its 'way of doing things'.

Staff commented on the importance of teamwork as a way of developing and sharing vision and values, and as a means of making sure that they shared the same values and adopted the same approach to the young people and to learning and teaching in the school. The whole idea of sharing and teamwork within staff groups could be difficult to foster at a time when external forces (e.g. pay differentials and performance management) could so easily encourage internal competition.

School leaders, especially heads, managed to promote and encourage shared values. They communicated their core values by:

- working with, managing and even searching out change
- paying careful attention to information management within the school – thus keeping staff constantly informed
- working very closely and sometimes seamlessly with their leadership groups
- developing leadership capacity and responsibility throughout their schools.

Each of these is briefly explored below.

Working with constant change

Most of the headteachers described mediating change, negotiating it effectively and adapting it to fit the school's values and ethos. Despite their different levels of acceptance of change, all the school leaders were clear that they responded to the changes they thought were important and necessary, fitting them into their own priorities for the school. They varied from those who

---

[1]This section draws heavily on Gold et al. (2003).

went to look for new challenges and new ways of extending the role of the school, to those who were selective about chosen changes, and made sure that the changes enhanced what the school was trying to do.

Several heads were generally proactive in their attitude to change, although for reportedly different reasons: one was good at 'environmental scanning', in order to anticipate 'what is coming along and preparing ourselves for it, so that when it does happen it's not such a shock'. Another remarked 'if you don't do something different, you won't move on'. At a school which had taken on lots of change the head explained that the new initiatives 'make the school feel good about itself and give people a chance to raise their own game and learn'. Yet another case study head used information and communication technology (ICT) to research and bring back new ideas to the school.

Several heads described the process of mediating new initiatives through the school's value systems as a reflective activity shared by all the staff: 'We're never stagnant ... it's because we never really leave things that long without review ... we're questioning all the time, it's constant review.' Another head who believed that 'change must be at the shop-floor if it is to be effective' and was seen by the staff and governors as a visionary, did not believe in change for change's sake – not all initiatives were considered to be good for the school, but all must go through a filtering process of 'a healthy disrespect for change'.

Keeping staff informed

The heads frequently referred to the importance of meetings as decision-making spaces and about the amount of information made available to staff. Meetings can be seen as the visible manifestation of a head's values system: clear ideals about respecting, transforming, developing and including staff can be evidenced by the importance given to meetings in a school and by the way they are run. The amount of information that is accessible to staff is also a values-led decision – notions of secrecy and exclusion from information do not encourage trust and empowerment or even informed decision-making. Many of the heads saw resources (in which they included information) as key to the development of their schools, and they either secured information (about funding, research and evidence about new initiatives) themselves, or encouraged other members of their school community to do so.

School leaders and other staff cited examples of how meetings and information were seen as important: in one special school, for example, teamwork was fostered and facilitated through meetings of the whole staff, team meetings and a programme of individual discussions between the head and all members of staff. The free flow of information within the school was referred to by many members of staff and was seen as contributing to the spirit of togetherness and the inhibition of any feeling of 'them and us'. In this school, good communication was not left to chance – there were systems in place, such as the staff-room notice board, the circulation of minutes of meetings and the weekly staff briefings, in order to ensure that information and ideas were freely shared.

In a large secondary school, a head showed her respect for her colleagues through the way she ran meetings: she constantly invited them to contribute their views, building consensus round the discussion and generally building agreement through the discussion. In another secondary school, teachers were encouraged to conduct research and enquiry, and most appeared to share a thirst for knowledge and investigation in the school.

In a smaller school, the headteacher used several strategies for encouraging a shared sense of purpose: staff meetings for discussions and review; a termly agenda-setting staff handbook which also included 'little articles ... depends on what the focus of the term is, or whether we've got problems or where we've got weaknesses'; and his way of spreading the use of ICT among his staff by giving them laptops.

Working closely with senior management and leadership teams

School leaders developed strong and effective SMTs or leadership groups which were accessible to other members of the school. Such teams were seen as strong, but consulting, respectful, listening and they could be trusted. The deputy head of a large primary school remarked that the school's SMT worked well together: 'we're all pulling in the same direction, sharing the same values'. The staff of that school held the head and deputy in very high esteem. Indeed, the relationship of mutual respect between the leadership team and the rest of the staff in the case study schools was strikingly similar.

The synergy of the parts of the whole SMT achieving more together than in isolation can be seen, for example, in a special school whose head commented: 'It's a bit like a machine – it's my job in particular to come up with good ideas, or to encourage the deputy head and the senior co-ordinator to come up with good ideas.' Another member of the staff of that school remarked: 'the head and deputy head are the school leadership ... the SMT is important, ultimately the headteacher is the boss, he makes the final decisions, he is responsible ... it's on his shoulders'. It was easier to trace the decision-making processes in this school because, although the headteacher worked creatively with his senior team to 'come up with good ideas', he ultimately took and was seen as taking, the final responsibility. However, in separate conversations with the school leader and his deputy, both of them stated that they did not always know which of them brought the new ideas to the SMT.

In an inner-city large primary school, the leadership team was made up of talented and committed teachers with high energy, where there was an over-riding ethos of consultation between the members of that team and between staff. It seems that this relationship was fostered by the school leader's beliefs and management style: 'a very personal type of leader. He practices what he preaches. He doesn't say one thing and do another. He knows everybody and will go above and beyond the call of duty'. Also, unusually for an inner-city school, the staff had been relatively stable and the school able to recruit and retain good teachers.

In the leadership team meetings of a large secondary Catholic school, individual members of staff were encouraged by the head to exercise full responsibility for specific areas of school policy. This entailed collecting data, taking decisions, developing schema and acting as an advocate. The head reinforced and reintegrated what they offered and invited everyone to pool their knowledge for the benefit of the meeting and for the school as a whole. There was an emphasis in the meetings of mutual appreciation, manifest in the careful, courteous way in which individual reports were listened to and discussed.

Developing leadership capacity in the school

Without exception, the heads paid great attention to the development of leadership capacity throughout their schools. For example, middle managers who had been apprehensive and lacking in confidence upon appointment to their present posts were well supported and the senior managers' reliance on them to manage their curriculum area gave them confidence, and shaped the rest of the staff's perceptions of them as experts in their fields. There was an expectation of continuing professional development for staff, both teachers and others. Forms of training and development were wide-ranging (such as reflective conversations, networking, role models and mentors) and more informal than in-service courses, but they set up an ethos or culture where people were prepared to take risks and to create a safe environment for others to do so.

In one secondary school, the headteacher had given key roles and responsibilities to the heads of faculty. Each had a devolved budget to run their subject area and was involved in appointing teaching staff. This challenged many of them, since these opportunities for leadership had not been delegated in the past. However, they welcomed the challenge and felt that the head trusted and supported them in the process, empowering them and giving them space to take risks, to try new things and to challenge decisions. As one long-serving member of staff remarked: 'The head trusts me to do more. I feel so much more valued now.' Staff at all levels within this school had opportunities for professional development: some were formal opportunities, others informal, such as being asked to lead on projects, to network and to work in other schools. Middle managers saw these opportunities as the most valuable form of professional development for taking on more senior roles. The fact that the school was widely networked within its locality and beyond gave staff and pupils the opportunities to experience leadership roles across a wide range of situations and school environments. The school was planning an 'Aspiring Senior Managers' residential course for staff.

Another large secondary school had a strong tradition of continuing professional development and training and ran a variety of in-school professional development programmes which included staff from other schools. Newly appointed staff were given individual mentoring sessions and were supported through the line-management system. Staff were developed by being involved in a range of initiatives and working parties, and often relatively inexperienced staff were promoted and given support for their roles. All were encouraged to think about career progression and were supported to take on responsibilities or to move to new schools if they chose. The headteacher 'gets a vast amount of pleasure from bringing staff on' and he hoped they 'never forgot learning their trade' at that school.

Since the case studies were completed in 2001, schools in England are continuing to contend with problems of staff recruitment and retention, as well as issues of workload and low teacher morale (e.g. PricewaterhouseCoopers, 2001). The ten schools visited showed how energetic and committed teachers stayed in the profession because they were given the opportunity to take on leadership roles, but with support and professional development.

VALUES-DRIVEN LEADERSHIP

All heads and other school leaders have – or should have – values, but what is not always clear from the relevant literature, including that published by the National College for School Leadership (NCSL, 2001), is their precise nature. This literature notes how successful school leaders are driven by personal, moral and educational values and are able to articulate these with total conviction, creating a clear sense of institutional purpose and direction (e.g. Fullan, 2003b). Such individuals have what Campbell et al. (2003) call a passion for the job. But what do their values look like?

Staff within the case studies were working in schools where the school leaders held a number of clear – and shared – educational values and beliefs. They were principled individuals with a strong commitment to their 'mission', determined to do the best for their schools, particularly for the pupils and students within them. They endeavoured to mediate the many externally driven directives to ensure, as far as it was possible, that their take-up was consistent with what the school was trying to achieve.

The origins of these values were not always clear (and this was not investigated as part of the DfES-funded research) but they might broadly be defined as social democratic or liberal humanist in nature. They were concerned with such matters as inclusivity, equal opportunities and equity or justice, high expectations, engagement with stakeholders, co-operation, teamwork, commitment and understanding. Related to these strongly held values, and mentioned by case study interviewees, were the personal qualities of the headteachers and other school leaders. These included, openness, accessibility, compassion, honesty, transparency, integrity, consistency, decisiveness, risk-taking and an awareness of others and their situations.

The case studies offer insights into how some of the above values and beliefs were demonstrated through the words, deeds and characteristics of heads and other school leaders. Their leadership was clearly values-driven and evidence from the case studies helps to provide a better understanding of the nature of those values and how they were most likely to be exemplified. This can be clearly seen in the next chapter which is a case study of leadership in action.

6

School Leadership in
Action – a Case Study

Keston Infants and Nursery School
Leadership style
Vision and values
Key themes and issues

In this chapter – school leadership in action – a case study of leadership in a primary school is used to offer a rich description of a highly effective primary head and her school.[1] Key themes and issues from the case study are identified.

KESTON INFANTS AND NURSERY SCHOOL

Keston Infants and Nursery School is located in spacious grounds, which it shares with the Junior school, in a residential area in the south of the London borough of Croydon. There are just over 300 pupils on roll, aged between three and seven, who come from a wide catchment area with most coming from a small local area of owner-occupied housing and a large council housing estate, part of which has been identified by social services as an area of social deprivation (13 percent of pupils are entitled to free school meals and a higher than average number of pupils for whom English is an additional language).

The school is very popular and its two reception classes are regularly oversubscribed (a third class has recently been created due to the number of children who had a successful appeal). The school has a good reputation for inclusion of, and provision for, pupils with special educational needs, although there is no designated provision for this. As a result the LEA directs a growing number of SEN children from outside the school's catchment area. Currently there are four children with autism and one with a cochlea ear implant (there are only two in the country in a mainstream school). One-quarter of the pupils, including four with statements, are on the school's special educational needs register. Attainment on entry to full-time schooling at age five, is wide ranging but generally in line with national expectations.

Keston school employs 11 teachers and 14 support staff, many of whom have been at the school for a considerable time. The staff is stable, secure and very experienced and in the first year of the scheme, all teachers who applied successfully passed the threshold.

Achievements

The school had a very successful Ofsted inspection in March 2000 when *no* key issues for action were identified. The report described Keston as 'an outstanding school' and went on to state:

> The school provides a high quality of education for all its pupils which enables them to develop self-confidence, very positive attitudes to learning and achieve their best ... together the whole staff work incredibly hard and are most successful in fulfilling the school's Mission Statement to 'create a happy, secure environment in which each child discovers the joy of learning, gains self-confidence, self-respect, and confidence in order to achieve high academic standards and to successfully meet the challenges and opportunities in their life'.

Keston is an improving and self-evaluating school which never rests on its laurels, improvements having continued to be made since the school's initial inspection in 1996. The head and staff are keen to improve the provision for all the children but the 2000 Ofsted report notes that:

> there are no areas in which the school could, realistically, improve further. High standards have been sustained in reading, writing, and maths and recent National Curriculum test results show the school to be in the highest five percent of schools in the country. Compared to 'similar' schools, standards are very high in reading, writing and maths.

The success of the school has been acknowledged and Keston (at the time of the research) was about to become a Beacon school (for literacy, SEN and inclusion, nursery provision; leadership and management and display).

The school offers a very friendly, open and supportive environment, the children are very happy and want to attend, it makes them feel successful in what they do, helps to raise their self esteem and makes them feel valued – 'Education is about more than SATs, it is for life'.

The staff and children work hard and pull together but the expectations of both are very high – much is expected and much achieved. Standards of teaching are described by Ofsted as very good with the staff, sharing with the headteacher and governing body, 'a tenacious commitment to sustaining high standards within the excellent range of curriculum opportunities provided by the school'. Teachers were said to have excellent knowledge of their pupils' strengths and weaknesses.

LEADERSHIP STYLE

The leadership and management of the school by the headteacher, governing body and senior management team are described by Ofsted as 'outstanding' and committed to sustaining the high standards achieved in the school.

Linda Hall, the headteacher, has been in post for over 12 years. She came from another school where she was deputy but also has experience of working outside education. The deputy headteacher, who has also been at the school for many years, was appointed by the new head having been acting deputy for one year prior to the head's appointment. The head and deputy get on very well with each other and work closely as the senior management team. Year Group leaders form the middle management team but the small size of the school and its egalitarian ethos meant that it was not considered hierarchical, with the weekly staff meeting being an important forum for debate.

This year neither the head nor deputy head teach (although the deputy is expected to return to the classroom in the near future) and their style is best described as 'management by walking about' (MBWA) – both are very visible and 'pick up things from classroom visits and share them with others', often at staff meetings.

Both work to engage and involve staff, their style of leadership being described as supportive and inclusive – regarding all that work at the school as part of the staff with each person having an important role to play. 'It's about being valued and being part of a team.' All the staff, including those in senior positions, are very approachable and advice can always be sought. A 'team approach' characterised the way the school and its leadership worked, there was no feeling of 'them and us', leadership was a shared notion although staff were also clear that the head was ultimately responsible and was trusted to act in the best interests of the school.

Those 'at the top' were seen as doing their jobs very well; they were highly respected and staff responded positively to any requests. The leadership was recognised as strong and purposeful but it was also seen as extremely good at delegating, facilitating and empowering others: 'You don't feel threatened by the leadership here – you're moved forward and in a positive way'. 'The head leads in a very positive but relaxed way'. 'She gives us space and respects our professionalism'. 'We're all involved right from the outset regardless of status – we're treated as equals.' 'Leadership is shared – the head involves everyone.'

The manner in which this approach was operationalised can be seen in relation to decision-making. The school was not a democracy, votes were never taken but all staff – from the very experienced to the newly qualified – were given the opportunity to contribute and were closely listened to. All were able, indeed encouraged, to make an input at weekly staff meetings, which were used to discuss and evaluate difficulties, successes and ways forward. For example, the decision to become a Beacon school was agreed once the consequences were clearly spelt out and a consensus reached after each individual's view was sought. Similarly, with the introduction of the 'literacy hour', the English co-ordinator presented the pros and cons, and staff were asked for their views and a decision made not to do it on every day of the week.

On other occasions decisions were made by the head alone – on some matters the staff felt she was better placed than they were to make informed judgements. But there was a sense of trust of the school's senior team and governing body, and a genuine openness in all that was done. 'We're kept in the picture – there's an openness about everything and their consequences are made known.' 'We're asked for our views about most things.'

Leadership at Keston was not 'in your face'. As described by one teacher: 'It's not so much an enabling or an empowering leadership as this implies a top down approach; it's more an approach that involves and includes you – it's involving or inclusive leadership.'

VISION AND VALUES

The most recent Ofsted report refers to 'a consensus and clarity of vision which is shared by all staff; they work extremely well together to fulfil the school's aims'. Ofsted had given the school public recognition but it was crucially important 'to recognise the good work that's going on and to say "well done", for after all there are no perks in education other than those who work around you'. It was important to say 'well done' to staff and children. This valuing of everybody involved in the school was a centrally held value but the head also believed that if a job was to be done then it should be done well.

The head's vision for the school had not changed very much since her appointment – she knew from the outset what she wanted to achieve for the school and this reflected her own background. She was very aware that different children had very different opportunities in different schools. She wanted her school to treat all pupils equally and to offer an all-round education. This had been a challenge but staff had been excited by this and were prepared to work towards its achievement. The school was very much the making of the head's vision but it was a shared vision. A centrally expressed value of the school was that 'Everything we do is for the benefit of the pupils'. The school had been successful in creating a disciplined environment, but one which was sufficiently relaxed to encourage creativity and learning – the children (as were staff) were always encouraged to question and to give of their best.

A core value of the school was valuing what people had to offer but to do this in a non-patronising way. Everyone was valued for what they brought into the school and everyone wanted each other to do well. Staff were given 'ownership' and constantly reminded that what they did made a big contribution to the school and its development.

Care was taken when appointing staff to ensure that they would fit into the culture of the school. Some staff referred to themselves as 'Kestonites' having absorbed the supportive and egalitarian ethos of the school. There were no status differences amongst staff and the whole-school community would, on occasion, socialise together. Opportunities were frequently taken up to celebrate and to give thanks, e.g. the head sent notes of congratulation to staff, flowers given in assembly to departing dinner ladies. Staff were happy to reciprocate and it was quite common for the head to receive tokens of appreciation for something she had done.

Working at Keston was variously described by staff as relaxed, happy, supportive, like a family or a team. Camaraderie was clearly evident and there was 'a joy at work' where 'everybody laughs a lot!' and there was 'never any tension in the staffroom'. There was a willingness to share good practice and knowledge, the atmosphere was relaxed and there was mutual respect and openness.

The head liked to be 'ahead of the game' and kept abreast of developments via such sources as consultation documents ('a good sign of what's coming up') and DfES websites. She was also a regular reader of the educational press and attended meetings of her professional association. The head was of the view that the school's high standards 'could only be maintained through effective leadership, management and self-review, always trying to analyse what we are doing in order to do it better'. She saw her responsibility 'to give a clear direction of what needs to be done and why, and how we can achieve this'.

Instructional or learning-centred leadership

Although the head did not have a regular teaching commitment she was determined not to divorce herself from the children and made concerted efforts to visit classrooms to both monitor and look at samples of pupils' work. Both the head-teacher and the deputy were in and out of classrooms regularly and the staff were used to this and did not find it threatening. Both were very much 'hands on' and demonstrated by example, e.g. the deputy showed how to teach the literacy hour (both had an LEA-wide role in relation to the literacy hour). Teachers were used to visitors (including the occasional governor). Monitoring was conducted by the senior staff and curriculum co-ordinators but it was mainly of an informal kind. (Teachers could expect to be observed at least termly.)

The staff showed a genuine interest in how children learn and develop, and even over lunch it was not unusual for the talk to be about teaching and learning (pedagogy). Good practice was regularly advertised and celebrated. The head had good knowledge and understanding of nearly all the children. The emphasis, for both staff and pupils, was on giving positive feedback. The senior staff were regarded with high esteem, afforded much respect and credibility, and seen as first-rate practitioners and as 'leaders of learning'.

Leadership and the community

Keston was seen as a village school and tried to be part of the local community, endeavouring to involve itself in community activities (e.g. visits to the local bakery and the library, floats, book trail). The school operated an open-door policy with parents, and parental involvement was seen as crucially important – parents were encouraged to share things with the school and to be aware of their role in their children's education. Home visits were made to every Nursery and Reception child prior to starting school. There were close links with the local church; the ex-curate was a governor and the lay reader conducted fortnightly assemblies.

Leadership and governance

Ofsted noted that the governing body fulfilled their responsibilities extremely well. They were seen by the school as very supportive, especially to the head, who had another group to turn to when help was needed. The head made a point about including governors and keeping them informed about everything – 'to ensure they were not divorced from what's going on in school'. There was a recognition that the governors' role might become a different one if the school was not succeeding but the aim was to 'go forward together' and to work in tandem with the staff.

Both the past chair and present chair of the governing body were former teachers. The chair had been a governor for nine years (since her retirement as a teacher at the adjacent Junior school for which until recently there had been a common governing body) and chair for the last three years. She spent about one day a week in school.

Each governor has a curriculum area or responsibility and was encouraged to visit and observe classes in action (they were asked to complete a monitoring form). Governors were perceived as very supportive and several currently worked in the school. They saw themselves as well informed about the school and its activities; they were made to feel at ease, each new governor attended an induction course and they were encouraged to be involved as much as they wished.

There was mutual trust and respect and the head was held in high esteem. As with the staff, governors were encouraged to state their views and were not afraid to disagree with the professionals. They were 'never made to feel unwelcome or unimportant'. This central value permeated the whole institution and the way it operated. The governors' role was one helping to make sure things ran as smoothly as they could – 'helping to take the pressure off people'.

Governors were invited to participate in a training day when the whole-school three-year development plan was formulated. Governors made every effort to attend with staff and to share ideas, ask questions and set targets. Curriculum planning, teaching methods and the vision for the school were all discussed at these INSET days.

Leadership and multiple innovations

The constant change of the last decade had helped to keep the head motivated – 'there's been so much change that you can never relax!' Her approach to leading and managing this welter of initiatives had been to make a judgement and decide what required instant attention and what could wait. Also – and this comes with a growing self-confidence and assurance – 'not jumping simply because someone tells you to jump!'

The head protected her staff, filtered external demands and tried to ensure that 'we do what we think is best for our children'. Her expertise in knowing how to pace change and not to overload staff was widely acknowledged. Staff were always given adequate time to respond. The head was also good at environmental scanning, being able to anticipate 'what is coming along and preparing ourselves for it, so when it does happen it's not such a shock'. The sooner something was known about then 'we can prepare for it and pick out the good points'.

The school was always looking at their own practice with a view to improvement (e.g. listening skills, questioning skills). The latest challenge was becoming a Beacon school and moving to three forms of entry. The school had a very positive approach to change – staff were not afraid of it and were very supportive of each other – 'there's always someone there to help you if needed'. The school tried to ensure change was seamless and built upon what it was already doing.

Leadership and professional development

Approaching change in this way was a powerful form of professional development in itself but many other forms were also found. The way the school operated meant that staff learned from each other through such things as joint planning and mutual observation. Staff were encouraged to avail themselves of all opportunities (e.g. in-house shadowing of curriculum co-ordinators; job sharing with a view to taking over in the future) and the head kept staff informed of CPD opportunities, specifically mentioning courses that were thought to be useful. There was a system of mentoring in place and lots of opportunities to observe good practice.

There was a subject focus each term, often identified through monitoring, and outcomes were discussed at staff meetings to improve provision in the focus subject. Staff were encouraged and enabled to monitor each other and findings from lesson observation fed back to individuals and discussed at staff meetings for subject development. This in turn developed whole-school provision, including strategies for teaching.

The school provided an excellent grounding for staff who were encouraged to take on a whole-school approach and to think about their career development. Many opportunities were available for staff but many did not wish to leave the classroom for promoted positions or even to undertake training during school time. Teachers were loath to leave their classrooms as with 'little ones' they 'needed to be there all the time'. Also so much change had been experienced in the last decade or so, that teachers did not want the further challenge of taking up senior posts. Teachers were happy at Keston, morale and job satisfaction were high, so it was asked 'why move?' It was not that life was cosy – far from it – it was hard work and much was expected, but importantly it was an enjoyable and relatively stress-free place to work. Some teachers did envisage moving on and were extremely appreciative of the learning opportunities that were being provided simply by working in such a well managed and led school. Newly qualified teachers (NQTs) became very rounded individuals and the school was seen as a good training ground, and young teachers were expected to gain promotion relatively quickly. Keston was an excellent place to work, offering high job satisfaction – 'I know I am at a very good school'. As such there was a reluctance to leave for pastures unknown.

The head's own professional development included being a mentor for new heads in the LEA, and she had experienced a short secondment as an Ofsted inspector of initial teacher training (the school had also been involved in the Articled Teacher scheme). The head had yet to undertake the LPSH but felt that feedback on performance was very important and would like her staff (rather than the governors) to set her performance objectives as they were well placed to know what she does well and not so well. However, whatever CPD opportunities were taken up by the head, they would have to relate back to her core principle – 'it would have to benefit the children and show some immediate impact'. The head and deputy often went on courses together, partly to develop the working partnership between them.

Leadership and evidence-based practice

Keston was very much a self-evaluating school, keen to improve but wanting to base this on evidence of what works (e.g. boys' writing; listening skills). New initiatives were always evaluated and the school was keen to move forward being able to absorb new ideas, evaluate them and adapt them to their best advantage.

Ofsted noted that the school undertook excellent analyses of National Curriculum test results, baseline profile information and other standardised testing. The senior team and the relevant co-ordinators examined data and looked for trends which were discussed with the whole staff. Co-ordinators were now doing this analysis without prompting. Such enquiry had led to changes in school policy or schemes of work. Why, for example, did boys do so well in writing and did this mean the girls were disadvantaged?

Leadership for inclusion

Inclusion was very high on the school's agenda and the intake included pupils from across the ability spectrum and a growing proportion with language difficulties and defined special needs. All the Nursery staff had undertaken speech and language training, and the headteacher and several teachers had formal qualifications or received training in special educational needs. The head's spouse worked in SEN and she had a personal and professional interest in inclusion. Staff had seen the benefits to mainstream children of having SEN pupils in class. But it was not inclusion for inclusion sake – 'only if we feel the child will benefit as a result'.

KEY THEMES AND ISSUES

- Having a non-teaching head and deputy was hugely helpful. The school was well resourced with excellent classroom support. The head was a great fighter for and acquirer of resources.

- Trust, honesty and openness – staff felt the senior staff were on their side and fighting with them to do all they could to provide a quality experience for the children. Keston was a very close knit community of which the governing body was a part.
- A stress-free atmosphere was found, largely created by effective management and leadership. The senior staff were recognised as 'putting in the hours and pulling their weight'. Stress was minimised and collaboration and mutual support created by a strong emphasis on teamwork and valuing everyone's contribution. There was laughter in the staffroom and the classroom – this showed people worked well together.
- Clearly the head was a key player, but it was not a 'one person show'. The success of the school was seen as related to its effective leadership – but there was a strong collaborative culture and distributed leadership, no marked hierarchy, no 'them versus us'. If the head left the school it was strong enough to continue to achieve high standards, etc. It has the capacity to continue to succeed but it would be a major challenge for any successor – Keston is a highly successful school, it can only go down!
- There was no desire on the part of most staff to take up more senior positions – preparation for deputy headship courses in the past had no take-up. Many staff wished to remain in the classroom, not wanting to be a manager but to stay with the children. The head's role had changed so much, taking her more and more away from the classroom. Even new teachers were slightly apprehensive about leaving such a good school.

NOTE

1. This case study is an extended version of the one first published in Earley et al. (2002, pp. 110–15).

7

Accountability and Ethically Responsible School Leadership

Induction of newly qualified teachers
'Rogue' schools
Professional responsibility and public accountability
What needs to be done?
Conclusion

This chapter considers the professional and ethical responsibility of school leaders to their staff. This is examined with reference to human resource development, particularly the provision of induction for newly qualified teachers, and in the context of central government mandated policies (e.g. the induction circular). Notions of professional responsibility and public accountability are used to analyse the small number of 'rogue' school leaders who, within the new legislative framework, treat newly qualified teachers unprofessionally and waste public resources. Drawing on research that one of us (PE) did with induction expert, Sara Bubb, we argue that ethically responsible leadership is more important than ever. The growth of site-based management, greater school autonomy and the devolution of resources make it crucially important that headteachers act morally and responsibly and develop a school culture that supports teacher learning and development. The notion of unethical leadership is examined and a typology of 'rogue' school leaders developed. The various sanctions that can be deployed against 'rogue' school leaders are also noted. How LEAs and school governing bodies handle their monitoring and accountability roles and manage such school leaders is considered. Finally, suggestions are made for improvements, such as the need to clarify professional responsibility and refine and strengthen systems by which headteachers are held to account.

INDUCTION OF NEWLY QUALIFIED TEACHERS

Between 1992 and 1999 there were no national regulations in place for the induction of new teachers. Hence, individual schools and local authorities were free to choose whether or not to offer their own model of induction and how extensive their programme of support would be. So, for seven years there was neither assessment of the first year of teaching nor a requirement for schools to provide induction. There were many instances of good practice by schools and LEAs but these were isolated from one another. It was up to the 'professional integrity of heads, teachers and advisers to sustain and encourage good practice' (Bleach, 1999, p. 2). Nevertheless, the broad agreement between the profession, LEAs and successive governments was that the induction of NQTs was inadequate and ought to be improved.

It is against this background that the induction of NQTs was made statutory in England in May 1999 with the issuing of the government circular 5/99. Induction to be 'a bridge from initial teacher training to effective professional practice' (DfEE, 1999, para. 1). It gives a reduced timetable and a framework of monitoring, support and diagnostic assessment. No longer should a successful first year of teaching be a matter of luck and favours: it is an entitlement that should be planned by schools, funded (in 2003) at £3,000 per NQT per year, and which headteachers are required by law to give. Now, all NQTs have to complete a statutory induction period of a school year (full time). The policy has two main principles:

- a national entitlement for NQTs to support and professional development
- assessment of NQTs against defined national standards.

Induction is therefore a mixture of pressure and support. Support comes from feedback after half-termly observations of NQTs' teaching, the individualised and structured support programme to meet specific objectives, induction tutor and ten percent reduction in timetable for professional development activities such as observing other teachers. Pressure comes from the observations but mainly from the assessments undertaken by the school at the end of each of the three terms that make up the induction period. Those who do not meet the induction standards at the end of the year are deregistered from the General Teaching Council and so can never teach in a maintained (or non-maintained special) school again. This dire consequence is a great inhibitor for new teacher development.

A large-scale research project into induction in England conducted at the Institute of Education found that the vast majority of NQTs, heads, induction tutors and representatives from LEAs believed that statutory induction was beneficial, particularly in helping NQTs to be more effective teachers (Bubb et al., 2002; Totterdell et al., 2002). Many heads and induction tutors thought that the structure of induction had accelerated the progress of their NQTs, enabling them to get to grips with aspects of teaching earlier than previously. The policy has also raised expectations of what should be achieved in the first year of teaching.

Contravention of induction regulations

Induction in England is a top-down government-led policy but it addresses a popular need and is based on ideas about what people know to be the important issues in induction, and has sought to address weaknesses in previous practices and policies. However, the variability of experience that was a feature before the induction policy is still a factor. The national evaluation found that a fifth of NQTs did not receive all their reduced timetable throughout the year, a fifth did not think their induction tutor gave useful advice, one in 11 had not observed any other teachers, three-quarters had some non-teaching responsibility and half considered that they taught classes with challenging behaviour (Totterdell et al., 2002). What we need to know more about is the 'patchy periphery'; the 'rogue' schools and their heads that do not conform to the regulations and what can be done to ensure that all NQTs receive their statutory entitlement to a good induction experience.

There are widespread contraventions of the induction entitlement reported by teachers in the *Times Educational Supplement* new teacher forum. Though there are meant to be procedures in England for NQTs to air dissatisfaction at both school and LEA level, research suggests they are rarely used. For who is going to complain about their assessor – the head and induction tutor – when these people can recommend a fail which would result in the NQT being forever barred from teaching in a school? Few NQTs aired grievances officially, but moaned informally. The tension is summarised well in this NQT's words:

> At the end of the day, no matter what structures are in place, it's actually very difficult to discuss problems. I want to pass my induction year and if this means keeping my head down and mouth shut that's what I'll do. The alternative is to highlight problems with my support and then have to face awkward times with my induction tutor or head, with the implications that might have on whether they pass or fail me.
>
> (Bubb, 2003b, p. 18)

Newly qualified teachers are dissatisfied with inconsistency of provision, which they see as unfair and bringing into question the status of induction as a whole. Individual new teachers appeared highly aware of the provision *other* NQTs were receiving because they stayed in contact with college friends through networking sessions and courses. Indeed, the most common area needing improvement identified by the NQTs surveyed was tighter monitoring of school provision.

'ROGUE' SCHOOLS

Of particular concern are the persistent offenders – what we call the 'rogue' schools and headteachers (Bubb and Earley, 2003) – and their accountability. If schools can be identified as at risk of not getting induction right, then something can be done to help the situation.

We considered looking at how much of the induction entitlement certain schools failed to give, but this did not provide a clear picture. The national evaluation found that NQTs highlighted that it was the *whole* induction package that mattered rather than being able to say that one element was more beneficial than another (Totterdell et al., 2002). The factors that seemed most common across schools whose NQTs reported weak provision centred around two features:

1 The level of management competence.
2 The degree of intent to flout regulations and guidance.

Level of management competence

The effectiveness with which schools are managed and led is an important factor for the implementation of any policy. Certainly the complexity of the induction regulations means that schools need to be knowledgeable about the rules and procedures, and proactive in organising the reduced timetable and nominating and training an induction tutor. Effective management of induction at school level was found to be essential. Newly qualified teachers highlighted the regularity and structure of various practical elements as beneficial. In schools where there was a teacher shortage, induction tutors had less time to spend with their NQTs and cover for the ten percent reduced timetable was difficult because the demand for supply teachers elsewhere was very high. Schools in difficulties were more likely to have inadequate induction provision. This in turn often led to new teachers avoiding or leaving the very schools that needed them most.

Degree of intent to flout regulations and guidance

The other dimension of induction compliance is that of wilful intent: the deliberate intention to flout the induction regulations and guidance. This concept allows one to distinguish between those schools that neglect their new teachers deliberately from those that do so out of ignorance, misunderstanding and incompetence. It is helpful to analyse compliance with the spirit of the guidance as well as with the actual compliance with its statutory elements. For instance, there are schools which do not manage to provide scheduled induction tutor sessions but whose ethos is so supportive that new teachers thrive through enormously helpful informal support networks. There are others that on paper appear to be complying with the regulations but where new teachers don't make the expected progress because everything is given at a minimum and a grudging level. In some the balance between support, monitoring and assessment is weighted towards the latter, with the result that NQTs get bowed down by pressure. In others the emphasis on support to the neglect of the other elements results in new teachers not making progress and being deceived into thinking that they are more effective than they are.

Schools with poor induction practice can thus be conceptualised in terms both of how well they are led and managed and how deliberately they decide not to comply with regulations (see Table 7.1).

Table 7.1 'Rogue' schools: a typology

High

	A. Well-managed school that is ignorant of the regulations and guidance	**B.** Well-managed school that deliberately flouts the regulations and guidance
	C. Poorly-managed school that is ignorant of the regulations and guidance	**D.** Poorly-managed school that deliberately flouts the regulations and guidance

Management competence (vertical axis)

Degree of intent to flout regulations and guidance

Low ➝ High

It is therefore possible to identify four broad categories of schools:

A The well-managed school that does not comply with the regulations and guidance out of ignorance.
B The well-managed school that deliberately flouts the regulations and guidance.
C The poorly-managed school that does not comply with the regulations and guidance out of ignorance.
D The poorly-managed school that deliberately flouts the regulations and guidance.

In our research (Bubb and Earley, 2003) we found examples of schools that fit each category.

Type A schools: well-managed non-compliers who are ignorant of the regulations

We found very few schools in this category, as might be expected. Contraventions of induction policy were rarely deliberate, but more due to key personnel in schools not being up to date, perhaps because the school rarely appointed NQTs. Those we did identify were quick to remedy weaknesses in provision when they realised the need.

Alpha is a successful and well-led secondary school, which gets good results. It has a stable staff, and has not needed to appoint an NQT since induction became statutory in 1999. Hilary, the NQT, was mature and highly qualified in her subject. However, these apparent strengths became her Achilles heel because staff assumed that she would not need as much support as the average NQT. Her classroom was isolated and she had no head of department to check her plans or drop into lessons. The school left her to her own devices. They considered that she must have been doing well because the extra-curricular activities that she organised were successful. Induction provision was at first non-existent but when the LEA monitoring pointed this out the school was quick to remedy matters. However, the harm was done: she was a poor teacher who argued with everyone who suggested that she had weaknesses, blaming the school's lack of induction compliance in the first half-term for all subsequent problems.

Type B schools: well-managed but who deliberately flout the regulations and guidance

This category is also rare, but much more problematic in terms of outsiders seeking to improve such schools' practice. The reasons why headteachers flout regulations are varied. Sometimes their maverick or eccentric behaviour is seen as part of their effectiveness and applauded. They may decide not to support NQTs because their priorities lie elsewhere: for instance, they may believe that pupils' education will be affected by giving new teachers a reduced timetable. However, the leaders of *Beta* school showed no such philanthropy.

Beta is a very well-managed primary school, which gets good results from a socio-economically disadvantaged group of students. However, its management of human resources is less impressive. It employs large numbers of NQTs: over a third of the staff in any year. The school gives NQTs half a day out of their classroom a fortnight rather than every week, meaning that they only have a five percent reduced timetable.

No staff have attended induction tutor training. There are NQT meetings with induction tutors but they are not supportive, nor are they intended to be – they are line-management meetings to ensure that the NQTs are conforming to school policies. The only induction is into the school's systems and procedures, not to meet any individual needs or interests. Newly qualified teachers have no choice in how to spend their reduced timetable but are told what to do and whom to observe. They are not allowed on any courses despite all other primary NQTs in the LEA attending the local programme. Each NQT has objectives but these are set for them rather than being negotiated. Observations are carried out by people within the school, but they are done to monitor and assess, rather than support and, so, NQTs dread them. All assessment reports are completed, but without any meeting with NQTs to discuss the content.

Almost all the NQTs (ten out of 11) left during or at the end of their first year at *Beta* school. The four NQTs whom we interviewed spoke of severe bullying: 'They (the SMT) made my life miserable.' They found the experience damaged their self-confidence enormously: 'I nearly left teaching altogether, and it took me six weeks to build up the confidence to start looking for work again.' We were unable to discover how many of the ten who left remained in teaching.

Type C schools: poorly-managed and not complying with the regulations out of ignorance

This category is more common than the other types. Sometimes there is genuine ignorance of the complexity of the induction requirements but more often it is simply that, where schools have many problems to deal with, induction provision falls to the bottom of the pile of priorities.

At the time of the research the head and deputy of *Gamma* secondary school had been suspended. Others within the school had to take on greater leadership roles. The school was in crisis for a long time, with staff leaving and replacements not being found. Student behaviour deteriorated. The suspended deputy had been the induction tutor but left without letting anyone else have the necessary information. The school was understandably in chaos.

For one and a half terms the NQT, Lucy, taught as full a timetable as other teachers. Induction was only arranged after she complained to the LEA in the second term. The LEA acted quickly, visiting the school and trying to ensure that this basic provision was in place. Unreasonable demands were made of Lucy. She taught classes that would challenge an experienced teacher and the SMT did not always back up the school behaviour policy. At the end of the first term her head of department left the school and was not replaced. The only other member of the department was a part-timer, so Lucy had to take on some of the tasks of a head of department and set work for the supply teachers who were taking the head of department's lessons. She had little help with students with special needs because the special needs co-ordinator was on sick leave for much of the second term. The NQT was also the form tutor for a difficult Year 9 group.

Lucy did not enjoy her first year. She left at the end of the year, without having another job to go to.

Type D schools: poorly-managed that deliberately flout the regulations

This category is rare but difficult to deal with due to the deliberateness of the contravention of the policy and because in a poorly led school it is invariably difficult to get to the roots of a problem.

Delta school is for students with severe learning difficulties. The LEA judged that the head's management of the school was poor and her leadership style was autocratic. John trained at the school on the graduate teacher programme. The headteacher considered that the school had supported him enough during his training year and that he did not need any additional support: induction would for him be unnecessary and the money could be better spent elsewhere. She deliberately flouted the regulations – John had no element of induction except for the three termly reports – but did not return the £3,000 the LEA provided for induction costs.

Unreasonable demands were made of John. He taught a very large class by special school standards – 15 nine-year-olds with severe and widely differing special needs. One boy was very violent. The climate in the school was not conducive to raising any points or making any criticism. John did not know any of the LEA personnel to complain to.

John enjoyed his first year as a qualified teacher, despite it being very tough. He was completely committed to his students and is still working at the school.

PROFESSIONAL RESPONSIBILITY AND PUBLIC ACCOUNTABILITY

In devolved education systems the counterpart of greater freedom at institutional level is an increased need for accountability to show how such freedom has been used. Accountability has been defined as 'a condition in which individual role holders are liable to review and the application of sanctions if their actions fail to satisfy those with whom they are in an accountability relationship' (Kogan, 1988, p. 25). Professional responsibility – a sense of being governed in one's conduct by professional answerability to colleagues about how one justifies the way one's work is done (Davis, 1991) – can be seen as one of several kinds of accountability. Indeed, teachers and schools have four kinds of accountability relationship:

- to pupils (moral accountability)
- to colleagues (professional accountability)
- to employees or political masters (contractual accountability)
- to the market – where clients have a choice of institution they might attend (market accountability).

Within England over the last decade, the accountability framework has been dominated by Ofsted, the government's school inspection agency. As part of its framework for inspection, Ofsted examines a school's provision for professional development, including the induction of NQTs. Where such provision is found to be a serious weakness, it would be identified as a 'key issue' and one which the school would be asked to include in its 'post-inspection action plan' (Ferguson et al., 2000).

Headteachers are therefore publicly accountable to Ofsted for the effective use of public funds and the overall quality of the school, but they are also accountable to others – most significantly, parents, governing bodies and LEAs. Indeed, one of the heads' professional associations has argued that there is a need for 'intelligent accountability' as currently their members are over-regulated (SHA, 2003). However, as far as NQT induction is concerned, LEAs have a key role in monitoring or quality assuring arrangements.

The role of LEAs

Local education authorities are accountable for ensuring that all their schools with NQTs carry out induction properly. They are meant to monitor the quality of:

- induction provision in schools
- assessment reports
- NQTs' teaching performance.

However, the national evaluation found that 14 percent of schools have very little relationship with their LEA beyond the submission of termly assessment reports (Bubb et al., 2002). Moreover, the turnover of personnel responsible for induction within LEAs is high. This is a concern because it takes time and experience to set up effective procedures and build relationships with schools. Some LEAs are proactive but most are more reactive. The above case studies of the 'rogue' schools illustrate different approaches. *Alpha* and *Beta* schools are in LEAs that can be described as proactive. They had systems that spotted problems, and then tried to remedy them, albeit unsuccessfully in the case of *Beta* school. *Gamma* school's LEA was reactive. It moved quickly when asked to remedy a problem but the NQT had to complain first. *Delta* school's LEA had quality assurance procedures but they came too late to help an NQT who had received no induction support or monitoring because they were not proactive in seeking information until the end of his first year of teaching.

Whilst LEAs have responsibility for induction, they have only limited powers to control what actually happens in their schools. This means that they need to ensure compliance by devising ways to encourage, guide and influence; they cannot impose change. Several did this by publishing induction newsletters and sending out questionnaires. The latter was effective not only in providing a picture of provision in the area but in reminding people about all the elements of the induction entitlement in the government circular.

Responsibilities and sanctions

Induction is a positive experience for most new teachers, and the current regulations in England are a distinct improvement on previous arrangements (Earley and Kinder, 1994; HMI, 1988). However, the 'habitat' in which they spend their early years is crucial. Induction can help their speed of development (Bubb, 2003b; Earley and Bubb, 2003) but also determine what sort of a teacher they become. It is in everyone's interests for new teachers to be highly effective as soon as they can and for as long as they can.

We have described England's induction arrangements as a carrot and stick policy for new teachers. Should there not also be some carrot and stick response to heads in terms of their induction provision? They are responsible, both morally and professionally, for the development of school staff, including NQTs. However, as resources are increasingly devolved to schools, there are few sanctions that can be effectively deployed against 'rogue' schools and heads. Local education authorities may decide that a withdrawal of funds is the ultimate sanction but these funds have increasingly been devolved directly to schools. As noted above, LEA advice and guidance can be easily ignored and whilst NQTs are free to raise their concerns with their union, the school or the LEA, few do so for obvious reasons – the school makes the decision about the success or otherwise of the NQT's first year and whether or not they have met the induction standards.

Neither do Ofsted inspections of schools provide an effective deterrent. They take place infrequently (every six years) and it is clear that unless the school is seriously failing to provide an adequate education for the students, the inspectors are incapable of exerting the pressure needed to ensure compliance. They identify key issues for action that schools are expected to respond to, but whether they do so or not depends on whether they are seen as important by the school (Ferguson et al., 2000). In some cases, inspectors appear to get it wrong. For instance, inspectors visited St John Rigby in 1996, 18 months after the headteacher began using the school funds as 'a personal bank' (Revell, 2003) for which in 2003 she was sentenced to five years in prison. Ofsted reported that 'the principal and the senior management team provide strong leadership and a clear ethos'. Financial planning and administration were 'good'. The school provided 'good value for money' and the auditors' report was 'excellent'.

School governing bodies, another body to whom heads are accountable, are being encouraged to act as 'critical friends' but they have been shown not to be a strong accountability mechanism, their effectiveness often hinging on the attitude and approach of the headteacher. The headteacher as chief gatekeeper to information about such matters plays a key role (see Chapter 12).

WHAT NEEDS TO BE DONE?

The sanctions for non-compliance at the moment are weak and there is little that can be done to counter the activities of unprincipled or 'rogue' school leaders. It is therefore essential for the preparation and training of heads and other school leaders to stress these wider responsibilities within a system of site-based management and, crucially, for those responsible for their appointment to give due attention to questions of values and ethical leadership (Gold et al., 2003). In order to ensure that headteachers act both accountably and responsibly, we suggest the following:

- LEAs identify potential 'rogue' schools.
- Ensure that all school leaders understand the regulations, the benefits of induction and the consequences of poor experiences.
- Tighten systems of accountability.

LEAs identify potential 'rogue' schools

Our typology of 'rogue' schools may help LEAs identify NQTs that are likely to suffer from poor induction experiences. This will enable them to use their finite resources efficiently by proactively checking that new teachers in 'at risk' schools are receiving a good induction experience – and to do so early on, before damage is done. 'Rogue' schools that are not complying out of ignorance or poor leadership can be fairly easily supported. Where non-compliance is more deliberate, tougher measures will need to be taken, as we illustrated in the case study of *Beta* school.

Ensure the regulations and guidance, the benefits of induction and the consequences of poor experiences are understood

In our research we found numerous examples of misunderstandings of the induction regulations by school leaders. Although NQTs for the most part are knowledgeable, some heads are not, particularly if they have not employed new teachers in recent years. Training and the clear dissemination of key information for all school leaders are imperative.

Research shows that there is a positive correlation between 'enjoyment' of the induction year and whether key elements of induction, such as an accessible induction tutor and ten per cent reduction in timetable, are in place (Bubb et al., 2002; Totterdell et al., 2002). Where NQTs perceived themselves not to be receiving a 'fair deal', they were quick to consider alternative opportunities – to leave the school and sometimes the profession. The consequences of poor induction experience have an impact on retention, and ultimately on recruitment. The cost to the profession of teachers whose self-esteem has been affected is huge – to say nothing of the effects of attrition.

Tighten systems of accountability

In the context of site-based management, devolved budgets and the absence of ring-fenced monies for induction with the new changes to the Standards Fund that the DfES implemented in April 2003, it is essential that school leaders be clear about their accountability in providing adequately funded induction arrangements. Heads are responsible for all arrangements and judgements concerning NQTs – though they can delegate tasks, they cannot shirk this important responsibility. They need to be held to account for how they spend the funds that the school receives for induction. This will mean that the money cannot be spent in other ways. 'Rogue' headteachers need to be accountable not only to their staff, governing body and their LEA, but also ultimately to the General Teaching Council – the professional body responsible for maintaining and judging contraventions of professional standards.

CONCLUSION

Ultimately induction is a matter of *professional accountability* – a professional and ethical responsibility – to students and staff working within schools and to the profession as a whole. Intelligent accountability, as O'Neill (2002) reminds us, is inextricably linked to a sense of trust requiring more attention to good governance and much less fantasying 'about Herculean micro-management by means of performance indicators or total transparency' (ibid., p. 58). Values-driven leaders or 'principled principals' (Gold et al., 2003) are concerned about the well-being of their staff and strive towards improving the quality of teaching and learning in their schools. Ethically responsible leadership is more important than ever but cannot be mandated or legislated for. The growth of site-based management, greater school autonomy and the devolution of resources make it crucially important that school leaders act responsibly and develop a school ethos or culture that supports both student and teacher learning (see Chapter 14). Efforts therefore need to be made through the preparation, training and professional socialisation of school leaders to ensure that they are responsible and accountable for their actions, both to their profession – including its recent recruits – and to the wider community. We need to ensure that the next generation of teachers is given the best possible start and that they are not lost from the profession. As one headteacher put it: 'If they don't succeed we're all going to fail because we won't have teachers to put in front of students ... if these NQTs now don't get the time to develop properly we're on a slippery slope – we've got to look after them.'

8

Images of Leadership

The research reported in this final chapter of Part 1 uses metaphors to explore conceptions of school culture and leadership. It reviews research on metaphors, the changing images of principals, and how heads and deputies see their roles. An awareness of these images can help people to become reflective practitioners who are better able to improve their ways of working.

METAPHORS AND IMAGES

Lakoff and Johnson (1980) believe that metaphors are 'pervasive in everyday life, not just in language but also in thought and action. Our ordinary conceptual system, in terms of which we both think and act, is fundamentally metaphorical in nature'. Metaphors always involve a sense of paradox because they invite people to think about themselves or their situations in ways that are patently false. For example, the metaphor 'my manager is a fox' invites us to see the fox-like aspects of the manager: their cunning, guile, craftiness and smooth image. But we have to ignore other ideas – about the black pointed nose, fur, four legs or tail. Metaphor works by playing on the pattern of similarity and difference. There is nothing self-evident in the meaning of the metaphor; meaning has to be created by those involved. They only have impact when they ring true: one cannot force a metaphor to work. When different people generate different metaphors that have a great deal in common, one knows that one is dealing with highly resonant insights.

In the US metaphors and images have been used to consider the nature of organisations (Morgan, 1986), conceptions of the school (Bredeson, 1988) and the nature of the principalship (Bredeson, 1985; 1987; Beck and Murphy, 1993).

In Australia, Grady (1993) presented a series of metaphors to teachers and asked them to rate how closely they represented their school.

In *Images of Organisation*, Morgan (1986) presented evidence to show eight main metaphors for organisations: machines, organisms, brains, cultures, political systems, psychic prisons, flux and transformation, and domination. In a later book, *Imaginization* (Morgan, 1993), he describes a technique to help people develop new ways of thinking about organisations and their management. He believes that managers need to 'read' the organisation through a set of frames because different images generate different insights. Morgan links this idea to Schon's (1983) notion of reflective practice. A reflective practitioner for Morgan is someone who is aware of how implicit images, ideas, theories, frames and metaphors guide and shape their practice, and how they can be used to create new possibilities.

In *The Fifth Discipline*, Senge (1990) believes that a new view of leadership is required in learning organisations. He feels that the traditional view of leaders is rooted in an individualistic and non-systemic perspective where leaders tend to be seen as heroes. 'At its heart, the traditional view of leadership is based on assumptions of people's powerlessness, their lack of personal vision and inability to master the forces of change, deficits which can be remedied only by the few great leaders' (ibid., p. 340). In the learning organisation the metaphors of the leader are those of 'designers', 'stewards' and 'teachers'. For Senge, the work of leaders includes the design of the organisation's policies, strategies and systems in a way that integrates all his five 'disciplines'. For him the new work for leaders is to design the learning process whereby people throughout the organisation can deal productively with the critical issues they face and develop their mastery. Senge says that effective leaders perceive a deep story and sense of purpose, which lies behind their vision. He calls this their 'purpose story', which gives unique meaning to the leader's personal aspirations and hopes for the organisation. From the story, the leader develops a unique relationship with their own vision and they become the steward of the vision. In learning organisations leaders may start by pursuing their own vision, but as they learn to listen carefully to other's visions they begin to see that their personal vision is part of something larger. It ceases to be a possession and becomes a *calling*.

The role of the leader as teacher is to help people achieve more accurate, more insightful and more empowering views of reality. Leaders need to teach people how to see the big picture – how the different parts of the organisation interact, and help them focus on the purpose story. These are the hows and whys. Senge believes that leaders talented in integrating both the story and the systemic structure are rare – one reason why learning organisations are still uncommon.

CHANGING METAPHORS FOR US PRINCIPALS

Beck and Murphy (1993) used a historical approach to determine how the image of the US principal in the literature has changed between 1900 and the

1990s. They found that in the 1900s principals were seen as teachers with administrative responsibilities and as the guardians of accepted values. By the 1920s the dominant view was of the principal as scientific manager, but there were also numerous references to spiritual and religious value images. These disappeared in the 1930s and the stress was on principals as business managers and school executives. For the 1940s and 1950s principals were leaders of democratic schools, while in the 1960s principals were asked to use proven strategies to promote excellence. The 1970s' principal should lead the way to solve social problems. In the 1980s principals were asked to manage schools to promote the development of a stable economy. The early 1990s were part of the second wave of educational reform – the restructuring movement. Beck and Murphy argue that this created new demands on principals that can be seen in metaphors:

- *Leader*: a move from the manager to the leader.
- *Servant*: how to lead not from the top of the organisational pyramid, but from within the web of interpersonal relationships. To use empowerment rather than control.
- *Organisational architect*: principals have to reshape the school to the changing external environment, and become proponents of change.
- *Social architect*: in this role principals have to bridge the connection between the conditions of education and the changing social fabric of society.
- *Educator*: the principal must become the head learner in the school.
- *Moral agent*: this concerns the fundamental issue of values and the moral issues of schooling and the principalship.
- *Person in the community*: principals must continue to remember that their work as an educational leader is first, foremost and always with people. The key concept here is that of equity.

FOUR FRAMES TO LOOK AT LEADERSHIP

Bolman and Deal (1991) devised an instrument to explore how school principals and other leaders perceive their leadership style in terms of organisational frames or lens. Using the frames provides a different perspective on what leadership is and how it operates in organisations. The four frames are called political, human resource, structural and symbolic.

1 The *political frame* points out the limits of authority and the inevitability that resources are too scarce to fulfill all demands. The principal is power broker or statesperson. The school is seen as a collection of special interest groups and the task of the principal is to mould these into a school-wide coalition. Conflict is seen as a natural by-product of collective activity and the principal confronts and encourages it.

2 The *human resource frame* highlights the importance of needs and motives. In the imagery of the school as extended family, the principal's

leadership role is concentrated on meeting individual needs. He or she gives praise and constructive feedback to promote both satisfaction and growth. The principal listens and helps teachers and students grapple with personal strengths and weaknesses.

3   The *structural frame* emphasises productivity and assumes that organisations work best when goals and roles are clear, and when the efforts of individuals and groups are well co-ordinated. The school-as-factory image emphasises the principal's role as engineer or supervisor. As an engineer, the principal focuses on designing a system of roles and relationships that uses the talents of staff, supports the instructional programme and allows the school to deal with the environment. As a supervisor, goals are clearly defined and the principal sees to it that these are translated into objectives for teachers and non-teachers.

4   The *symbolic frame* centres attention on symbols, meaning and faith. Seeing the school as drama or theatre requires the principal to be a poet or symbolic leader. The principal spends time building the culture of the school – shaping and articulating shared values, celebrating heroes and heroines, orchestrating key rituals dramatising the school's identity, spreading its merits in stories, working hand in hand with the priests and priestesses, storytellers and gossips to keep the spirit of the school alive and the core values and beliefs intact. As poets the principals articulate visions, speak about the school in artful prose, capturing the emotion and passion of the classroom or playground.

Bolman and Deal use metaphors to type effective and ineffective leadership within each of the frames.

- Effective leaders are seen as:

Structural frame:	social architect
Human resource frame:	catalyst, servant
Political frame:	advocate
Symbolic frame:	prophet or poet.

- Ineffective leaders are seen as:

Structural frame:	petty tyrant
Human resource frame:	wimp, pushover
Political frame:	con artist, hustler
Symbolic frame:	fanatic, fool.

In later work Bolman and Heller (1995) reviewed research on school leadership and suggested that views of leadership for each frame have changed in the following ways:

Frame	From	To
Structural	Autocrat	Analyst and social architect
Human	Good father	Catalyst and servant
Political	Great warrior	Negotiator and advocate
Symbolic/cultural	Hero as destroyer of demons	Hero as creator of possibilities

Deal (1987, p. 244) stresses the importance of using each of the four lenses or frames as a means of understanding schools as organisations:

> By becoming instructional leaders principals may very well jeopardise the leadership they need to provide as counsellors, engineers, power brokers or poets. Effective schools meet human needs, get things done, negotiate an arrangement between existing factions, and create meaning for those who learn, study, support, or appreciate them. Effective principals are those who focus time and attention on each of these areas. They see the school as a family, as a factory, as a jungle, and as a carnival. They rotate their lens like a kaleidoscope, finding different patterns in the social world they are asked to administer. They enjoy providing leadership for each. They know better than to concentrate their efforts on one view – even if researchers and policymakers tell them that they should.

Frames and UK primary schools

Lee Bolman kindly gave us permission to use his leadership frames questionnaire in the UK study of leadership in large primary schools, and 25 of the heads we visited completed the self-assessment instrument. As a comparison, we were also able to work with a group of 75 heads of smaller primary schools (Southworth and Weindling, 2002). The data from the frame questionnaires were analysed for schools with over and under 400 pupils. As Bolman and Deal had previously found, the heads used all four frames. But the heads of the large schools had significantly higher mean scores than those of the smaller schools on the political ($p = .006$), and structural ($p = .003$) frames. The results for the human resource and symbolic frames did not show statistically significant results. This indicates that while all heads use the human resource, or interpersonal style the most, the size and complexity of the larger primary schools means that the relative importance of the structural and the political frame increases for these heads.

EMPIRICAL WORK ON EDUCATIONAL METAPHORS

Researchers have employed both qualitative and quantitative methods to study the use of metaphors in educational settings. One of the early examples was by Blumberg and Greenfield (1986) who, to describe their case studies of eight effective principals, used the metaphors of the organiser, the value-based juggler, the authentic helper, the broker, the humanist, the catalyst, the rationalist and the politician.

Bredeson (1985) interviewed and shadowed five principals and found that they operated within three broad metaphors of 'maintenance', 'survival' and 'vision'. These US principals (unlike UK headteachers) saw few substantial changes in what was currently going on in their schools. The survival metaphor overlapped with that of maintenance and manifested itself through crisis management and short-range planning. The metaphor of vision was the ability of the principal to view holistically the present, reinterpret the mission of the school to all and use imagination to think of a preferred future.

In a second study, Bredeson (1988) obtained over 40 different school metaphors from graduate students in an introductory class on educational administration. He then discussed six of the metaphors and their implications: an assembly line, a ticking clock, a garden, a candy machine, a mirror of society and a museum. The assembly line and the ticking clock convey the notion of a well-oiled machine and the stress on timed activities which dominate schools. The garden metaphor evokes the notion of growth and careful nurturing. The candy machine analogy suggests the reliance on extrinsic motivators. The mirror of society emphasises the notion of cultural reproduction, while the museum metaphor suggests that schools house a variety of artefacts and living relics which represent a rich historical past.

Steinhoff and Owens (1989) developed the 'organisational culture assessment inventory' (OCAI), which they piloted with 56 graduate students, including elementary and secondary teachers and some administrators from schools and districts. They later obtained data from 50 teachers in two elementary schools, which produced four main groups of metaphors.

- Family – about a third of respondents referred to the school as a family, home, team or womb. The principal was seen as a parent, friend and coach.
- Machine – about a third of the metaphors saw the school as a well-oiled machine, beehive, rusty machine. The principal was seen as a workaholic, a General, Charlie Brown and the slug!
- Cabaret – almost ten percent used images of a circus, Broadway show, banquet, ballet. The principal was seen as a master of ceremonies, tightrope walker, whirlwind, mentor and clown.
- Little Shop of Horrors – about eight percent used images of the unpredictable such as, nightmares, closed boxes, prisons. The principal was seen as Jekyll and Hyde, and walking on eggs.

Grady (1993) examined Australian teachers' use of metaphors. Teachers were asked to indicate how strongly they thought each metaphor applied to their school. Grady used factor analysis to analyse the data from 283 teachers to produce six clusters, which he called:

- co-operation – the school as family, forum, artist's palette, team negotiating arena
- suppression – prison, mental straitjacket, military camp, ghetto

- constrained activity – beehive, traffic jam, Olympic Games, living organism, theatre
- celebration – culture, exhibition, orchestra, garden, forum
- basic needs – hospital, crèche, shopping mall, labour ward
- mechanistic – machine, museum, herd.

UK STUDIES

In research by Day et al. (2000), heads, teachers, students and governors in 12 case study schools were asked for their metaphors for leadership. Many of these were similar to those found in a series of workshops conducted by one of us (Weindling, 1995). School leaders were individually asked to produce metaphors to describe their school, the headteacher and the senior management team. The instrument used was based on the OCAI developed by Steinhoff and Owens (1989). School leaders were asked to complete a number of sentences such as: 'My school is like a ....' and to explain why they chose the metaphor. (Examples and guidance were not provided in advance.)

Completed questionnaires were obtained from 128 heads and deputies in different schools (73 primary and 55 secondary). Although a few found it difficult to think in terms of images, the large majority of school leaders said they enjoyed the exercise and a considerable number of different metaphors were produced. As part of a workshop on leadership and school culture, the generation and discussion of the metaphors helped the heads and deputies to talk about their own school and the role of leaders within it. The exercise proved both powerful and highly enjoyable for the participants. The most frequently used metaphors for the school, the head and the SMT are given below.

The school

The most frequently mentioned metaphors for the school concerned the idea of a family, home and community. For example: 'My school is like a family. We aim to support, extend and share experiences with each other. We establish trust and confidence within a framework of relationships. Individuals have scope to discover different aspects of themselves with the same framework.' Other common community metaphors were the school as a beehive or ant hill. Although more primary school leaders used the metaphor of family or community, this was not exclusively so as a number of secondary school leaders also used these types of images.

A second group of metaphors emphasised development and growth. One of the primary heads said: 'My school is like a competition garden. The whole is set out well and each plant is in place but at different stages of growth and flower. Hopefully they will be perennials!' In contrast, a secondary deputy head wrote: 'My school is like a rather poorly managed garden centre. Some "plants" are tended better/more than others. Some are ignored and left to wither. One particular type of plant is cherished and nurtured even though it has probably outgrown its usefulness.'

Many images were related to movement, conveying the rapidly changing context of government-imposed national reform. While some of these metaphors were machines, others consisted of organisms and natural events. Examples of the first group were a 'storm-tossed ship', a 'roller coaster', a 'hot air balloon' and a 'locomotive'. Metaphors from the second group included a 'swan', a 'tree' and a 'tornado'.

As a primary deputy wrote:

> My school is like a hot-air balloon. Sometimes there is a lot of hot air! Sometimes floating high looking around with a clear sense of what is going on, on the ground, sometimes with people baling out of the basket, lots of jostling and pushing, some accommodation. It dips perilously close to the ground when I fear the pilot will bale out, and where will that leave the rest of us? Then it rises up again, hopeful and optimistic. It's hard to maintain a steady height.

Another said: 'My school is like a swan. It seems to be gliding along, but we are paddling like mad underneath. Parents and visitors to the school are generally complimentary, but teachers are aware that they are having to work incredibly hard to keep the thing going. Expectations are high.' A secondary school leader thought that their school was like a winding, fast flowing river: 'Going in the same direction but not at the same pace and so we develop bends. Everything is fast moving and some people can't swim – but those who learn are exhilarated by their achievements. I think we have life belts.'

Another cluster of metaphors concerned the idea of a 'safe haven', a 'refuge', and a 'little oasis', where the children were protected and sheltered from the problems of the outside world. For example: 'A little oasis! The school is calm and secure and children feel valued. All this is for real despite the location of the school. The majority of the children come from deprived and difficult home situations.'

The headteacher

Remembering that the family was the most frequently used metaphor for the school, it came as no surprise that the most common image for the head was that of 'parent', 'father' and 'mother'. Another cluster related to control, for example, a 'benevolent despot', and a 'ringmaster', while a linked group was more concerned with direction: an 'architect', a 'navigator' and a 'film director'. For one person their school was like a building site and the school leader was like an architect: 'Involved in the design work and creation. But with fixed boundaries, constraints and limitations – it is not open-ended.'

A number of people used the same metaphor of the headteacher as a 'juggler' who has to keep all the plates spinning. A smaller group of related metaphors emphasised the central role of the head as a 'pivot'. A headteacher who said that the school was like a mobile, and she was like a pivot, explained: 'The headteacher is like a pivot or fulcrum. One part of the mobile – but also influenced by change. I have to be there and be seen. I have to observe and identify the need for change. Elusive after imbalance, stability returns.'

A rather sad metaphor was used by one head that seemed to sum up how stressed he was feeling at the time: 'The headteacher is like a punch bag. Ensuring that I soften the blows directed at various points of the school.' One of the more unusual metaphors was: 'The headteacher is like a pizza. There is a firm crust with different toppings: which reflects what I perceive is the need for a strong foundation with the capacity for change (flexibility).'

The SMT

Many of the metaphors illustrated the idea of an effective team: an 'Italian football team', a 'team of huskies', a 'volleyball team' and a 'team of super heroes'. One of the secondary school leaders said that their SMT was like: 'A team of super heroes. The fantastic four: the human torch, the thing, invisible woman, and Mrs Fantastic. There are lots of internal differences and arguments, but in the end they save the world!' In a primary school the SMT was seen as: 'A volleyball team – managing to keep the ball up, just. We're not always successful in moving the school forward, but we seem to be surviving what is thrown at us. Meetings seem to deal with coping, rather than making progress. We seem to be defending rather than attacking.' Another set of metaphors was linked with the notion of an inner-planning group, such as: a 'cabal', a 'think tank' and a 'selection committee'. Some images also carried the notions of status and power: 'the ace, king, queen etc.', a 'board of directors' and 'The White House Office'.

In contrast to the effective SMTs, a few of the heads and deputies indicated a lack of cohesion and direction in the team. A secondary deputy wrote: 'The senior management team is like a ship with eight rudders, but a captain who can't decide on which course to take and which rudder to manoeuvre, or even how to stop the crew from mutinying. We lack clear direction and leadership.'

A few of the images for secondary SMTs suggested rather aggressive actions to drive the school. For example: 'The SMT is like a Chieftain tank crew. The commander knows where he is going. Some of the crew are hot, busy and not able to see the view' and 'The SMT is like a sword. Cutting, sharp, dangerous, threatening. Reaches the point too quickly. You need training in using it effectively.'

In general, the metaphors for primary schools suggested more tightly knit teams. For example, a primary deputy described the SMT in her school as: 'A speedboat. Powerful, high powered? A bit scary? We stick closely together to manage the stress, making decisions, accommodating. We hang on to anybody threatening to fall (or jump) overboard. Rushing ahead, slowing down occasionally to consolidate. Can everybody swim?'

HEADS OF LARGE PRIMARY SCHOOLS

Further data on heads' metaphors were available from the study of leadership in large primary schools – those with over 400 pupils – conducted by

Southworth and Weindling (2002). At the end of the questionnaire the heads were asked to provide a metaphor or simile to encapsulate what it felt like to be the headteacher of a large school. We also asked for some notes to explain why they had chosen the metaphor. Three-quarters of the heads (304 of the 404) provided a metaphor, making this the largest ever study of school metaphors. Table 8.1 shows the type of metaphors, the number and percentage, and some examples produced by the heads.

The key factors expressed in the metaphors were to do with performing on stage, co-ordination, steering and guiding, motivating, absorbing problems and dealing with adversity. Many of the images show the intensity and pressure on the heads and the need for constant activity switching. The most common metaphors, such as the juggler who has to keep lots of plates spinning, and the captain of the ship, are perhaps not unexpected, as people have often used these images for headteachers. The image of trying to steer the large oil tanker, which is not easy to turn quickly, is very revealing for the heads of large schools. There are surprisingly few examples of the parent, the visionary and the chief executive, despite their prevalence in the literature.

Overall, there seemed to be more negative images in the secondary schools, and primary school leaders appeared to have found the exercise easier and to have been rather more creative than the secondary school staff.

CONCLUSION

The metaphor of the school as a family is a commonly found image with UK school leaders (although this was less so in the large primary schools). This matches the empirical findings of both Steinhoff and Owens (1989) and Grady (1993). The images of the oasis, warm duvet and cosy bedroom, where the school was a haven for children from disadvantaged homes, does not seem to have appeared in previous literature. The metaphor of the beehive/anthill was also frequently used, but discussion with the school leaders indicates that they saw this as a form of community, rather than as a 'machine'.

Various machine images were found but these tended to be used to indicate movement, e.g. ships and trains. Perhaps surprisingly, given the emphasis in the previous literature, very few metaphors were produced about the school as a 'business' or an 'industry'. Considerable numbers of metaphors for living organisms were used but there was an almost total absence of images such as prisons, ghettos and straitjackets. The closest was one secondary deputy who said 'my school is like a treadmill' – representing the constant new initiatives that were falling on the heads of the small number of people in the SMT.

Other metaphors showed the difficult role of the plate-spinner and juggler. Some people used terms such as, architect, navigator and developer, which match the suggestions of the 'new leadership' from authors such as Senge, Bolman and Deal, and Beck and Murphy. Most of the metaphors for the headteacher concerned the idea of direction and control – issues which school leaders are required to do with site-based management, strategic and school development planning, and the implementation of national reforms.

Table 8.1   Headteachers' metaphors of their role in large primary schools

No.	%	Metaphor	Examples
51	16.8	Circus performers	Juggler trying to juggle with porridge/cross eyes/heavy cannon balls; tightrope walker; quick change artist; ringmaster
40	13.2	Captains	Captain of a ship or a large oil tanker; cricket or football captain; Captain Furrillo in *Hill Street Blues*
23	7.6	Animals	Hamster on a treadmill; octopus; swan; chameleon; leading dolphin – Flipper; meercat
21	6.9	Jack of all trades	All things to all people
18	5.9	Dealing with adversity	Headless chicken; whirling dervish; one-armed paper hanger; knight without a sword
16	5.3	Conductor/band leader	Conductor of an orchestra; leader of a marching band
12	3.9	Pilots or navigators	Helmsman at the wheel of a large ship; pilot of an aircraft; cox on a rowing team
11	3.6	Energisers	Dynamo; Eveready battery; bundle of dynamite; yeast
8	2.6	Growth and gardeners	Roots of a tree; head gardener
8	2.6	Guiding the journey	Lighthouse; leader of expedition to Mount Everest
8	2.6	Swimming/water	Surfer; cross-Channel swimmer attached to piece of elastic; bubbling spa
7	2.3	Parent	Father of a large family; penniless godfather; single parent to a family of 50
7	2.3	Central linkage or hub	Cog at the centre of a wheel; an important link in a web
7	2.3	Sponge	A rolling sponge
5	1.6	Roller coaster/big dipper	Mountain biking down a roller coaster; riding the big dipper
5	1.6	Chief executive/managing director	Managing director of a company
5	1.6	Fountain of knowledge	Fount of knowledge
4	1.3	Visionary	Oracle; look-out at prow of boat
4	1.3	Ball	Ping pong ball; rubber ball
3	1.3	Magnet	Magnet gleaning ideas and solutions from a variety of sources; magnet attracting everything nobody wants
3	1.3	Car	Formula 1 racing car; VW beetle car
35	11.5	Other	Benevolent autocrat; chess player; data processor; fast-food outlet; prime minister; wizard in *Harry Potter*

Key points to emerge from the studies show that the use of generative metaphors is a powerful means of exploring leaders' perceptions of the school, their role and the nature of team leadership, which have developed to cope with the massive changes in the educational system. Metaphors can help people change. For instance, Bubb (2004, p. 107) describes how in trying to manage a very difficult class she had to 'change tack' and became a different sort of teacher – Hitler-like rather than caring and democratic.

Metaphors are useful for presenting an alternative lens through which to look:

> The use of metaphors in the field of educational administration is more than a creative exercise for workshops and classrooms. It is more than a trivialisation of the complexities of leadership in schools to earthy and clever analogies. The challenge in educational leadership is not to find 'the perfect metaphor' but rather to seek a better understanding of schools, their organisation, operation, and administration.
>
> (Bredeson, 1988, p. 309)

PART 2

DISTRIBUTED LEADERSHIP FOR SCHOOL IMPROVEMENT

9

Senior Management and Leadership Teams – Three Research Projects

Historical perspective
NFER secondary heads project (1982–94)
The effective management in schools project – 1993
Leadership in large primary schools project – 2002
Conclusions

Over our 20 years of research we have worked on several projects that provide insights into the way the head and senior management teams, or to use the latest nomenclature – leadership teams – work. After a brief introduction, this chapter uses data from three separate but related studies – the first examines the NFER secondary heads project, the second uses data from a study of effective management in 57 primary, secondary and special schools, and the third – and most recent – presents the findings from research on leadership teams in large primary schools.

HISTORICAL PERSPECTIVE

Traditionally in English grammar and secondary modern schools there was a headmaster or headmistress and a single deputy head. In 1956 the Burnham Committee established the role of deputy in all schools over a minimum size. Senior management teams emerged in secondary schools in the early 1970s, following the establishment of large comprehensives that had at least two deputies. During this period legislation created the additional posts of senior master/mistress and senior teacher. By the 1980s it seemed that most secondary schools had SMTs and in 1987 the term deputy head replaced the gender-specific senior master and mistress. In 1992 the School Teachers' Review Body recommended the abolition of a statutory number of deputies for schools of specific sizes and nationally this led to a reduction in numbers, as school budgets could not afford to replace deputies who left. It is not exactly clear when primary schools began to use senior management teams but the evidence suggests these emerged following the national educational reforms of the late 1980s and early 1990s. The notion of leadership teams or the leadership group became more common in the early 2000s, especially in secondary schools. The term 'leadership group' was introduced by the DfEE in September 2000. It specified the new category of 'assistant head teacher' and brought heads, deputies and assistant heads together on a single pay spine (DfEE, 2000d). The members of the leadership group within a school were normally those who formed the senior management team.

Given the importance that is attached to teamwork it is perhaps surprising that there have been very few empirical studies of leadership teams or SMTs in education. Wallace and Hall (1994) provide a detailed, observation-based study of six in secondary schools, two of which were followed over a year in 1991–92. In another empirical study, Wallace and Huckman (1999) looked at management teams in four primary schools over four terms. Wallace, drawing on the work of Bolman and Deal (1991), developed a theory of the combined cultural and political metaphors to examine these data. He argued that SMTs are high risk or 'high gain, high strain' strategies. If they work well there is much to be gained, but if they do not there is much to lose:

> The heads needed other SMT members to commit themselves to the team approach as much as the latter needed the head's sponsorship for the opportunity to be in the team. Failure of teamwork stands to make a bigger dent in the credibility of heads with other staff and governors than in the credibility of their SMT colleagues, since heads are accountable as SMT leader. Therefore adopting a team approach in more than name is a high-risk strategy for them.
>
> (Wallace and Hall, 1994, p. 186)

NFER SECONDARY HEADS PROJECT (1982–94)

Our research with the 1982–83 cohort of heads found that secondary school management was seen as too large a task to be undertaken successfully by one person and so it was important for the new head to establish a good working relationship with the existing management team.

Many secondary schools appeared to operate a two-tier system for their senior management, that is, some meetings only included the head and deputies, while others involved the senior teachers. In some schools policy decisions were made by the head and deputies and then taken to the larger group for ratification. Several heads indicated that such a two-tier system could cause tension between the members of the SMT. Whether the SMT consisted of the deputies or included the senior teachers was an important decision for the head to make and seemed to be largely based on the personalities involved.

In most cases – nine out of ten – the new heads came from outside the school and inherited an established team or group of senior staff. Some found themselves in situations where all the deputies had been at the school for a considerable length of time: in one case the three deputies had given 'over 100 years of loyal service to the school'. New heads in this position found that it was sometimes difficult to introduce change without the full support of their

SMT. The new heads relied considerably on the team to implement the many changes they had initiated. However, the problem of inheriting one or more 'weak' senior staff was found to be quite widespread.

Difficulties with senior staff

Coping with a weak member of the senior management team was an issue for 38 percent of new heads and after ten years over one-quarter (27%) of the heads still said they had problems. Some senior staff were defensive about their areas of responsibility and displayed rigidity and narrow interpretation of their tasks or lacked management training in dealing with comprehensive schools, and could make only minor contributions to pastoral care or the curriculum.

A number of senior staff were felt by the heads to be promoted beyond their ability and unable to cope. Some were near the end of their careers and suffering from 'burnout'. Where this occurred it put extra pressure on the head and the rest of the SMT, who had to 'carry' or 'patch around' the person concerned. Obvious difficulties also occurred where members of the management team did not get on with each other and 'personality clashes' arose, sometimes casting the head in the role of referee.

One head had inherited three deputies all of whom had been at the school for more than 30 years when it had been a grammar school. He soon decided that they were trying to block his initiatives and he began to work around them by going directly to the heads of year and heads of department. After about 18 months the situation came to a crisis when the deputies made a vote of no confidence in the head to the chair of governors. This went to the Director of Education who set up an inquiry. The Director and chair of governors spoke to the head and deputies and confirmed the head's authority. The first deputy then resigned, followed six months later by the second deputy. Thus after a very difficult period the head was able to recruit two new deputies with whom he is very satisfied: 'As a team we are now much more in line with the comprehensive approach.'

Making new senior appointments

An obvious advantage for new heads was to be able to appoint a new deputy or (as they were then called) a senior master/mistress. 'New appointments have revolutionised the way in which I can work. We now have a team of relatively young deputies all appointed in the last 18 months and committed to working as a team.' Half of the heads were able to appoint at least one deputy during the first two years of their headship. Sixty percent of these appointments were external and 40 percent were internal promotions of a teacher already at the school. This provided a valuable impetus as the head was usually able to appoint someone who shared their philosophy and provided another source of ideas and support for the head's plans. Privately we began calling the new heads 'vampires' because so many wanted 'new blood'! A mix

Table 9.1 Number of changes in senior staff after five years

0	1	2	3	4	5	6	7	8
8%	21%	18%	22%	17%	7%	4%	1%	2%

n = 122 schools (total changes of senior staff = 334)

of both new and experienced deputies was seen as the ideal combination in the SMT, as it provided a balance between innovation and stability.

Those heads who were unable to appoint any or only one new member of the SMT frequently expressed frustration about being the only innovator. Some schools still had elderly deputies who had only taught at the one school and whom heads considered were simply waiting for retirement. A head who had not been able to make any new senior appointments remarked:

> The deputy has been at the school for more than 25 years when it was previously a secondary modern. The two senior teachers are incapable of making any contribution to the development of the school, again having spent the whole of their careers at the school. I have abandoned the SMT.

Table 9.1 shows that only about one in 12 (8%) of the cohort of heads had had no changes of senior staff in the five to six-year period they had been in office (1982–83 to 1989), while at the other extreme two percent of schools had eight changes. Most schools had between one to four changes of senior personnel. About half were appointed from outside the school but external appointments were more frequent for the post of deputy head than for other senior staff. Just over 70 percent of the 160 deputies appointed came from another school, compared with 49 percent of the 41 senior masters/mistresses and only 23 percent of the 133 senior teachers.

Team approach

Most of the NFER heads favoured a team approach to school management and where positive comments were made about the deputies they usually referred to how well they worked as a team in terms of joint planning and decision-making. For this to function effectively the head had to delegate clearly defined areas of responsibility to the senior staff. While many new heads found it difficult at first, they began to delegate more confidently during the first year, although this largely depended on the ability of their deputies. During the new heads' first year they became aware of the strengths and weaknesses of their senior staff. In most cases, deputies were able to act as a valuable link between the head and the staff. New heads particularly relied on their deputies to provide feedback on staff attitudes and feelings. Some heads were clearly aware of the danger of drawing the deputies towards them and creating a large gap between the SMT and the rest of the staff.

Where heads praised their deputies and senior staff, they usually spoke of them as being reliable, dependable and efficient. They also valued people who were open and frank and did not 'sit on the fence' but spoke up and told the head when they did not agree with something.

After five years just under half the heads felt they worked well as a team, some saying the teamwork was excellent. However, over half expressed dissatisfaction and said they were definitely not a team, but a *group* of senior staff each with defined areas of responsibility. So five or six years after the new head's appointment, many schools had not been able to establish a fully effective team.

The heads saw most of the problems among the SMT as related to individual personalities, which overrode any structural factors. For example:

> The team functions moderately well. It is hindered by the character and personality of the senior deputy. He appears to be so terrified of being wrong that he is quite unable to take a decision, but he also feels threatened by the other colleagues who all make decisions and display an initiative he doesn't possess. He has never offered a suggestion on anything in six years. He will give no opinion other than to imply he works harder than his senior colleagues.

Sometimes heads were inspired to reorganise the SMT by an inspection:

> One of the principal HMI recommendations was that we change the composition of the SMT which consisted of the head, two deputies and three senior teachers and represented the tradition of the old school. In a week HMI picked up the discontent among the staff. The senior teachers' message to HMI was totally different from the deputies and mine. The senior teachers were being subversive. They were hostile to mixed ability teaching but not in an open fashion. I brought in the senior teachers and told them what I was going to do and why. I gave them two weeks to respond but they didn't come back to me. I have taken away the senior teachers' responsibility for sections of the school and now one deputy is in charge of Years 1 to 3 and the other has Years 4 to 6. The deputies now have a higher profile than they did. I delegate more and meetings are chaired by them. HMI said restructure, so I did.

After ten years in post

When the cohort was surveyed for a third time in 1994, after ten years in post, the heads indicated their views on the effectiveness of the school's senior management team and the results are shown in Table 9.2. The answers are, of course, highly subjective and only reflect the views of the headteacher on the functioning of the team, but it is reassuring to note that over three-quarters of the cohort thought their SMT functioned well or very well.

The head of the school with a poorly functioning SMT, wrote: 'Weak deputies and weak curriculum co-coordinators. Too keen to let me make the important decisions.' In the three schools where the heads felt the SMT did

Table 9.2 SMT effectiveness after ten years as head

SMT effectiveness

Please indicate the extent to which you feel that the SMT functions well as a team	%
Very well	34
Well	43
Moderately well	18
Not very well	3
Poor	1

(n = 100)

not function very well, the following reasons were given: 'The SMT are reluctant to deal with the challenges and problems facing schools today'; 'They are very effective at their separate jobs but there is not a lot of teamwork or team spirit'; and 'Three of the four people function well. At least the fourth retires early this year.'

Teams that were only moderately effective usually had one member of the group who was 'out of step' or 'pulling in a different direction', which meant that the rest of the team had to carry the weakest member. Some – but not all – of the heads who thought their SMT worked well as a team, had been able to appoint them themselves.

It was clear that the heads did not want a group of 'clones' or people who simply agreed with everything they said. Differences were important, and heads believed strongly that to be effective the team members needed to complement each other. Deputies and senior teachers were key appointments and trying to get the right balance in the team was specifically mentioned by one head who said: 'We built the team on Belbin lines to cover all the functions. We are all very different.'

The ability to trust and support each other and present a common view to staff was seen as very important. Also necessary was the opportunity for members to be able to speak their mind and to express contrary views but still work well as a team. Sharing a common purpose, clear roles, collective decision-making, joint responsibility and presenting a united front, were all factors mentioned with regard to successful teams.

THE EFFECTIVE MANAGEMENT IN SCHOOLS PROJECT – 1993

The previous section has shown how the situation changed for the NFER cohort of secondary heads over the ten-year period from 1982–83 to 1993–94. The involvement of one of us (DW) in another research project, 'Effective Management in Schools' (EMIS) (Bolam et al., 1993), provides evidence on staff views about effective leadership and management in a self-selected group of 57 primary, secondary and special schools. This group of schools volunteered to take part in a DfEE-funded project that looked at effective management. A total of 643 questionnaires were returned from the staff in these 57 schools (an excellent 84 percent response rate) and visits were made to 12 case study schools and interviews conducted with the heads, chair of governors and a cross-section of staff.

One of the most striking findings was that patterns of team or collegial management appeared to be emerging and, in some cases, to be firmly established. This was as true of primary as secondary schools, and is in sharp contrast to the traditional idea of a single leader – the headteacher. The educational reforms from 1988 onwards required heads to involve senior colleagues to a greater degree as schools attempted to cope with multiple innovations.

Primary management teams

The concept of the SMT was normally associated with the secondary sector yet there was clear evidence of a 'management team' in five of the seven case study primary schools, though these were often the larger ones. In the remaining two schools no such team was readily identifiable, although in one the headteacher stressed that in effect the staff as a whole functioned as a close-knit team. Where a distinct team was discernible, typically this comprised the headteacher, the deputy and teachers with senior allowances, making a group of between four and six people. This group would usually meet on a regular basis, every two or three weeks, for about an hour at the end of the school day, to discuss matters relating to school policy.

In those schools where the team was perceived to be effective, the positive features mentioned by teachers were that the team members worked well together, there was good management and decision-making which kept the school on course, and that the overall style of management was consultative.

In the schools where the team was perceived not to be working well, the main reasons appeared to be a breakdown in interpersonal relationships and poor communication. In one of the schools, the team comprised the head-teacher, deputy and three team leaders, but it was proving impossible for them to work together effectively because of a serious clash of personalities involving the head and the deputy. (Indeed, there was some indication to suggest that the headteacher had deliberately enlarged the team, partly with a view to acquiring allies, but also in an attempt to reduce the deputy's influence on policy-making.) The head and the deputy gave sharply differing accounts of the reasons for their inability to work together, which appeared beyond resolution as long as they both remained in the school. Staff were well aware of this division, and some voiced concern about it.

In a second school where the SMT was reported to be experiencing problems, much of the difficulty was attributed to a combination of lack of explicitness and poor communication coupled with interpersonal difficulties. Here, according to the headteacher, the team consisted of the headteacher, the deputy and two 'B' post-holders. However, three 'A' post-holders were under the impression that they, too, were members of this group, having been present on specific occasions in the past. They had anticipated being regularly involved but, in the event, had been excluded without any explanation, which led to frustration and disenchantment. Consequently, the group was regarded by some of the staff as a divisive force. One teacher referred to a wedge having been driven between the SMT and the rest of the staff – 'It is divide and rule'.

One primary school had no obvious management team and little by way of delegation. The head appeared to devote limited time to management tasks. She emphasised the role of lead teacher – and saw the managerial role in terms of shielding staff from external pressures and from policy-making, so that they could concentrate whole-heartedly on classroom work. 'I am there to protect staff and they are there to teach.' The majority of the staff in this school were content with this. Most were highly supportive of the head, and any criticisms were quite minor.

A possible explanation for this state of affairs, which is consistent with a contingency perspective on leadership and effective schools, would be that the approach was appropriate for the context. This was a small school serving a middle-class catchment, where the emphasis was firmly on pupil achievement, and where there was a long-established and very stable staff whose objectives closely matched those of the parents. The teachers were able classroom practitioners (in the traditional sense), had no great aspirations to an enlarged or reconstituted role and were content to be left alone to get on with their teaching.

Secondary management teams

In all four secondary case study schools, responsibility for formulating and deciding school policy was clearly vested in teams of senior managers, which ranged in size from three to five people. Additionally, in at least two of the schools, there was an extended group of mainly senior staff whose remit was to shape policy in specific areas. Over and above these formal structures, in every case efforts were made to build a sense of ownership of school policies by extending the circle of people who were involved in reviewing current practice and debating the nature and merits of new initiatives. This was particularly pronounced in one school where every effort was made to consult staff, and give them opportunities to challenge ideas or to put forward their own ideas for consideration.

Each SMT appeared to be functioning effectively, and while some staff voiced specific criticisms, overall, considerable satisfaction was expressed. Senior staff were especially positive: 'There's a feeling of immense support within the group'; 'I think we work effectively as a team' ... 'We complement each other' ... 'I don't think there are any holds barred between us.'

In three of the four schools, whilst staff acknowledged that their views were canvassed on most whole-school issues, invariably their response was invited to a specific proposal, and only when a good deal of groundwork had already been carried out. As a teacher in one of the schools put it: 'Of course you can have a say, but by the time it reaches us it is not whether we should do it but how we should do it.' Moreover, not everyone was convinced that senior managers really took account of staff views and opinion. The feeling that decisions had already been reached and that consultation was something of a charade persisted in three of the schools. 'It's cosmetic', was the reaction of one teacher to the school's much vaunted system of internal consultation. In another school a teacher spoke about the senior management meetings which, unusually, were open to anyone who wished to attend. 'You can input things there but you still get the feeling that several people have decided that this is the way we're going.' Where then did the real influence lie?

> It's mainly the SMT who decide how we are going to do things and then it's passed on to us to implement it, albeit in a very nice way. It's not a democracy – in that we don't all make decisions in a corporate way. Someone makes a decision and we can discuss it ... but if they have decided this is the way we go, then this is the way we go.

The other general criticism voiced of senior management was of what was perceived to be their over-enthusiasm for taking on new initiatives without always having consolidated existing developments. Even allowing for the multiplicity of government-led changes it was felt that some headteachers and SMTs were over-disposed to innovate.

The team approach to management

The following is a summary of perceptions about an effective SMT – it is a composite across the 57 schools.

The head and SMT:

- work well together as a team; have roles and responsibilities which are clear to staff; are highly visible and approachable
- take the key policy decisions but consult widely before doing so; face up to differences of opinion and work for a negotiated solution and a sense of joint ownership of school developments
- set out a broad strategy for change and thereafter encourage and facilitate teacher autonomy, supporting teachers during the implementation stage
- think and plan strategically, paying attention to current practice as well as to the medium and longer term. They specify priorities, phase in developments, and allow time for consolidation
- are proactive and keen to stay in the forefront of change. They are adept at anticipating future developments and the implications these might have for the school. They display the capacity to avoid crisis management
- model desired behaviours and attributes, e.g. hard work, commitment, mutual support and teamwork; behave with openness, honesty and integrity; acknowledge that they are accountable to staff by providing clear evidence of the outcomes of their actions; are ready to admit mistakes and to consider alternatives

- are adept at managing people, including identifying and mobilising individual talents and energies and delegating meaningful tasks in order to develop and empower staff
- have high expectations of staff and demand a lot from them; but are sensitive to the teachers' mood, morale and their workload
- convey to staff the sense that the school is being actively steered and is under control, thereby providing reassurance; provide good and consistent support to the staff.

One of the most interesting findings of the EMIS study in 1993 was the emergence of patterns of team or collegial management in the primary schools. Indeed, no one thought that there was anything strange about discussing the role of an SMT in the context of the primary school. Implicitly, it was widely agreed that the scale and diversity of the management tasks merited some form of collegial arrangement. This would seem to represent a significant shift from the position where, traditionally, headteachers in primary schools had exercised somewhat autocratic leadership.

LEADERSHIP IN LARGE PRIMARY SCHOOLS PROJECT – 2002

Data from a third research project (Southworth and Weindling, 2002) enables us to look at leadership and management in large and very large primary schools – those with over 400 full-time pupils. The research involved questionnaire surveys (n = 404) to heads, and visits made to 26 schools, where the head and senior staff were interviewed.

The management structure

The size, composition and even the title, of the SMT varied considerably across the 26 large primary schools visited. The smallest consisted of a group of three (headteacher, deputy and senior teacher), while rather surprisingly, the largest numbered 11 people including head, deputies, assistant head and senior teachers. However, several of the schools used a two-tier system so that in addition to the larger SMT, there was an 'inner cabinet', a 'star chamber' or a 'headship team', which consisted of the head and deputies who often met informally before school and sometimes more formally once a week. In some schools the senior teachers were also invited to these weekly meetings, but in other cases the larger SMT might meet only monthly or three times a term.

The basic unit in these large schools was the year team of three or four teachers plus their classroom assistants, who would meet weekly. Each team usually had a named leader but this was not always the case. In addition to this horizontal strand, the schools also had the vertical structure of the curriculum, where curriculum managers usually had whole school responsibility for their subject area. So in some ways this matrix model of management mirrored that commonly found in secondary schools. However, heads were generally insistent that they wanted to maintain the primary school ethos. Looking across the schools it was difficult to find a clear pattern to the roles and titles allocated to the members of the SMT. The most frequent model was a phase structure, where each of the senior staff took responsibility for two year groups. But it was also common to divide the school into Key Stages. In addition, there were various combinations so that senior staff might have a curriculum responsibility and oversight of some of the year teams. The most unusual structure, found in one case, was to divide the school into three vertical teams so that each of the three senior staff had a team of seven teachers (one from each year).

It seems there has been a move from the past when the structure was based strongly on the curriculum, due to the introduction of the National Curriculum, to a structure which is now predominately based on the year group and the phase or Key Stage (with the curriculum taking a less prominent role in the structure).

In some cases the shape of the building (with a senior manager on each floor) or two separate buildings, influenced the structure and function of the SMT. A key decision was the amount of non-teaching time for the members of the SMT and the co-ordinators. This varied considerably across the schools and was not simply related to school size, but depended to some extent on historical precedent, and the views of the head and the governors.

About half of the 26 heads we interviewed thought that their SMT was very effective. As we found in our other studies, they saw the importance of getting a good balance of youth and experience in the team, and they wanted 'ideas people' not just a group of 'yes men/women'. At one end of the continuum a head said: 'It's a bit too comfortable: three long-serving, non-ambitious staff. Not a major contribution to the school's development.' In other schools there were new members of the SMT, who needed more experience of whole-school management, before they could become fully effective. The heads also recognised the value of internal appointments which were good to show staff promotion, and external people who brought in new ideas to the team. They wanted the team members to have a range of experience from all phases. The best teams had complementary skills, and were seen to be hard working with no negativity or disillusionment, who were respected by the staff. In all the schools the SMT needed to be seen to speak with one voice in public. As one head said: 'Agree in public, disagree and discuss in private.' Another expressed the same point: 'We work as a cabinet and have collective responsibility.' A third head said: 'Trust is essential. The SMT must be leak-proof.'

All the heads wanted the SMT to undertake whole-school strategic planning as well as the day-to-day management for their areas of responsibility. The heads wanted to be kept informed by the SMT, and they valued a member of the team who had 'the ear of the staff' and was able to bring their views to the meetings. The importance of two-way communication to and from the SMT to the staff was stressed by many of the heads.

Table 9.3   Size of the SMT

Number of people	Number of schools	Percentage of schools
2	8	2.0
3	42	10.4
4	91	22.6
5	99	24.6
6	82	20.4
7	49	12.2
8	22	5.5
9	5	1.2
10	1	0.2
12	2	0.5
19	1	0.2

n = 402 Missing data 2

Survey data

The questionnaire enabled us to look at the size of the SMT and the numbers of senior staff in large primary schools, including the head (see Table 9.3).

The mean size of SMT across all the large primary schools was 5.25. But schools with under 600 pupils had an average of 5.09 in their SMT, compared with 5.73 for the schools with over 600 pupils. Thus, not surprisingly, larger schools had larger SMTs.

The great majority of schools had one deputy head. This finding should be compared with secondary schools of similar size which often have more than one deputy. As might be expected, the larger schools, with over 600 pupils, had more deputies and assistant heads, and the differences were statistically signif-icant. However, the average number of senior teachers was *not* significantly different. The use of assistant heads was uneven and difficult to interpret given the shift in nomenclature in the last few years. Whereas some people have argued for deputy heads being called assistant heads, now assistant head is a position in own right (DfEE, 2000d) indicating the number two or second deputy. All of which means the position of deputies is even more unclear.

The data suggest that leadership and management of large primary schools are now more shared, distributed and interactive than in previous years or smaller-sized schools. This shared work is less about heads and deputies working together, than heads, deputies and other senior staff being involved. Thus there are, today, more staff involved in running the primary school than was formerly the case and the SMT plays a major role in strategic planning and there are more effective phase/key stage leaders.

CONCLUSIONS

The findings from our three research projects spread over 20 years (1982 to 2002) show the changing nature of school leadership from the single headteacher and one deputy, perhaps working through shared leadership, to the development of management and leadership teams and the greater use of distributed leadership. The use of senior teams is now commonly found in primary, secondary and special schools.

The NFER national study of new secondary heads showed the crucial importance of good working relations with senior staff. However, almost a fifth of the new heads reported that they had very serious problems with at least one member of the SMT, and a further 20 percent said the problem was 'serious'. Over time the heads were able to appoint new senior staff – after two years about half the schools had appointed at least one deputy and after five years only about one in 12 had not made any changes to their senior teams. The majority of heads had appointed between one and four new senior staff during the five-year period. Fashioning an effective team to lead the school was of great importance to the heads. They relied on the senior staff to introduce and manage innovation. However, after five years in post over half the NFER heads said they still did not have a fully functioning team. By the ten-year mark, with further changes and new members of the team, three-quarters of the heads thought their SMT functioned 'well' or 'very well'.

The second research project (EMIS) looked at the SMT in 57 secondary, primary and special schools where the head thought the school was effectively managed. The staff generally agreed that the SMT worked well and supported the staff, with more positive results coming from the primary phase. The case studies illustrated those teams which worked in a collegial fashion and others where problems arose with one or more members and the group did not really function as a team. A set of features of an effective SMT was derived from the staff perceptions across the schools.

The third study of leadership in large primary schools clearly demonstrated the importance of a team approach and the use of distributed leadership. Although some of the schools had developed structures similar to those in secondary schools, the heads were very keen to maintain what they called the primary ethos even in large schools. Almost all the heads thought the SMT played a major role in strategic planning and 90 percent said their team was highly effective. The heads of these large primary schools considered that they had good middle and senior managers.

The three projects show that a team approach to management is important across both phases, and would seem in part a reflection of the greater complexity of the task of managing and leading schools in the wake of the Education Reform Act 1988. The number of innovations that have had to be introduced in a short time period is so large that no one person could reasonably hope to manage their implementation. Moreover, the technical complexity of some of these innovations has also made it imperative that traditional managerial responsibilities and procedures be reconsidered. There was clear evidence of local management of schools in particular having had direct consequences in terms of the headteacher's role, this in turn triggering further change to the managerial responsibilities of other staff. Heads increasingly have found themselves being propelled toward a role more akin to that of chief executive, exercising oversight of the work of leaders and managers – in effect, functioning as leaders of leaders – rather than being directly responsible for every aspect of management related to the various discrete areas. They increasingly also have to be 'leaders of learning', exerting an effect indirectly and through various 'avenues of influence'.

The role of the deputy headteacher seems to have been considerably enhanced too, embracing both new and greater areas of responsibility, and more autonomy. In particular, the head's focus having become broader and longer term, has led to the deputy head assuming greater control of day-to-day matters within the school. This represents change of considerable magnitude in the primary sector in particular, where, historically, deputies all too often remained under-extended in terms of managerial functioning.

It was, however, teamwork that most characterised the management and leadership function in the majority of the schools. In the secondary schools, although responsibility for policy-making invariably remained in the hands of the four or five members of the SMT, it was increasingly common to find a wider group who had a critical function to serve in terms of policy shaping. With a backward glance toward the isolation of the traditional headship, several headteachers said how much they appreciated the benefits deriving from collegial working. The synergy of effective teamwork should not be underestimated, it is crucial to the success of any organisation; but, unlike their counterparts in the private sector, not all new heads were able readily to achieve the teams of their choice!

10

The Heart of the School?
Middle Leaders

The key to school success
Middle managers or leaders?
National Standards
Teaching and learning
Strategic direction
Tensions
Summary

The focus of this chapter is middle management, or what in the light of the new discourse is increasingly called, middle leadership. After a brief introduction suggesting middle managers and middle leaders are the key to school success, their main roles are outlined and reference is made to the National Standards for Subject Leaders. Two key aspects of the role relating to school improvement are considered – that which relates to the improvement of teaching and learning, and that relating to the strategic, both of which are conceptualised as 'leadership' roles rather than management.

THE KEY TO SCHOOL SUCCESS

Middle managers have long been recognised as crucial to an organisation's success. Schools and educational establishments are no different from other organisations in this respect, but it is only comparatively recently that the importance of middle managers – they have a variety of names in schools: subject leaders, department and faculty heads, year heads, pastoral heads, curriculum co-ordinators, Key Stage managers, special educational needs co-ordinators, heads of ICT or literacy, or numeracy – have attracted the attention of policy-makers and educational researchers, particularly those interested in school effectiveness and school improvement. This is perhaps surprising given that middle managers or middle leaders – of which there are around 220,000 in English schools (NCSL, 2003b) – are uniquely placed to have a major impact on a school and the quality of its teaching and learning. As Lofthouse et al. (1995) note:

Curriculum area managers, be they head of department, subject co-ordinator or course leader are, in many instances, best placed to influence the sharp end of teaching and learning – what goes on in individual classrooms. As such, it is they who should be able to ensure a high degree of consonance between whole-school or college values, curriculum policy and individual practice.

(Lofthouse et al., 1995, p. 22)

In the late 1980s a research study into department and faculty heads (Earley and Fletcher-Campbell, 1992) was initiated by the NFER, largely as a result of our earlier research project into secondary headship in which it had been very apparent that so much of a new head's success in implementing desired change – or what might now be called their strategic vision – hinged on the quality of the school's middle managers (Weindling and Earley, 1987). Clearly, effective leadership and management at all levels is important but the NFER research suggested that middle managers were the driving force behind the organisation and the key to improving the quality of teaching and learning. They are the 'kingpins', 'the boiler house', 'the engine room' or 'the hub of the school' and Her Majesty's Inspectorate (HMI) went as far as to say that schools 'rely more for their success on the dynamism and leadership qualities of the head of department than on any other factor' (HMI, 1984, pp. 3). Much more recently the National College for School Leadership has stated that effective middle leaders are at 'the heart of the matter' representing 'a critical base of knowledge and expertise for schools' noting that heads 'talk about them as "the engine room of change" and a repository of expert, up-to-date knowledge capable of transforming and energising learning and teaching' (NCSL, 2003a, p. 1).

There is a growing body of empirical research evidence that points specifically to the key role of middle managers in effective and improving schools. The first such study – a detailed quantitative study of a small number of multi-racial comprehensive schools in England – found that rates of pupil progress differed widely within the same secondary school *between* subject areas. Different departments were shown to have achieved substantially different results with children who were comparable in terms of background and attainment at an earlier time (Smith and Tomlinson, 1989). Significantly the researchers suggested that explanations of school success, at least as measured in terms of pupil attainment, could not be confined to managerial or organisational factors that involved the whole school, but had to take account of management and leadership at the department level.

In the mid-1990s a study of secondary school departments made use of 'value added' data to delineate some of the key characteristics associated with effective departments (Harris et al., 1995). These included such factors as a shared vision, a central focus on teaching and learning, a collegial approach, scrutiny of results, record-keeping and effective resource management and organisation of teaching. In a follow-up study Harris examined departmental ineffectiveness and pointed to a number of common features, some of them the opposite to what had earlier been found for effective departments, such as inappropriate leadership styles, lack of vision for the subject, poor communication and organisation, inadequate monitoring and evaluation systems and lack of professional development and learning (Harris, 1998, p. 274).

In the most detailed study to date, a team of school effectiveness researchers from the University of London's Institute of Education, has made similar claims about what constitutes departmental effectiveness and ineffectiveness, although they did note that in some schools it was much easier for all departments to function effectively (Sammons et al., 1997, p. 99). This ESRC-funded study made reference to high expectations, an academic emphasis, a shared vision, consistency in approach, high-quality teaching, parental support and a student-centred approach. An effective senior management or leadership team was also considered to be a significant factor. They led by example, promoted high staff morale, had high expectations and helped to create a shared vision. The way senior staff worked with their middle manager colleagues was crucial, especially in relation to such matters as role clarity, whole-school policy implementation and involvement in decision-making.

The overriding attribute of an effective department head is often said to be team leadership and the ability to motivate and inspire other members of the team – 'what you get out of others is more important than what you do yourself' – the welding together of a group of individuals into a team was the hallmark of a truly effective department and effective department heads 'create climates in which people grow and the curriculum could develop' (Earley and Fletcher-Campbell, 1992, p. 62).

However, despite its obvious importance, research and inspection evidence have consistently shown that the leadership role of middle managers continues to be variable (Earley et al., 2002; Ofsted, 1997) and although examples of good practice can be found, as a group, middle managers are said to be less effective than they could be (Jones and O'Sullivan, 1997).

MIDDLE MANAGERS OR MIDDLE LEADERS?

The definition of middle management itself is not unproblematic. All teachers are managers in that they are responsible for the management of pupils or students, resources and the management of the learning process. Only some, however, have responsibility for the work of other adults – the key factor in any definition of management. Management, at senior or middle management level, is about getting things done by working with and through other people, and it is likely to consist of a combination of activities such as planning, organising, resourcing, controlling, monitoring and evaluating. It will also involve *leading*.

Middle managers are now seen as having a key leadership role – as middle leaders. It is not the case that previously leadership was unimportant, it has always been necessary to lead a subject or a department or a year group, rather it is more a matter of emphasis. The importance of leadership is reflected in the national standards, which as we will see, are for subject *leaders*. Before their publication in 1998, 'subject leader' was not a standard term with (in primary schools) subject or curriculum co-ordinator, or (in secondary schools) department head being more commonly used. The NCSL also prefers to use the term 'middle leader' rather than 'middle manager'. As was noted in Chapter 1, this reflects the dominant discourse which is now about leadership not management, and distributed or shared leadership where anyone in an organisation can function as a leader outside their formal position as such. The use of such language helps shape the focus and is an attempt to move away from traditional, hierarchical forms of school organisation to those that better reflect forms of distributed leadership. This shift, however, is problematic. As Field and Holden (2004, p. 4) note: 'The term "leader" carries with it connotations. It implies vision, direction and inspiration. It is more exciting than the word "manager", which suggests concepts of maintenance and the implementation of policies devised by others.' The change of label is important but it is not clear in an education system whose curriculum is increasingly controlled from the centre whether subject leaders are more concerned with curriculum management and implementing someone else's agenda, be it the head's and the governors' or that of the government. As Field and Holden go on to note: 'the challenge to subject *leaders* as curriculum *managers* is then to establish a balance between leadership and management roles – to provide a vision and direction, yet also to ensure the implementation and monitoring of pre-determined policies and procedures' (ibid., p. 13, emphasis in original).

NATIONAL STANDARDS

As part of a much wider initiative to establish a professional development framework for teachers (Green, 2004) and to define standards of performance within the profession at a number of key points, in 1998 the Teacher Training Agency (TTA) published a set of national standards (TTA, 1998b). In the description of the role (for both primary and secondary schools) offered by the TTA, the term 'subject leader' is preferred to either middle manager or curriculum co-ordinator.

The TTA defines the core purpose for subject leadership as: 'to provide professional leadership and management for a subject to secure high quality teaching, effective use of resources, and improved standards of learning achievement for all pupils' (TTA, 1998b, p. 4). It goes on to state that:

> A subject leader provides leadership and direction for the subject and ensures that it is managed and organised to meet the aims and objectives of the school and the subject. While the headteacher and governors carry overall responsibility for school improvement, a subject leader has responsibility for securing high standards of teaching and learning in their subject as well as playing a major role in the development of school policy and practice. Throughout their work, a subject leader ensures that practices improve the quality of education provided, meet the

needs and aspirations of all pupils, and raise standards of achievement in the school.

(TTA, 1998b, p. 4)

Most importantly, it is assumed that subject leaders work within a school-wide context, are able to identify subject needs but recognise these have to be weighed against the overall needs of the school.

The TTA lists four broad categories of *skills and attributes* which subject leaders should possess. These are:

- leadership skills, attributes and professional competence: the ability to lead and manage people to work towards common goals
- decision-making skills: the ability to solve problems and make decisions
- communication skills: the ability to make points clearly and understand the views of others
- self-management: the ability to plan time effectively and to organise one-self well.

Attributes listed as required for the successful enactment of subject leadership include: personal presence, adaptability, energy and perseverance, self-confidence, enthusiasm, intellectual ability, reliability and integrity, and commitment.

The key areas of subject leadership and management are set out in detail under the four headings of:

- *Strategic direction and development of the subject* (within the context of the school's aims and policies, subject leaders develop and implement subject policies, plans, targets and practices)
- *Teaching and learning* (subject leaders secure and sustain effective teaching of the subject, evaluate the quality of teaching and standards of pupils' achievements and set targets for improvement)
- *Leading and managing staff* (subject leaders provide to all those with involvement in the teaching or support of the subject, the support, challenge, information and development necessary to sustain motivation and secure improvement in teaching)
- *Efficient and effective deployment of staff and resources* (subject leaders identify appropriate resources for the subject and ensure that they are used efficiently, effectively and safely) (TTA, 1998b, p. 9).

TEACHING AND LEARNING

Turner (2003) in a useful review of research on subject leaders in secondary schools identifies the ways in which they can influence effective teaching and learning outcomes. With reference to an ESRC-funded project conducted with Bolam, he identifies the main school-related factors that influence the methods subject leaders use in departments to improve teaching and learning. These factors included:

- the overall school policy on teaching, learning and assessment as expressed in the school's development plan
- the school's financial position and its system of allocating resources
- the extent to which subject leaders felt they could influence the appointment of departmental staff
- the characteristics of the student intake, especially in terms of their performance at Key Stage 2
- the ways in which pupil grouping was organised within the school
- the organisation of the timetable (Bolam and Turner, 1999, p. 254, cited in Turner, 2003).

In an earlier publication Turner (1996) outlined several ways in which department heads influence teaching and learning outcomes. These included discussion of department vision and how to achieve it; encouragement of teamwork; informal discussions; use of meetings to plan the curriculum, share good practice, discuss marking policy and teaching methods used; engage in staff development; feedback on performance; direct classroom observation and classroom appraisal.

Turner's most recent research amongst departmental heads in Welsh secondary schools points to six methods or strategies used to improve the quality of teaching and learning in their subject areas. These were the use of school-based in-service training; planning the curriculum and sharing good practice in departmental meetings; promoting team spirit; monitoring pupils' work and encouraging pupils' work to be displayed (Turner, 2003, p. 19).

In the summer of 2003 the National College for School Leadership published a practical guide to what middle leaders can do to improve learning in secondary schools (NCSL, 2003a). Although not based on research findings, the guidance and advice was derived from a series of 'leading-edge' seminars attended by middle and senior leaders. It states that the guide, entitled *The Heart of the Matter*, 'confirms a shift of role from managers of resources to leaders of people' and sets out to:

- illuminate the relationship between effective middle leadership and school improvement
- recognise the practical ways in which schools can harness the potential of middle leaders and develop their capacity to work as a team
- explore how senior leaders can provide support and enable middle leaders to be as good as they can be (ibid., p. 1).

The message of the guide is that schools need clarity, consensus and senior staff support 'in identifying what makes a difference in building schools' capacity to improve learning for all' (ibid.). It asks how can middle leaders be enabled to have maximum impact on the quality of learning in schools?

The guide sets out eight areas in which middle and senior leaders can make a difference to learning. These are:

- a focus on learning and teaching
- generate positive relationships
- provide a clear vision and high expectations
- improve the environment
- provide time and opportunities for collaboration
- distribute leadership: build teams
- engage the community
- evaluate and innovate.

For each area a list is provided of what middle leaders can do and how senior leaders can support and enable them to work effectively.

The first area, teaching and learning, is the specific focus of this section and it is not intended to list in full all 17 strategies or suggestions for middle leaders or the 18 for senior leaders. The reader is advised to consult the document which is readily available on the College's website. At the end of this first area – by far the lengthiest in the document – is included some comments from practitioners ('Practitioner voice') which note:

> In our school we felt there were three key tasks that we needed middle leaders to fulfil:
>
> - *Teaching* – make sure that the teaching delivered by those you line manage is of the highest possible quality;
> - *Learning* – make sure that pupils achieve at least to their potential as established by baseline testing, and preferably, beyond;
> - *Becoming involved in, or initiating, a whole-school activity related to school improvement* – help to drive the school forward.
>
> (Ibid., p. 10)

The message is to focus on these three essentials – 'deliver well in these key areas and you'll be doing a good job' (NCSL, 2003a, p. 10).

The practitioner voice notes that the third requirement is especially important as it made sure that middle leaders 'got their heads above the parapet of their own departments and developed an understanding of the vision of the school and contributed to taking it forward' (ibid., p. 10). It is to the strategic aspect of role that we now turn.

STRATEGIC DIRECTION

In broad terms the notion of 'strategy' has been seen as being concerned with the long-term future of an organisation – with *planning for a successful future*. As Weindling notes: 'The business literature uses a variety of terms such as "strategic management", "strategic planning" and "strategic thinking", but in essence, strategy is the process by which members of the organisation envision its future and develop the necessary procedures to achieve that future' (Weindling, 1997, p. 220).

Strategy is about forward planning and Fidler (1996) suggests that possibly the most important part of strategy is *strategic thinking* – the attitude of mind by which strategy is formulated. This, he notes: 'encompasses the long term, is constantly researching the external factors which may influence the school in the future, thinks in whole-organisation terms and is aware of, and tries to fully use, organisational capabilities' (Fidler, 1996, p. xvi).

Clearly such activities, reflecting as they do the importance of a vision or future state for the *whole* organisation, are largely seen as being a key responsibility of senior staff, particularly the headteacher and leadership team *and* the school's governing body (see Chapter 11). This does not mean, however, that middle managers/leaders and other staff will not be able to contribute to strategic thinking; there will be a need to make use of all the resources at the organisation's disposal. School staff, regardless of level or grade, are likely to be perceived by organisational leaders as an important source of information about the external world and its likely impact, particularly on their areas of responsibility or expertise. In the secondary school sector, for example, effective middle managers have been seen as contributing to whole-school issues, keeping senior staff informed of developments as they affect their subject and the school, and to have a role in decision making at both department and school levels (Brown et al., 1999; Earley, 1998; Earley and Fletcher-Campbell, 1992). Their main role however – both as delineated in job descriptions and as carried out in practice – has tended to focus predominantly on matters closer to the classroom. Traditionally, the prime concern of middle managers has been with the successful implementation of the organisation's strategy rather than with its creation.

It has become increasingly apparent that for organisations to survive in an increasingly turbulent and changing environment, issues of strategy can no longer be seen as the exclusive preserve of senior staff. For strategy to be successfully implemented, staff at all levels in an organisation increasingly need to be involved in decision-making and policy formulation – albeit to varying degrees – and be encouraged to develop a sense of ownership and share the organisation's mission. As Tom Peters, writing within a business context, remarked many years ago: 'The essence of strategy is the creation of organisational capabilities that will allow us to react opportunistically to whatever happens. In the fully developed organisation, the front line person should be capable of being involved in strategy making' (Peters, 1988, p. x).

Middle managers/leaders working with their teams are very much in the front line but capability, in itself, does not necessarily mean involvement in strategic matters or organisation decision-making. Levels of involvement are likely to vary according to a number of factors, including the nature of the organisation and the attitude or predisposition of staff. Much is likely to depend on such factors as:

- the structure of the organisation (is it hierarchical or relatively flat, for example?)
- the leadership and management style of senior staff (is it predominantly participative or directive?)
- the culture of the organisation (how are things done and what are the expectations of each other?).

Strategic planning must become embedded in the culture of the organisation if all staff are to work together in the same direction towards common goals. An individual's willingness or desire to become involved in such matters will also need to be taken into account, and these in turn are likely to be shaped by the culture of the organisation or sub-unit (e.g. department, section, year group) and, most importantly, the time and opportunities that are created for such activities to occur.

Schools might not always be able readily to find the required financial resources but are they always making the best use, strategically, of their most valuable resource – their staff, especially their middle managers?

Floyd and Wooldridge (1996) in their study of 250 managers in 25 organisations in the USA, stressed the importance of middle manager involvement in the formulation of new strategies as well as in the implementation of existing strategies. They identify four strategic roles for middle managers:

- championing innovative initiatives
- facilitating adaptability to new behaviour
- synthesising information (both within and outside the organisation)
- implementing strategy.

In their view the performance of these roles has a direct bearing on a company's overall ability to pursue its strategies and maintain its competitive advantage.

Middle managers' involvement also depends on how the term 'strategy' is defined. Johnson and Scholes (1993) usefully differentiate between strategy at the corporate level, competitive strategy and operational strategy. The former they associate with what types of business the organisation as a whole should be in, whilst competitive strategy is about how to compete in a particular market. Operational strategy is concerned more with how the different functions of the organisation contribute to the other levels of strategy. Thus corporate strategy might be perceived more as a senior management or governing body responsibility, with middle managers and other staff being involved more at the other levels.

Middle managers' prime focus in any organisation, however, is therefore likely to be on short-term tactical planning and operational strategy rather than the wider strategic direction or vision for the organisation as a whole (at the corporate level). Although middle managers in schools are essentially curriculum managers or leaders of teaching and learning, they will be expected to play a role in policy development at both subject level (broadly defined) and at whole-school level. Involvement in the production and implementation of school improvement/development plans and strategic plans will also be important but planning processes will be undertaken, for the most part, at the level of the section or unit – the department, the curriculum area or the year team. These plans will be expected to fit in or dovetail with those of the school as a whole.

The delegation of resources and the growth of decision-making powers, through local management has meant schools, more than ever before, need to plan strategically and to think in strategic terms. Strategic planning enables organisations to develop and act in a proactive manner. Rapid change and uncertainty in the environment makes it ever more difficult to predict future external trends. With such a scenario in mind strategic management and planning increasingly become everybody's responsibility.

TENSIONS

Studies of the actual practice of middle management point to the considerable discrepancy that exists between what actually takes place 'on the ground' and that outlined in job descriptions and role definitions. It is to the research literature that attention is now given.

It must be stated at the outset that there are very few studies that are based on what middle managers actually do, compared to those that report what middle managers (or others) claim they do or, more commonly, should do. The few observational studies that have been conducted – and these are almost totally secondary school focused – demonstrate that the work of middle managers, like their more senior counterparts, tends to be characterised by fragmentation and involves them in a myriad of interactions with both pupils and staff. Routine administration and crisis management seem to be the norm with middle managers having little time for strategic thinking and planning, either within the department or across the school as a whole (Earley and Fletcher-Campbell, 1992). Also, of course, it should not be forgotten that middle managers spend the bulk of their time teaching, they have little non-contact time; indeed, most primary practitioners have none!

Earley and Fletcher-Campbell

In the NFER study which included shadowing and observation of practice, middle managers were often criticised by senior school staff for their rather limited or subject-bound perspectives (Earley and Fletcher-Campbell, 1992). Involvement in whole-school decision-making was seen as highly desirable; indeed, all the schools participating in our research had systems and structures in place which permitted staff involvement in decision-making processes. Although this level of involvement was seen as desirable for heads of department, it was reported to be an essential attribute for heads of faculty. If middle leaders were aiming for senior posts, then they were expected to develop a whole-school perspective. Staff, from their perspective, liked to be consulted about major issues and welcomed the opportunity to put forward ideas and suggestions.

In general, however, many teachers felt they had little say in whole-school decision-making and particularly objected to being consulted after a course of action had been decided on. Senior staff were seen as having responsibility and the right to make decisions but 'pseudo-democracy' was something to be avoided and could contribute to low staff morale. Expectations did vary according to the importance of the matter being discussed, but indecisiveness and slow decision-making were criticised. Staff looked for genuine opportunities to participate in decisions about school issues but much did depend on the significance of the issue under discussion, the level of commitment required and teachers' own views about their preferred level of involvement. Some teachers and middle managers, for example, saw their priorities as attending to classroom rather than whole-school matters. This was likely to be more commonly found where consultative structures were perceived as little more than 'talking shops' with minimal or no influence on decision-makers.

Brown and Rutherford

In their research study, which included the shadowing of eight heads of department, Brown and Rutherford (1996) report a similar tendency for senior managers to look for the wider perspective. They note the comments of a deputy who remarked of an otherwise effective department head:

> He makes little contribution to the management of the school. He does not discuss the wider issues of where the school is going with the senior management team and so lacks a 'whole school' perspective. He is too tied up in his own department, perhaps because the role of the head of department has expanded so much over the last few years ... Nevertheless he should make a wider contribution to the school.

> (Brown and Rutherford, 1996, p. 9)

Brown and colleagues' more recent work (Brown et al., 1999) note a similar situation with wide variation reported in relation to middle manager involvement in whole-school decision-making. In a random sample of 21 secondary schools in North-West England they identified three levels of participation with varying degrees of collaboration concluding that middle managers wanted 'a greater say in decisions about the school ... subject leaders want bureaucratic approaches to leadership to be replaced by distributed leadership throughout the school' (ibid., p. 329).

As noted earlier, the contributions middle managers are likely to make to whole-school decision-making will be affected by a variety of factors: those specific to the organisation, its structure and culture, and those related more to the individual and the degree to which the role is perceived in strategic and whole-school terms. Certainly the research evidence over the last 15 years or so from the secondary sector suggests that there is still some way to go before many middle managers define their role largely in terms of management and leadership. The NFER report, for example, was entitled *The Time to Manage?* not only because of the very real difficulties created by the fact that middle managers had so little non-contact time to conduct their 'management' role, but also because the role, for many, was still being conceptualised in non-management terms. In other words it was suggested that it was time for middle managers in schools to reconceptualise the role away from seeing themselves as 'senior subject teachers' towards that of a manager and subject leader with responsibilities for developing people as well as resources and pro-grammes. Strategic management and an interest in whole-school issues was seen as part of that broader conceptualisation. Whether the work of the NCSL, including its innovative training programme *Leading from the Middle*, and the change of title from middle manager to middle leader, will alter such attitudes and mind-sets will be interesting to observe.

Ofsted findings

If this is the situation for secondary schools – and recent Ofsted inspection reports suggest that although there have been changes, the middle manager's role has still to be developed in many secondary schools (Ofsted, 1997) – then it is hardly surprising that evidence from the primary sector shows a similar pattern. As noted earlier, there is often limited or no non-contact time for middle managers in primary schools to perform their leadership and management functions, even if they wished to do so (although this situation should change in the light of the government's workforce remodelling agenda).

A summary of Ofsted findings on subject co-ordination in primary schools (Ofsted, 1996) for example, states that essential though the role is, there are few schools in which the management of all the subjects is effective. It continues:

> In Key Stage 1, the quality of management of subjects is weak overall in over a quarter of schools; for individual subjects, this figure ranges from one-fifth to well over one-third. In Key Stage 2 the situation is worse: it is weak overall in almost one-third of schools, and in individual subjects from a quarter to well over two-fifths.

> (Ofsted, 1996, p. 34)

Clearly, many subject leaders or curriculum co-ordinators in primary schools have difficulty, due to limited time and/or a reluctance to see themselves in this way, in performing the role of curriculum manager or leader with whole-school responsibilities for other staff and subject areas. The monitoring role in particular is often seen as the responsibility of the headteacher and not that of one's professional peers or colleagues (Webb and Vulliamy, 1996).

The smaller size and collegiality of the primary school has usually meant that headteachers who wished to consult staff were able to do so relatively easily, although the culture of the primary school has been found to be an important factor in determining levels of involvement in whole school decision-making (Nias et al., 1989). Research suggests that recent educational reforms in relation to the curriculum and its assessment may have created more team-work within primary schools (through, for example, joint planning) whilst also, paradoxically, setting up possible divisions through the establishment of senior management teams (Wallace and Huckman, 1996), and less *direct* consultation as many heads attempt to 'protect' staff from matters that take the teachers away from their main focus – the classroom.

SUMMARY

A central theme of this chapter has been to show that middle managers are in a key position to help shape the future direction and continued success of their schools. The 'school improvement' function of middle management or middle leadership is crucial and is likely to increase in importance over the next few years. This increasing significance is reflected in the recent growth of research and writing on middle management (e.g. Bennett, 1995; Blandford, 1996; Brown et al., 1999; 2000; Busher et al., 2000; Field et al., 2000; Gold, 1997; Kitson and O'Neill, 1996; Sammons et al., 1997; Turner, 2003; West, 1995), along with the development of training programmes, particularly the NCSL's *Leading from the Middle*. With restructuring and the general move towards flatter management structures and shared and distributed leadership, the pressure at the middle manager level for attitudinal change and the need for a range of new skills are critical issues in quality improvement for schools.

11

Governors as Leaders

Do governing bodies matter?
Governors' leadership role
Headteacher selection
Ways forward

This chapter argues that governors have an important leadership role to play in schools.[1] It attempts to define that role and draws upon recent research to illustrate the extent to which governors are demonstrating leadership in their activities. A comparison is also made with the independent school sector. Governors are critically responsible for the appointment of headteachers and the final section of this chapter uses the findings from a recent study to examine the process. The role of the governing body in school improvement is considered in the following chapter. This chapter begins however by drawing on research and inspection evidence to address the difficult question of ascertaining the impact an effective governing body has on a school and its overall effectiveness, including its performance and leadership.

DO GOVERNING BODIES MATTER?

Methodologically it is extremely difficult, if not impossible, to ascertain the precise contribution a governing body makes to its school. It could be argued that some schools are effective with little or no help from their governors. There is a view, held by some heads, that governing bodies are yet another level of accountability, leading to 'meetings, reports and work' and that their role should be drastically reduced as the benefit they bring to schools is outweighed by the work they generate (Revell, 2002). For those heads struggling to recruit a full complement of governors (let alone giving consideration to their quality) it may seem like a great deal of effort expended for little reward; indeed, priorities may lie elsewhere, especially if there is much to do with little time to do it!

However, there is a growing body of evidence to suggest that there is a link between school effectiveness and governing body effectiveness. It may be possible to have a successful or effective school with an ineffective governing body but how much more successful might that school be with an effective governing body, working in close partnership with the school and the community?

Important empirical studies of school governance were published in the mid-1990s – for example, Bullock and Thomas (1997), Deem et al. (1995), Levačić (1995), Shearn et al. (1995a; 1995b) and Thomas and Martin (1996) – but the focus of these research studies was not specifically on the governors' role in school improvement or school leadership. The emphasis was more often on the effects of delegation, the local management of schools, and the role of governing bodies in decision-making and resource allocation. The first major research study to explore notions of effectiveness and the link between schools and governing bodies was that undertaken by Scanlon et al. in 1999. This was followed by a study from Ofsted based on inspection findings and published in 2002 (Ofsted, 2002b).

The Scanlon et al. (1999) research (funded by the government and directed by PE), as part of a much larger study, specifically explored the relationship between effective schools and effective governance. A small sample of matched pairs of schools, similar in a number of important ways (phase, size, free school meals entitlement and denomination) was studied in detail. One group of schools was deemed by the inspectors to be 'very effective' and the other 'less effective' (but not subject to special measures). The researchers found a strong association between the inspectors' judgements of a school's effectiveness and their judgements of its governing body. The researchers asked the governors of these schools to rate the overall effectiveness of their governing body. Questionnaire data from the governors showed a statistically significant difference between their view of governing body effectiveness and the school's effectiveness as defined by Ofsted. It appeared as though there was a positive relationship between effective schools and effective governing bodies, although the causal direction could not be determined.

The second piece of evidence, provided by Ofsted, suggests that where governance is good, standards of attainment are more likely to be higher than in other schools (Ofsted, 2002b). There was found to be a clear association between effective schools and effective governing bodies, although again the direction of the association was impossible to ascertain. A marked correlation was found, although as the report notes: 'It is not possible to prove that good governance leads to good schools, as the cause and effect evidence is impossible to isolate. However, there are very strong indicators to show that where there is good governance the school is more likely to be successful' (Ofsted, 2002b, p. 11).

Research has shown that the attitude of the headteacher is a crucial factor in 'good governance' or governing body effectiveness, but even the most 'governor friendly' head may have their request for greater governor involvement politely rejected. Heads of schools with governing bodies that are reluctant or incapable of acting 'effectively' will be disadvantaged. It is not that such schools will also be ineffective, indeed they may be seen by Ofsted and others as highly effective but, as earlier noted, how much more effective might that school be with an effective governing body? The importance of good governance becomes more apparent when consideration is given to the benefits that are said to accrue from it.

GOVERNORS' LEADERSHIP ROLE

The roles and responsibilities of the governing body have developed over the years to the present position in England where it is increasingly expected, especially in the light of the new inspection framework, to have a significant leadership role. This can be seen especially in relation to strategic leadership and helping to provide and shape the school's direction and be clear about its core values and vision for the future (DfES, 2002b; Ofsted, 2003a). Recent guidance is clear; governing bodies are 'to carry out their functions with the aim of taking a largely strategic role in the running of the school' (DfEE, 2000b, p. 1). Similarly, the developing framework of national standards for school governance gives prominence to such matters as strategic planning and ensuring progress (Little, 2002).

It could therefore be argued that governing bodies have a leadership role and that this is expressed largely in terms of the enactment of the three roles – strategic direction, critical friendship and accountability (see Chapter 12), especially the first, the strategic. Advice and guidance to governing bodies is increasingly conceptualised in terms of carrying out these roles (e.g. DfEE, 2000a), whilst a DfES national conference for governors was simply entitled 'Steering or Rowing?' (DfES, 2002b). The latest inspection framework gives a similar message (Ofsted, 2003a).

Martin and Holt (2002), drawing on the Audit Commission's *Lessons in Teamwork* (1995), attempt to describe what 'acting strategically' means in practice. They suggest that the governing body's steering or strategic role is to agree aims, values and policies for the school, and they note how it is about 'setting a course, deciding on a route, looking to the future for the school, thinking about what the school needs to achieve and plotting how to get from where it is now to where you would like it to be in the future' (Martin and Holt, 2002, p. 17).

This is not a role however to be performed in isolation, it's very much about sharing and distributing leadership. Operating and thinking strategically is done in conjunction with the head and other school staff, indeed 'strategy must be worked out in partnership – and the vast majority of headteachers who choose to be governors, together with governors representing the teaching staff, have a legitimate role to play as part of the corporate body in setting the course' (Martin and Holt, 2002, p. 17). As government regulations and advice make clear, 'creating strategy is the essence of the governing body's role. It produces the strategy for the school's development' (Martin and Holt, 2002, p. 17). Martin and Holt provide helpful advice on what being strategic actually means in practice and refer to a three-stage process of agreeing aims and values; planning how to put them into operation; and ensuring that they are put into practice (Martin and Holt, 2002, p. 18).

Of course the degree to which governors are said to be leaders depends on how the concept is defined. The notion of *governors as leaders* has recently been explored by Jane Phillips, chair of the governor association, National Association of Governors and Managers (NAGM). She draws on the work of

Dave Ulrich (1996) to define leadership in terms of the five 'A's – namely: Assessment; Articulation; Allocation; Attention and Accountability – and she looks at each of these in terms of governors' key roles: strategic direction, critical friendship, and monitoring and accountability (Phillips, 2003).

• *Assessment* – leaders assess their personal and organisational strengths and weaknesses. Acknowledging weaknesses and making best use of strengths enables leaders to know themselves and their organisations well enough to make progress. Phillips notes that for governors:

> having an understanding of the school's strengths and weaknesses depends largely on their having an open and honest relationship with their head – so that the head is confident that his/her governors will act as true 'critical friends' when hearing the bad news as well as the good. However, governors must not rely on the head as their sole source of monitoring information. Alternative sources of information include governors' visits, reports from other staff members and reports from sources beyond the school (primarily their LEA link adviser, LEA comparative data and Ofsted Panda and inspection reports).
>
> (ibid., p. 1)

• *Articulation* – leaders articulate their personal and organisational goals so that this vision becomes a useful means of setting direction. For governors, as Phillips notes:

> this wholly encompasses their strategic role. This role goes far beyond involvement in production of the SDP/SIP (important as that is). It includes defining the ethos and values of their school community and deciding the priorities for their school – and deciding whether these priorities will align with priorities imposed from above.
>
> (ibid., p. 1)

• *Allocation* – leaders allocate resources both financial and human. The personal resources of leaders include their time and accessibility. As people are seen as the most important resource their deployment, development and happiness are all seen as leadership issues. Phillips sees this as most problematic for governors as they neither have the time to undertake all these responsibilities with sufficient rigour nor are they accessible during the school day. The NAGM's own research (of their members) suggests that 'personnel responsibilities cause governors substantial angst' and Phillips suggests that this is the part of the leadership role where governors need substantial support.

• *Attention* – leaders focus attention and gain credibility by having a passion about a few priorities. They help organisations to focus attention by specifying a few key priorities, relentlessly pursuing those priorities and building an organisational culture of resolve. Phillips sees this as part of the strategic role of the governing body and argues that:

> deciding, with the head and staff, the priorities for the school and monitoring and evaluating their implementation – again with the head and staff – are strategy personified. The unique role of governors in this task relies on their perspective as representing a variety of stakeholders. This additional perspective can add real value to the outcome.

> (ibid.)

- *Accountability* – leaders ensure accountability and are themselves accountable. Without reporting procedures, goals tend to become wishes, not realities. Phillips sees the performance management system as a key accountability mechanism where behaviours are accounted for. She notes:

> For governors, there are several important reporting mechanisms by which they are kept informed, but of greatest importance for their leadership role is the accountability of staff. The role of governors in performance management is largely confined to the performance review of the headteacher. In the head's review, there are two specified areas for objectives, pupil progress and leadership and management and these should relate to school priorities. So, this is a real opportunity for the governing body, through its appointed governors, to support the head, to focus on priorities to and hold him/her to account.

> (ibid.)

In this way Phillips argues that all three governing body key roles – strategic, critical friend and accountability – are involved and in enacting them governors are demonstrating leadership, albeit *shared* leadership.

But what do we know about how governors and headteachers actually perceive and enact these key responsibilities, and do they conceptualise their role as one of leadership? Also are there important differences between the state and independent sectors?

An Ofsted report on the work of state school governors drew on inspection evidence to note:

> Governors in about 90 percent of schools have a satisfactory or better understanding of the strengths and weaknesses of their school, but they are less effective in shaping the direction of the school … Where governors do not contribute effectively to shaping the direction of the school, they often have little knowledge of the school's main development priorities, agree plans and policies unquestioningly, and rely too much on the headteacher as the source of their information about the school.

> (Ofsted, 2001, p. 10)

Table 11.1 The degree governing body *should* play in strategic leadership: state schools (percentages)

	Major role – 1	Moderate – 2	Minor – 3	No role at all – 4
Headteachers (n = 606)	22	58	18	2.5
Chairs of GB (n = 197)	57	39	4	0

Table 11.2 Extent of governing body's *actual* role in strategic leadership: state schools (percentages)

	Major role – 1	Moderate – 2	Minor – 3	No role at all – 4
Headteachers (n = 608)	13	52	31	4
Chairs of GB (n = 197)	29	56	15	0

The leadership role of governing bodies was an issue also explored in the 2001 DfES school leadership study (Earley et al., 2002) and in a similar study undertaken for the independent school sector (Earley and Evans, 2002a). The findings of each are outlined briefly below.

State school governors and leadership

Headteachers in 2001 seemed to have a limited concept of the role of the governing body as can be seen in Tables 11.1 and 11.2. Over one-fifth of the heads agreed that governing bodies should play a major role in the strategic leadership of schools – but far fewer (only 13%) judged that their governing body actually did so. A third of headteachers thought that their governing body actually played a 'minor role' or 'no role at all' in the strategic leadership of their school. Of the one in eight heads who thought their governing body did play a major strategic leadership role, most were from secondary (15%) or primary schools (13%) with special school heads (4%) being much less positive about their governors' strategic role in practice. One in six heads indicated that governing bodies were a main source of ideas and inspiration about their work as school leaders.

Over 500 heads provided further comments about how the work of the governing body relates to their leadership role. About a quarter made reference to the governing body giving support and encouragement, with a further quarter mentioning the governors' role as a 'critical friend' or a 'sounding board'. About a tenth of headteachers providing comments made a negative remark about governors such as their lack of time and knowledge and/or inadequate skills.

Table 11.3 Significance of governing body's role in state
school leadership (percentages)

	Very signif 1	2	3	No signif 4
Chairs of GB (n = 197)	32	57	11	0

As part of the DfES study a questionnaire was also sent to chairs of governors (to a different sample of state schools from that of the heads) who were asked a similar set of questions about the leadership role of the governing body. A third regarded its leadership role to be 'very significant' (see Table 11.3), whilst not a single governor was prepared to say it was of 'no significance'.

State school governors were also asked how the work of the governing body related to the leadership role of the head. A similar set of themes and comments was offered as was found for the heads. For example, the governing body's work was largely seen in terms of providing direction, being supportive, acting as a sounding board and ensuring the school's resources were well managed.

Interestingly, several comments included notes of caution about what governors were not able or willing to do.

> Supporting the head, occasionally offering advice but we are *not* teachers and cannot always understand fully.

> The governors do not and should not, be involved in the day-to-day leadership role of the head. The best analogy is that governors carry out the role of non-executive directors in a large corporation, monitoring and advising the chief executive.

> We're supportive – but it is unrealistic to expect that non-qualified governors can do anything more than oversee in a general sense.

> Lack of time for most governors means that the head makes most decisions without reference to governors.

Chairs of governors were also asked to indicate the degree to which they thought their governing body should play a strategic leadership role, and the extent to which it actually did. The results, shown in Tables 11.1 and 11.2, present a far more positive picture than that for the headteacher sample. Perhaps unsurprisingly, no governor was prepared to agree that their governing body played 'no role at all', although 15 percent were of the view that their actual role in strategic leadership was 'minor'. Secondary school governors were more likely than their primary counterparts to state that the governing body should play a major strategic leadership role in the school's affairs.

Chairs of governors saw their role as providing support and encouragement; planning, decision-making processes and providing strategic direction;

monitoring role; being a 'critical friend' and sounding board for new ideas. However, comments often had a qualifying or cautionary note: 'Effective support (critical, practical, reflective) of the head, and of staff. In practice, this is an ideal rarely achieved'; 'It is not possible for part time volunteers to be realistically engaged in day to day leadership.'

The role of the governing body and issues around leadership and governance were also considered in each of the 2001 DfES research project's case study schools. They provided further examples of how headteachers and governors were able to work closely and effectively together. Some governors in the case study schools – in particular the chair of the governing body – appeared to have a strong influence and to be able to act as a mentor or a 'critical friend' to the leadership team. Important and strategic decisions, such as whether the school should apply for Beacon status or become a specialist college, were fully discussed with the governors and they were actively involved in decision-making. However, it was not clear whether the role of the governing body, as opposed to the role of one or two key influential governors, was generally one of strategic leadership (see Earley et al., 2002 for an account of each of the ten case studies).

The research also explored the main source of ideas and inspiration for school leaders. About one in six heads (16%) indicated that 'governing bodies' were a main source of ideas and inspiration about their work as school leaders. A very high percentage of chairs of governors (81%) pointed to the head as a significant source which highlights the key role that heads can play in the operation of their school's governing body. The degree to which governors are likely to be involved in strategic leadership and perceive of themselves as leaders is going to be shaped to a considerable extent by the approach and attitude of the headteacher. As one chair of governors noted: 'The governing body may have great vision and motivation but if the head is not receptive this energy is wasted.' The head has got to have a view of leadership that is shared or dispersed and that part of that dispersal includes the governing body.

Independent schools

What is the picture of governors in independent schools? The vast majority of independent schools that we sampled operated with a governing body (Earley and Evans, 2002a). As can be seen from Table 11.4, in nearly one third of schools with governing bodies, heads considered that they should play a 'major' strategic role. Just over one half of heads thought they should play a 'moderate' role. In only one school was the governing body seen as playing 'no role at all' in strategic leadership. Like their colleagues in state schools, governors' actual leadership was not as strong as heads would have liked.

However, on the whole, most heads (61%) were content with the level of involvement of their governing body in strategic leadership. In nearly one third of the schools, the head would have welcomed more involvement by the governing body in strategic leadership, and in eight percent of the cases, the head would have preferred the governing body to play less of a role.

Table 11.4 Heads' views on degree governing body *should* play and *actually* does play in strategic leadership: independent schools (percentages)

GB's role in strategic leadership	Major role 1	Moderate 2	Minor 3	No role at all 4
Role should play	31	53	16	0.6
(n = 155)	(22)	(58)	(18)	(2.5)
Role actually plays	25	40	29	6
(n = 157)	(13)	(52)	(31)	(4)

Notes Figures in brackets refer to the survey of state school headteachers.

Again, the governing body's role was seen as providing support and back up for the head and offering expert advice on non-educational issues, such as legal and financial matters. The expertise and experience offered by governors was most valued. As one head wrote: 'The governing body should support the work of the head and SMT, deferring to their understanding and experience of education but offering an objective perspective.' However, very few comments made reference to the governing body's role in monitoring the school's or the head's performance or as an accountability mechanism.

One independent school head spoke of her governing body as 'senators' who 'took advice from us but also gave advice – they're excellent at this and we listen carefully to them'. Another felt that the governing body should lead from the front as far as policy was concerned but, once decisions had been made, then it was up to the head and the management team to implement policy without interference. One head said that the school's governing body 'feels that heads are executives to manage. The governing body sets the policies and allows us to do our job'.

Another said the governors' policy should be to 'back me or sack me'. Others stated that they did not have particularly proactive governors but 'they would soon tell me if things were going wrong'. Some independent school heads were not convinced that governors should have a strong leadership role or be 'school leaders', rather they should act more as advisers: 'Yes they do have a leadership role but they rely heavily on me about the way they should be thinking e.g. updating corporate plan but looking to me for input.' One independent school head was most clear on this matter when he said:

> The governing body is there to oversee the finances. Their key task is to appoint the head and support him on such things as accounting, finance, law and property. They're experts in these (areas). Their fundamental job is to protect the school's assets and optimise resources. They don't have a leadership role: if they do it's because things have gone wrong in the school.

Whatever independent school heads' views were on the governing body's leadership role it was clear that the relationship with its chair was a crucial one.

Interviewees spoke of regular meetings with the chair and of the very good open relationships they had with them. This was not always the case, however, with one head noting that his was: 'not an easy, cordial relationship and as mutually supportive as I'd like. The governing body see themselves as employers of the head. The chairman has been a member of the governing body for a considerable number of years and a pupil before that. That has caused friction at times'. However, in general there were very few negative comments about governing bodies (less than one in 50).

HEADTEACHER SELECTION

The appointment of a new head is a major event in the history of a school and is a crucial decision for the governors – some say it is the most important job they do. However, the last piece of research on this topic was conducted over 20 years ago (Morgan et al., 1983), so in 2003 the NCSL commissioned a pilot study to explore the process and one of us was involved in the research (Weindling and Pocklington, 2003).

Twenty schools that had appointed a new headteacher in the previous year were chosen as case studies. Interviews were conducted separately with the chair of governors and the newly appointed head.

A model of the whole process was developed to show how the events and players interacted (see Figure 11.1). The main elements were: the school context; the perceived need for change or continuity; the production of the advert, and the job and person specifications; long-listing and short-listing; various types of exercises and activities for the appointment process; and final decision-making. The key players were the selectors (a sub-group of governors and LEA representatives) and the candidates.

The process was triggered when the incumbent head told the chair of governors that they wished to leave (most of the heads in the sample left after 10–30 years in post). The chair then informed the governing body and a sub-group of governors was set up to select the new head. The LEA link adviser first met with the governor sub-group and helped them to produce an advert, a job description and a person specification. The adviser usually offered guidance on the characteristics that were considered 'essential' or 'desirable' and these were discussed by the selectors. A critical decision was the degree to which the governors and LEA wanted the new head to introduce major change, maintain continuity, or work somewhere in-between. This was dependent on the school context and influenced by the governors' and LEA's perception of the outgoing head, pupil performance and the results of recent Ofsted inspections.

The chair of one secondary school said that governors had wanted someone to maintain the ethos and values established by the previous headteacher, and told of how they had reacted negatively to the views expressed by one of the candidates during the interview. In contrast, the idea of change was wanted in a number of the schools, for example: 'We were a school causing concern.

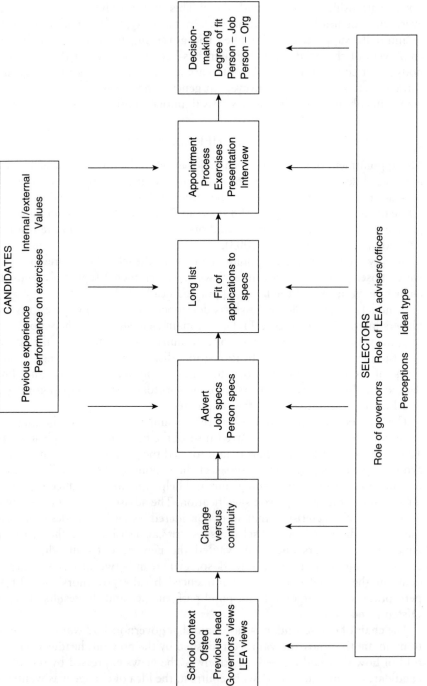

Figure 11.1   Headteacher selection

There was a long-serving staff and some weak teachers ... We wanted to raise standards ... We wanted a culture change.'

The secondary schools in the sample attracted more candidates than the primary or special schools. The average for the secondary phase was 20, with only six candidates for the primaries and 4.5 for the two special schools. A few schools had great difficulty in obtaining more than one or two candidates. The number of applicants has dramatically declined over the last 15 years (Earley and Baker, 1989) and Howson, who conducts an annual survey of advertisements, has reported that one-third of all primary and one-quarter of all secondary headships are re-advertised (*Times Educational Supplement*, 9 January 2004).

If they were interested, candidates responded to the advert and then submitted an application form and curriculum vitae (CV). The selectors read through the applications and compared them with the job and person specifications to produce a long list. These were discussed and a number of candidates invited for interview. This stage varied in length from a minimum of a half day, to one school that spent three days on the process. Most schools used one or two days. The process of appointment showed some variation in the number and type of exercises used, but the central elements consisted of a presentation by the candidates (usually their vision for the school in three to five years' time) and a formal panel interview. In addition, some schools used in-tray exercises, panels of selectors, exercises with the pupils and students, and perhaps meetings with the SMT. The secondary schools generally used more elaborate procedures that the primary or special schools.

The research showed that the key to decision-making was the 'degree of fit' – how the selectors perceived the qualities, values, skills and experience of the candidates against the 'ideal type' of headteacher for 'their' school. The concept of fit was clearly expressed by the chair of governors in a secondary school who said: 'In my mind I knew what I wanted for the school, and he said what I wanted to hear.'

A notable finding was that the majority of successful candidates were local – either from within the school or the LEA. Only four of the 20 new heads were appointed from outside the LEA. Eight were internal appointments, from deputy of the school to head, and another eight were deputies or heads from other schools within the authority. The large majority of candidates were deputies: for only two people was this their second or third headship.

The importance of being an acting head was also shown to have influenced the selectors. Twelve people had been acting heads for various periods, either of the school in question or at their previous school. There was a prominence of acting heads in the primary schools in the sample (eight of the 11 schools), who went on to be confirmed as headteacher. This would appear to suggest that acting heads have a definite advantage over other candidates.

Under current legislation school governors have the crucial responsibility for appointing a headteacher. Our interviews showed that they were very aware of the importance and significance of selecting a new head: 'that we were going to decide the destiny of the school'. Despite the changes in legislation which have given more responsibility to governors, they actively sought and greatly valued the advice and guidance they were given by the LEA. The school link adviser usually supported the governors throughout the process and a senior LEA officer sometimes joined the panel for the final interview.

The pilot study demonstrated the need for a larger research project which the NCSL were considering. This would need to examine selection processes in other countries and in business and industry. The pilot study indicated a reliance on 'one best model' which was suggested by the LEAs. Are there better models? There also appeared to be a tendency to choose someone already known to the selectors. The extent to which this could be seen as a 'safe choice' also needs to be explored.

WAYS FORWARD

If, as the National College for School Leadership (NCSL, 2001) and others state, the best leadership is shared then heads have a key role to play in shaping the nature and distribution of that leadership, and this must include the development of trust and the sharing of information with governors. For school leadership to be shared with the governing body a real partnership needs to develop, one that is equal and includes all stakeholders. When this is the case, governing bodies are enabled to fulfil their key roles, to be co-leaders and to contribute in meaningful ways to the processes of school improvement. Of course the degree to which governors are said to be leaders depends on how the concept is defined.

This chapter has presented data that indicate the degree to which governing bodies could be said to be operating strategically and sharing the leadership function with headteachers. As governors were reminded at a recent DfES national governors' conference, 'acting strategically means ensuring that the school was managed in keeping with the strategic framework, by requesting reports and reviews' (DfES, 2002b, p. 27). Also, as Ofsted has noted, where governors are operating well they will contribute to the shaping of the school's direction and be involved in the development of the school improvement plan. Furthermore: 'although the plan is invariably written by the senior staff of the school, effective governors discuss the plan and ask questions in a way that helps their understanding of where the school is going. This allows them to test the clarity of vision of the senior staff' (Ofsted, 2002b, p. 10).

For many governing bodies, leadership is still something that is largely perceived and practised through the head and senior school staff. Our research studies suggest that both state and independent school heads had a rather limited concept of the role of the governing body but that many welcomed governors and wanted them to play, in collaboration with themselves and others, a leadership role. It is also apparent, however, that there is a clear gap between the desired state and the actual practice on the ground. It is not always easy for governing bodies to operate strategically. It is often said of governors that they feel more comfortable giving support and offering advice than they do in helping to decide the school's strategy and direction. Therefore, in conclusion, four questions are asked of school governors as leaders:

- Is too much governor training currently focusing on the wrong things?
- Does more of it need to centre on the whole governing body, including the head and other senior staff?
- Should governors focus their efforts more on ensuring their schools are effectively led and managed and that its policies are successfully implemented?
- Are the current responsibilities and expectations of governors simply unrealistic or too high? Is too much expected from a group of part-time (or, more correctly, occasional time) unpaid volunteers?

This last question has been explored elsewhere (Earley and Creese, 2003) where it is asked if the role is best fulfilled by the present pattern of untrained, volunteer, 'lay' school governors, or whether it is time to adopt a more professional approach. For governing bodies to become more effective – more 'professional' in the way they work – the role clearly needs to give greater emphasis to strategy and accountability. Training is needed, preferably but not exclusively school-based, which helps governing bodies to operate in this way and ask 'the awkward questions' about the school and its performance. The training materials for newly appointed governors and for heads and chairs, funded by the DfES, should prove most helpful.

Perhaps governing bodies should focus their attentions, more than they currently do, on headteacher performance, school strategy and policy, with even greater management delegation being given to the head. Should governors concentrate most of their efforts, as Rowan and Taylor (2002) suggest, on ensuring their schools are effectively led, not so much seeing themselves as leaders but rather ensuring the SMT or leadership team, including the head, are doing the 'right sort of leading … otherwise there is a danger of crossing the line into an operational role' (Pollock, 2003, p. 27). Similarly, should more emphasis be given to the performance management of the head and the leadership team with an enhanced role for the external adviser to the governing body (Earley, 2004a)?

When governing bodies are working well they can help provide direction (be leaders?) and not merely be followers, operating under the guiding hand of the head or chief executive. As noted at the beginning of this chapter there are strong indicators to show that a school is more likely to be successful where there is evidence of good governance – and the latter, by definition, is concerned with steering and not merely rowing under the direction of the head and the leadership team.

The degree to which governors are likely to be involved in strategic leadership and perceive of themselves as leaders is going to be shaped to a considerable extent by the approach and attitude of the headteacher. Yet as Rowan and Taylor (2002, p. 20) unequivocally state: 'There is no escaping the fact that, since the 1986 and 1988 Acts promoted enhanced powers for governors and local management of schools, the head is seen as the main leadership figure in schools.' Similarly, Whitty et al. (1998) conclude that professional interests continue to dominate and that this is hardly surprising if one considers:

> that educational self-management allocates increased managerial powers to head-teachers who, by virtue of their new roles, become the main conduit for all significant information coming into and going out of the schools. This capacity enables them to manage and out-manoeuvre lay governors should they so wish to do so.

> (ibid., p. 101)

Governing bodies are not always helped in gaining access to the information they need to perform their role. A recent study, for example, notes that 40 percent of LEAs did not circulate monitoring and evaluation reports to chairs of governors with some LEAs seeing the provision of such information to governing bodies as 'a very hot issue' (Bird, 2002, p. 36).

Culturally embedded notions of power and authority vested with headship are difficult to alter but the relationship between the professionals and governors needs to move to one of interdependence – a leadership that is shared and a real partnership, one that is not unequal and includes all stakeholders. In the next chapter we continue this theme and look at how governing bodies can contribute to school improvement.

NOTE

1. This chapter draws on Earley (2003), Earley and Creese (2003) and Earley and Evans (2002a).

12

Governors and School Improvement

Governing bodies and school improvement
What inspectors look for
How governors help
Benefits to heads
The effective governing body
Critical friendship
Monitoring and evaluation
Governor training
Conclusion

School improvement and the raising of standards continue to preoccupy many heads and teachers, and are currently high on both political and educational agendas. Governors, too, are expected to play their part in the drive to raise the overall performance of our schools. This chapter draws on recent research and inspection findings to consider the part governing bodies can play in school improvement.[1] It explores notions of effective governance and how a governing body can 'add value' to the work of the school, especially to the headteacher and senior staff.

The role of governors in school improvement was first highlighted in *Improving Schools* (Ofsted, 1994). The 1998 Education Act states explicitly, that the purpose of governing bodies is to help to provide the best possible education for the pupils in their schools. To do this effectively the governing body 'should have a strategic view of their main function – which is to help raise standards – and clear arrangements for monitoring against targets' (Education Act 1998) (see also DfEE, 2000a).

Perhaps inevitably, some schools are better served at present by their governing bodies than others – certainly the evidence points to a range of practices. If all governing bodies are to become effective and to have a significant impact upon improvement within their schools, then some changes in the present pattern of operation would appear to be necessary. This seems to be recognised in the national strategy for governor support and training which, having devised training materials for newly appointed governors and for clerks of governing bodies, has developed a national training programme for chairs of governing bodies and headteachers (*Times Educational Supplement*, 3 January, 2003).

However, in spite of the importance attached to governors and their involvement in school improvement, there has been very little research in this area and very few official documents offer specific guidance to governors as to how they should fulfil their responsibilities in this field. The aim of this chapter is therefore to draw upon what we know about effective governing bodies, with a view to examining the many ways in which such bodies are able to contribute to the improvement of their schools.

GOVERNING BODIES AND SCHOOL IMPROVEMENT

As we noted in the previous chapter, it is very difficult to establish a direct causal link between effective governance and school effectiveness. There is, at present, little empirical evidence of how governing bodies actually contribute to school improvement in practice. An NFER study found that governors generally had a rather restricted view of their role in school improvement, tending to concentrate instead on the part played by the teachers (Earley, 1994). As with studies of school effectiveness, the school improvement literature usually makes only a passing reference to governors, if indeed they are mentioned at all (Earley, 1997a). What then is the role of governors in school improvement and what benefits do they bring to their schools and particularly their heads and senior staff?

The first official publication, specifically aimed at governors, which mentioned the governors' role in school improvement, was the broadsheet produced in the mid-1990s entitled *Governing Bodies and Effective Schools* (DFE/BIS/Ofsted, 1995). This suggested that governing bodies have three main roles: to provide a strategic view, to act as critical friend and to ensure accountability. This way of conceptualising the governing body's role has since been enshrined in legislation (the Education Act 2002) and the three roles also underpin the inspection framework when examining the leadership and management of schools (Ofsted, 1999a, p. 92; 2003a, p. x). Training materials produced by the DfES and available for LEAs to use with newly appointed governors, have also centred explicitly on the above three key roles (DfES, 2001).

The seminal 1995 pamphlet, produced by the Institute of Education, was issued to every school in the country. It recognised that governors have limited time and resources available and stated that, therefore, the governing body 'should focus on where it can add most value – that is in helping to decide the school's strategy for improvement' (DfE/BIS/Ofsted, 1995, p. 2).

More recently, *The Guide to the Law for School Governors* (DfEE, 2000a) sets out the powers and duties of governing bodies – nine in total – the first of which is 'conducting the school with a view to promoting high standards of educational achievement' (DfEE, 2000a, ch. 5, p. 1). The guide goes on to state that 'a good governing body will take mainly a strategic view through setting suitable aims and objectives, agreeing policies, priorities, plans and targets and monitoring and evaluating results' adding that 'the School

Development Plan, Ofsted action plan or School Improvement Plan will generally provide the main mechanism for the strategic planning process' (DfEE, 2000a, ch. 5, p. 2). The guidance document, *Roles of Governing Bodies and Head Teachers* (DfEE, 2000b), also argues for a strategic role for governors but uses the word 'progress' rather than 'improvement'.

WHAT INSPECTORS LOOK FOR

As was shown in Chapter 1 the most recent inspection framework, which has applied to schools since September 2003, gives further emphasis to the governors' role. Under the section entitled 'How well is the school led and managed?' inspectors are instructed to assess the extent to which the governing body:

- helps shape the vision and direction of the school
- ensures that the school fulfils its statutory duties
- has a good understanding of the strengths and weaknesses of the school
- challenges and supports the senior management team (Ofsted, 2003a).

In evaluating governance the new inspection framework states that the governing body has statutory responsibilities for the school, which includes responsibility for its improvement. Its main roles are to:

- provide a strategic direction for the work and improvement of the school
- support, monitor and evaluate the effectiveness of the school
- hold the school to account for the standards achieved and the quality of education (Ofsted, 2003a).

It offers advice to inspectors on how to pitch judgements on the effectiveness of governance and Table 12.1 illustrates what a range of governing body practice – from very good to poor – might look like.

For the governors to be influential there must be a good working relationship with the school, particularly between the head and the chair of governors, with frankness and mutual respect. Governors should know the school's strengths and weaknesses, and whether they have a clear sense of the priorities for its development. It is suggested that the involvement of the governing body in school self-evaluation is a useful indicator of its place within the school's leadership.

The key question is whether the governors know the strengths and weaknesses of the school well enough and what they do about them. Inspectors are advised to assess the extent to which governors:

- help to shape the direction of the school and how they do this
- understand the challenges faced by the school
- set appropriate priorities for development and improvement

Table 12.1   Judgements on governance

Very good (2) Creativity and dynamism in reflecting upon performance, promoting change, and capitalising on links with the local community suggest excellent (1) governance.	The governing body makes a major contribution to the leadership of the school, including its sixth form, and its successes. It is fully involved in strategic planning and formulating policies, and supports staff in implementing them. Governors keep in close touch with the school's work across all stages, and this cements the partnership between the governing body and the school. The pattern of the governing body's work meshes well with the school's development cycle, so that both are very influential, Governors are well aware of the school's strengths and weaknesses and deal with them openly and frankly, contributing fully to development planning. Performance management procedures are very effective and are monitored closely by the governing body.
Good (3)	The governing body influences the work of the school and its policies through challenge and support. It has a good grasp of the school's strengths and weaknesses and has a significant, strategic influence in leading the school's development, with a clear focus on raising standards and improving the quality of provision. The governing body is prepared to take difficult decisions where necessary. It is well organised and it improves its own performance through appropriate development activities or training.
Satisfactory (4)	The governing body ensures that the school meets its statutory responsibilities, and has clear aims and policies. Its performance management policy operates effectively. Corporately, it sets an overall direction for the school and formulates policies that reflect the individual character of the school. It reviews performance data to monitor the whole school's work and its recommendations for action are followed up. All governors understand their role and any specific responsibilities. There is a businesslike relationship between governors and senior staff in leading the school.
Unsatisfactory (5)	The school fails to meet one or more statutory responsibilities and lacks some of the policies that are required. The governing body relies too heavily on the headteacher. Although they are supportive, governors play a slight part in leading the school and do little to hold the school to account. Their work lacks focus and influence. They have insufficient knowledge of one or more of the stages. There is little corporate agreement about the school's strengths and weaknesses. The governing body has a limited grasp of the performance of the school and only modest effect on its development.
Poor (6) High vacancies, poor attendance, hostile relationships and almost total reliance on the headteacher are indications of very poor (7) governance.	Important statutory responsibilities are not met. The governing body is remote from the school. Relationships between members of the governing body or between it and the senior staff are at best indifferent and may be hostile or acrimonious. Governors' business is badly organised and their conduct presents a barrier to school improvement. Governors are largely unaware of the strengths and weaknesses of the school and, in particular, of the effectiveness or otherwise of its senior managers. They have a limited influence on the work of the school. The governing body presents no challenge. Standards and quality are not assured and it fails to set a clear direction or priorities for the school's work.

- find out for themselves how things are going
- take responsibility for the good and poor aspects of the school.

Inspectors also have to enquire whether governors both challenge and support the SMT and explore how the governors set objectives for the head as part of their responsibilities for performance management.

So much for inspection criteria and guidance on judgements, but what do we know about how governors contribute to school improvement?

HOW GOVERNORS HELP

A national study (Creese and Earley, 1999) based upon case study data gathered from 23 schools in differing situations found that governors were able to contribute to school improvement in a variety of ways. However, governors are not at the 'chalk-face' and their direct contribution to the raising of standards in their schools may not be immediately obvious. One of the difficulties facing governors wishing to raise standards in their schools may be their unfamiliarity with the curriculum and current teaching methods. Many governing bodies have set up curriculum committees and often governors are linked to specific subject areas or departments. This seems particularly helpful in secondary schools with a complex curriculum and a large number of teachers. Individual governors then need to pool their knowledge in order to obtain an overview by reporting to their colleagues either orally or in writing.

Governors may more easily be able to make a direct contribution to the quality of the education offered by their schools, for instance by using their specialist expertise in the classroom, particularly in small schools, to broaden the curriculum. They may be able to work on the enhancement of the pupils' environment or to use their contacts within the community to enrich, for example, the school's work-experience programme. Governors can certainly influence the quality and standard of the education provided through their involvement in policy-making and such policies can be an important aspect of accountability within the school.

Virtually every governing body now has a finance committee that monitors the school's budget and its expenditure. Governors are able to use their financial experience and expertise to assist the head and staff in budget setting; indeed, individuals with financial expertise are not infrequently brought onto the governing body for that specific purpose. Governors can help to ensure better monitoring and tracking of expenditure and can advise on more sophisticated aspects of financial management based on their experience outside the world of education. Governors may well have experience of development planning, quality initiatives and the management of change, which they can use to enhance the effectiveness of these processes in their schools.

The ethos of a school depends on a wide range of factors and this is another area in which the governors' contribution to improvement may not be always immediately obvious. However, governors' input can range from their discussions with pupils when they visit the school through addressing school assemblies to helping to develop school policies. Where there is some form of student forum or School Council, it can be very helpful if governors either occasionally attend its meetings or invite representatives to meet with them. Extra-curricular activities such as plays and concerts contribute significantly to the ethos of the school and governors should be keen to support these, recognising the importance of these in the pupils' overall education.

The climate for improvement

Hopkins and his colleagues (1996) suggest that getting the climate right is an essential prerequisite for school improvement. The factors that they suggest should underpin the school's improvement efforts are:

- a commitment to staff (and governor?) development
- practical efforts to involve staff, students, parents and the wider community in school policy- and decision-making
- a management style which fosters leadership at all levels within the organisation and which focuses on people as much as on outcomes
- effective co-ordination strategies
- spending time upon enquiry and reflection (asking 'How is it going?')
- planning collaboratively.

It might be argued that governors can contribute more easily, and more usefully, to establishing a *climate* for school improvement than they can to improvement directly. How then might this be done?

Creese and Earley (1999) found that effective governing bodies acknowledged that successful change is founded on appropriate staff development and also recognised their own need for development and training. Some governing bodies arranged for joint staff–governor training/planning events, which helped to foster the governor–staff partnership and also increased the degree of co-ordination between staff and governors.

Governors can play a key role in enabling parents and members of the wider community to contribute to the formulation of school policies as they themselves are members of that community. Effective schools have a clear vision of where they are heading and governors should have a full share in the development of that vision. This can be done by providing the governing body, or sub-group, with time and space to discuss the school's long-term aims. Governors may sometimes lay more emphasis upon the school's involvement in the local community than do the staff.

Almost all governing bodies have set up a series of committees and working parties. The work of these needs to be co-ordinated through strategies such as holding meetings of these groups in a logical sequence, thus ensuring that ideas could be progressed without back-tracking. Alternatively, there may be a co-ordinating group consisting of the chairs of the other committees. Whatever approach is used, it is important that there is a system for reporting back from the sub-groups to the full governing body so that the governors are kept fully informed.

All too often, governing body meetings become bogged down in petty detail that could be better dealt with either by the head and/or a governors' sub-group. Lack of time then prevents the governors from asking about the school's progress towards its key objectives and reflecting upon the answers. Many governing bodies now hold two meetings a term in order to allow governors time to discuss key educational issues in detail. It can be helpful, for instance, for a governing body to spend a little time at the last meeting of the year reviewing its own performance. The results of this review can then inform the governors' development plan which itself should form part of the overall school development plan.

Questions governors might ask about the 'climate for improvement' in the school include:

- Is there an acceptance that the governing body has a role in discussing matters to do with school improvement?
- Can governors raise challenging questions without being perceived as confrontational or unsupportive of the school?
- How does the head keep governors informed about the school's performance?
- Can governors discuss performance issues without being seen as intruding on the ground of the professionals?
- Do governors still feel as though they are being critical if they want to talk about improving on past performance or raising standards?
- Is a balance achieved between discussing the school's performance and ensuring the governing body does not interfere in the responsibilities of the school's managers?
- Are there areas of the school, which are highly valued, but where information about how it's doing is not collected (Creese and Earley, 1999, pp. 50–1)?

BENEFITS TO HEADS

There are clear benefits of having a good governing body, which offer many advantages to the head and the school (see below). These advantages could be said easily to outweigh any extra work generated as a result of governors' increased responsibilities. Both Creese and Earley (1999) and Scanlon et al. (1999) reported that headteachers stated positively that they now had to explain more fully to lay people what the professionals had too often taken for granted. They were also being required to make things more explicit, translate the coded language and jargon of education, and fill in background details so that governors could make informed decisions. One headteacher explained: 'Because I have to communicate with my governing body, it helps me to analyse and make explicit why I would like to see things changed', adding: 'having to explain has made me a better manager'.

The benefits of an effective governing body are:

- a critical and informed sounding board for the headteacher
- offering support for the school
- helping to break down the isolation of the head
- being a link with parents and the community
- working with the staff to provide direction and a vision for the school
- provide a forum within which the teachers can explain their work
- bringing to the school a range of non-educational expertise and experience (Scanlon et al., 1999, p. 27).

A common thread running through the heads' responses was their appreciation of the support, often personal as well as professional, which they received from their governors. Support from the governing body can go some way to help remove the feeling of isolation that is commonly recognised as being an integral part of headship. The expectations laid on the 'school leader' can be very great and these pressures, along with the notion that 'the buck stops here', mean that the job is often very stressful. The governing bodies involved in our research were conscious that headship could be a very lonely and highly pressured job. For their part, heads were grateful for the opportunity to share the responsibility of the running of the school with their governors who were prepared to listen to and support them.

The relationship between the headteacher and the chair of governors is crucial and affects how the whole school operates (Sallis, 2001). A headteacher in the Creese and Earley (1999) study noted how the chair provided 'an ear to bash, a shoulder to cry on and someone to bounce ideas off'. The heads suggested that the chair of governors required certain key qualities: they needed to be accessible, keen and interested. One head frequently offloaded his problems on the chair and used her as a sounding board: 'She is very sharp and with-it. That's really useful; it helps me to crystallise my thinking.' In many cases the good relationship between the head and the chair was cemented by mutual respect and a common view of the way the school should be run and on education in general.

Support from the governing body was sometimes described by the heads in terms of 'protection'. The governing body could take away some of the responsibility, the worry and the criticisms. A head commented:

> It is useful to have a body rather than individuals making agreements and decisions – it both protects and strengthens the school. I personally find it easier to deal with situations when I know there is a clear policy made by the governing body and I know I have implemented that policy.

Most governing bodies recognised the importance of their role as a critical friend to the head and to the school. One chair defined a critical friend as one who, 'asks the questions in order to get the best answers'. Heads commented that governing bodies could help to clarify issues by posing probing questions or requiring more detailed answers. Searching questions could sometimes be painful.

One of the most important attributes of a governing body was said to be that it is largely composed of individuals who bring different perspectives to the headteacher and the school, 'a knowledge of the world outside, of where education is going, of the world of work and unemployment'. Governors felt they 'added in areas of expertise and avenues that were not necessarily open to the school'. Sometimes the professionals were too close to the issues or had trammelled vision: 'you simply can't see the wood for the trees'. Having a group of people with a variety of skills and experience was an added resource for heads. This could enhance their role and make their jobs easier.

Overall heads are beginning more fully to appreciate the benefits of having a good chair and an effective governing body in what could, otherwise be a lonely and, at times, vulnerable position. They can find sympathy and understanding, as well as challenge and stimulus, from a body of hard-working and committed lay people who had the best interests of the school at heart. Heads can take comfort from the comment of the headteacher who said: 'As I'm accountable to everybody they (the governing body) take some of that responsibility off me because it's ultimately the governing body that carries the responsibility for the school.'

It is sometimes said that heads get the governing bodies they deserve. Wise heads put as much effort into the development of the governing body as they do into staff development. They recognise that an effective and efficient governing body can be invaluable to themselves, and make a significant difference to the effectiveness of their schools.

THE EFFECTIVE GOVERNING BODY

Effective schools and effective governing bodies make a difference – they add value. There is already a considerable body of research into what makes a school effective – see Chapter 13 and Sammons et al. (2004) and Teddlie and Reynolds (2000) for useful summaries. Although there has been less research into the effectiveness of governing bodies, it is possible to identify a number of factors that are present in effective governing bodies. These include:

- a positive attitude towards governors on the part of the headteacher
- efficient working arrangements
- effective teamwork within the governing body
- governors who are committed to the school (Scanlon et al., 1999).

Governing bodies which make a conscious effort to improve their performance in these areas *do* become more effective as can be seen from the six case studies described in Creese (2000).

Many research studies (e.g. Bullock and Thomas, 1997; Earley, 1994; Scanlon et al., 1999) have identified the key role which the head plays in determining the effectiveness, or otherwise, of the governing body. The nature of the relationship between the headteacher and the chair of governors in particular is crucial. As noted by Joan Sallis, a well-known governor trainer and agony aunt, schools will boast about their governing body's quality because the quality of the governing body, like the quality of the staff, gives evidence of the head's leadership and management (Sallis, 2001). Relationships between staff in general and the governors are also important. Governors should be encouraged to visit their schools regularly and so become well known to the staff who trust them and respect their input.

Efficient working arrangements, which allow governors time to concentrate upon the key issues for their school, are a feature of effective governing bodies. The setting up of a pattern of meetings, and delegation to sub-groups, enables governors to give time to the important issues. The second aspect of enhancing efficiency appears to be ensuring that the meetings are run well with all governors being given the opportunity to contribute. Including timings for the various items on agendas and indicating clearly specific responsibilities for follow-up in the minutes of meetings are two examples of good practice in this area. Good teamwork can be strengthened through having sound procedures and good communication systems, which were known to and understood by all.

The chair of governors is often the prime mover in enhancing the effectiveness of the governing body: 'It is difficult for a governing body to improve or become more effective if the role of the chair is poorly enacted' (Scanlon et al., 1999, p. 5). It is not always easy effectively to chair meetings of a group of disparate volunteers, such as a governing body. It may include some governors with little or no experience of meetings, who find difficulty in expressing their views, whilst at the other end of the spectrum there are those with considerable experience of serving on committees. A good chair will be able to ensure that all governors are able to contribute to meetings which have clear objectives and outcomes achieved within a reasonable space of time.

Governors, who may be parents, teachers or members of the local business community, come onto the governing body from a variety of backgrounds and with a range of experience and expectations of education. In general, therefore, there is no reason to suppose, indeed the opposite is more likely to be the case, that governors will automatically form themselves into a team with shared beliefs and a common sense of purpose. Some form of team-building process must take place if the governing body is to become an effective team. Many governing bodies arrange training sessions of one sort or another for the whole governing body, in addition to the training attended by individual governors.

Ofsted in a study of schools that have been removed from the special measures register are clear as to 'where governors make a difference' (Ofsted, 2001, p. 4):

- Governors are clear about the aims of the school and the values they wish to promote.
- The governing body and all its committees, have clear terms of reference, and an interrelated programme of meetings.

- Governors bring a wide range of expertise and experience, and attend meetings regularly.
- The chair of governors gives a clear lead.
- Meetings are chaired well, and efficiently clerked.
- There is a school plan, understood by all, which focuses on improving the school.
- Relationships between the governors and the staff are open and honest.
- Governors' training is linked to the school's priorities, and the needs of individual governors.
- Individual governors are clear about their role.
- The school's documentation is systematically reviewed.
- Governors have rigorous systems for monitoring and evaluating the school's work.

Although the study was based on a particular group of schools, *all* governing bodies should aim to achieve the above. The key question that an effective and efficient governing body will want to ask at all times is: 'Is the way we operate as a governing body allowing us to focus on making our school more effective?'

CRITICAL FRIENDSHIP

As the DfE/BIS/Ofsted 1995 broadsheet, *Governing Bodies and Effective Schools*, explains, governors can make a considerable contribution to the improvement of their schools by acting as 'critical friends' and promoting a climate in which questions about performance – including their own – are openly and honestly discussed.

A useful way of conceptualising governing bodies in terms of their effectiveness is in terms of where they are located on the pressure and support spectrum. Effective governing bodies are those that provide high pressure but with high support. As seen in Figure 12.1, these are referred to as 'critical friends' or as working in the partnership mode. Governing bodies have to offer both support and challenge to the schools, but getting the balance between these two is not always easy.

Governing bodies are '*critical* in the sense of the governing body's responsibility for monitoring and evaluating the school's effectiveness, asking challenging questions and pressing for improvement. A *friend* because it exists to promote the best interests of the school and its pupils' (DFE/BIS/Ofsted, 1995, p. 2).

Critical friends:

- provide an independent voice
- promote open and healthy debate
- work in the best interests of the school
- offer mutual respect.

To work effectively as critical friends there is a need for trust, sensitivity and openness. This cannot be legislated for, or introduced overnight (Creese and

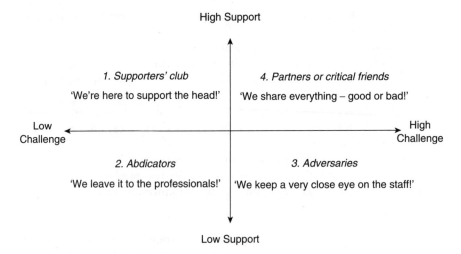

High Support

1. Supporters' club

'We're here to support the head!'

4. Partners or critical friends

'We share everything – good or bad!'

Low
Challenge

High
Challenge

2. Abdicators

'We leave it to the professionals!'

3. Adversaries

'We keep a very close eye on the staff!'

Low Support

Figure 12.1   The effective governing body

Earley, 1999, p. 50). What is more, once achieved there is no guarantee that such qualities will persist – changes of personnel mean that they have to be continuously re-established. Effective governing bodies are not heads' *supporters' clubs, abdicators or adversaries* but, as shown in Figure 12.1, the *partners* or *critical friends* offering 'high support – high challenge' (Creese and Earley, 1999, p. 8).

MONITORING AND EVALUATION

'Two of the most important functions of governors are their monitoring and evaluation of their school's performance, yet in many schools these are often the weakest areas of their work' (Ofsted, 2001). Ineffective governors are insufficiently informed about the day-to-day running of their schools and depend too heavily upon the head for information on how the school is performing (Ofsted, 2002b). Bird (2002) suggests that governing bodies which are failing in this area are either unaware of the importance of this aspect of their work, or are not carrying out the role effectively. For Carver (1990) governing boards should be deciding policy, allowing managers to get on with implementing them and receiving feedback on their effectiveness.

Monitoring and evaluating play an important part in helping to raise standards and in several of the schools in the study by Creese and Earley (1999), governors were directly involved in the monitoring process. In one secondary school, the governors 'monitored the monitoring'. Members of the school's SMT were linked to departments as line managers and saw every teacher teach at least six times a year. The governors oversaw this aspect of the work of the SMT. In two other secondary schools governors were directly involved in three-day faculty/departmental reviews which were, in effect, mini-inspections operating on Ofsted lines. The governor fulfilled the role of the lay inspector in an Ofsted inspection team, observing lessons, looking at samples of pupils' work, talking to staff and contributing to the final written report.

Governors taking part in such exercises need careful briefing and training and some form of 'protocol' for the review process to be helpful to all concerned. These reviews required a considerable investment in time and effort on the part of governors and senior staff but there were clear benefits for governors, staff and pupils in those schools.

In yet another approach, in a school for children with severe learning difficulties, the subject co-ordinators gave presentations to the governing body explaining the aims and content of their subject areas. The governor linked to the subject area then arranged to visit a class in order to see the policy in practice. In this way, the governors felt that they were aware of the curriculum and associated schemes of work in the various subjects, that they had seen them being delivered in the classroom, and that they were able to relate practice and theory.

A policy review process has been set up by some governing bodies whereby each of the school's policies is reviewed on a rolling programme (Walters and Richardson, 1997). In one secondary school a forthcoming inspection had encouraged the head, senior staff and governing body to look carefully at every aspect of the school's functioning, including its many policies, with a view to setting up a system of monitoring and evaluation through its committee structure. Each committee was serviced by a senior staff member who took the lead in presenting to that committee evidence about the effective performance of the school, including the implementation of its policies. The school's managers welcomed this degree of detail as it provided them with a clear focus and direction about what information was needed, and by when.

The way different school governing bodies are undertaking their monitoring and evaluating role – which is generally recognised to be *the* most difficult and problematic area of their work – can be further explored on the DfES's governors' website (www.dfes.gov.uk/governing/gpmonit.htm).

Thomas and Martin (1996) suggest that there should be a dialogue of accountability between governors and staff, and highlight the need for governors to have access to high-grade information about their schools, which does not come directly from the staff. Apart from the impressions they form during their visits, governors rely heavily upon the head to provide them with information about school performance. Lack of independent information on their schools remains a serious problem for governors. A recent survey (Bird, 2002) found that only six out of ten LEAs sent copies of the reports produced by link advisers, following their visit to the school, to the chair of governors and less than one in six sent copies to all members of the governing body. If governors are to fulfil the strategic role, and especially the monitoring function, set out for them in *Roles of Governing Bodies and Head Teachers* (DfEE, 2000b) and in the latest inspection framework (Ofsted, 2003a), then this information must go to them as of right.

GOVERNOR TRAINING

Training is important in helping governors to understand and enact their role, including a leadership role. The recent training materials for new governors, devised by the DfES (2001) for use by LEAs, focus on the aforementioned three key roles. School governing bodies are being urged by official pronouncements and government guidance to act more strategically in the way in which they work and avoid becoming involved in school matters that are not their prime concern. Training materials being developed for heads and chairs of governors, again supported by the DfES, should prove helpful here.

The vast majority of the school governors (95%) in our research in 2001 for the DfES had received training for their role. A high proportion (43%) found it 'very useful' with only three percent claiming it to have been 'not very useful'. Much governor training focuses on what might be termed the 'nuts and bolts' of governance – issues such as governors' legal responsibilities, budget management, etc. The wider but more fundamental issue of governors' involvement may receive less attention. As one chair of governors noted: 'Training needs to be less about procedures, policies and guidelines and more about visioning, leadership, effective teamwork, motivation and culture.'

A further difficulty lies in the constant turnover of governors. With new governors being appointed on a regular basis, there is an ongoing need for induction programmes, a need that has been partly filled by the national programme (DfES, 2001). New governors inevitably take time, perhaps as long as two years, to get to grips with their role. If they only serve one four-year term, they can only offer two years when they are in a position to undertake the sort of tasks which governors' involvement in school improvement requires.

As earlier noted, the chair has a crucial role in determining the effectiveness, or otherwise, of the governing body. The majority of LEAs offer training specifically targeted at chairs, in the form of briefings about forthcoming issues and/or guidance on how to run meetings, etc. Greater stress may need to be laid in training sessions for chairs, upon the factors linked to the effectiveness of the governing body, and the steps necessary to enhance effectiveness. In particular, chairs may need reminding of the importance of good teamwork, and of having working arrangements which allow governors time to concentrate upon the key issues in their schools. These are aspects of the work of the governors that should be stressed in any evaluation of the effectiveness of the governing body.

In many LEAs, governor trainers already offer training sessions aimed at the whole governing body. Such collective training sessions are invaluable as part of the essential team-building process. It is also worth noting that social events, of various sorts, contributed to helping governors get to know one another and to find a common sense of purpose. There is no reason why governing bodies should rely solely upon external agencies for developmental work in team-building. Experienced headteachers and governors can gain in terms of their own development by organising training sessions for their governing body.

Good relationships between governors and staff are also fundamental to improving the effectiveness of the governing body. The difficulty for governor trainers is that they cannot influence these relationships directly. What they can do is to stress to governors the importance of visiting the school during the day to see pupils at work and talking to, and getting to know, the staff. This should have a high priority within the limited time which governors may be able to devote to their schools. Governors can also be offered guidance on how best to get the most out of their visits. Many governors still find it difficult to find time to visit the school during the day. Unfortunately the House of Commons Education and Employment Select Committee report on school governors (1999) did not recommend that governors have a right to a reasonable amount of time off work with pay.

In their small-scale study of the role of governors in school improvement, Creese and Bradley (1997) suggested that some form of catalyst is necessary to bring about significant change in the way in which governing bodies operate. If a catalyst is required to bring about change, how far is it possible to provide such a stimulus without waiting for a change of chair/headteacher or an inspection? Can less effective governing bodies be identified and invited to review their practice? A number of LEAs already have in place self-evaluation programmes for their governing bodies (e.g. Parkin, 2003) and there are moves to promote a national (albeit voluntary) model (Little, 2002). However, it may be that the less effective governing bodies will not take advantage of such opportunities, and more direct intervention may be required.

CONCLUSION

Governing bodies are contributing to improvement in their schools in a wide variety of ways. Importantly, they can be helpful in enhancing the climate for improvement. Indeed, it may well be, that their contribution to getting the climate right is actually more significant than any direct impact which they may have upon the raising of standards, and that this is an issue which governing bodies should address as a starting point. However, recent inspection evidence (e.g. Ofsted, 2002b) suggests that a significant proportion is still failing to do so. There are a number of possible reasons for this. The recruitment of suitable persons to be governors can be problematic, especially in inner city areas (Bird, 2002; Bird, 2003; Scanlon et al., 1999). The attitude of the head towards the governing body can hinder governors' efforts to contribute and governors may lack the necessary information on which to base a judgement regarding the effectiveness of their schools (Bird, 2002).

In the past, quite understandably, considerable time and effort has been expended by trainers in providing governors with what was seen as the essential knowledge necessary to enable them to become effective. More recently, there has been a shift towards providing governors and the governing body as a whole with appropriate skills. More time is being devoted to team-building and to enhancing relationships between governors and between governors and staff. There is some evidence that these activities are enhancing governing body effectiveness (Scanlon et al., 1999). These efforts need to be continued and developed further. All heads and governors need to be reminded that having a governing body which is functioning as an effective team, with sound working practices and which works in a genuine partnership with the staff, is essential if it is to be in a position to contribute, in any meaningful way, to school improvement.

NOTE

1. This chapter draws on Earley and Creese (2003).

13

Effective Schools and Improvement Strategies

School effectiveness
School improvement
NFER heads' views
'Failing schools'

The previous chapter examined governors' role in school improvement. This chapter provides a summary of the research on school effectiveness and describes the factors associated with effective schools. The second part shows the kind of strategies that can used to bring about school improvement. Whereas school effectiveness is concerned with comparing schools at a moment in time, school improvement draws together the effectiveness research and the work on managing change to show how a school can improve over time.

SCHOOL EFFECTIVENESS

Considerable problems arise if attempts are made to compare schools on various performance indicators without taking into account the obvious fact that their intakes, as well as other factors, differ. When the DfES performance tables were first published in the mid-1990s they caused concern among heads and staff because the data do not take the context of the school into account. The term 'school effectiveness' is used to describe studies which measure and relate intake, process and outcome variables. In this country a more recent term is 'value-added' and the latest performance tables (2003) now show a measure of how the pupils' average achievement has changed between one key stage and the next.

The early work on school effectiveness began in the US and consisted of large-scale input–output studies of student achievement, such as that by Coleman et al. (1966) and Jenks et al. (1972). The depressing conclusion drawn from this work was that schools made little, or no, difference. Home background, IQ and rather surprisingly, luck, were found to be the main variables determining student achievement. However, some researchers refused to believe this and began to search for effective schools. An essential technique was to disaggregate the student achievement data so that it became possible to compare various groups of children for example on, gender, socio-economic status (SES) and race. It was also important to look inside the 'black box' and find out what schools actually did.

The most influential advocate of the effective schools movement was a black superintendent and researcher, Ronald Edmonds, who died in 1983. He defined an effective school as one that 'brings the children of the poor to those minimal masteries of basic school skills that now describe minimally success-ful pupil performance for the children of the middle class'. An effective school 'must bring an equal percentage of the highest and lowest social class of students to minimum mastery' (Edmonds, 1979, p. 3). Lezotte, who worked with Edmonds, suggested that when a school achieves a figure of 95 percent of all groups of students reaching mastery of basic skills, and maintains this over three years, it can be called an effective school (Levine and Lezotte, 1990). More recently, Gray and colleagues working in England, have defined an *improving* school as one which increases its effectiveness over time – the value-added it generates for pupils rises for successive cohorts (Gray et al., 1999).

Working in Detroit and New York, Edmonds identified a number of 'corre-lates' which were associated with effective schools, and this became known as the 'Five Factor' model. The schools where children achieved 'more than expected' tended to have the following:

- strong leadership
- high expectations for children's achievement
- an orderly atmosphere conducive to learning
- an emphasis on basic skill acquisition
- frequent monitoring of student progress which is used as feedback.

Critics pointed out that the main focus of effective schools was too narrow and that schools had other aims as well as academic achievement. Methodological concerns were also raised about the small numbers of schools and the fact that the US research was largely based on urban elementary schools serving disadvantaged children.

In the UK, in contrast to the US emphasis on elementary schools, most of the studies (apart from Mortimore et al.) have looked at secondary schools using 16+ exam results as outcome variables rather than standardised tests of reading and maths. The main studies which have looked at school effectiveness in this country are:

- Reynolds et al. (1976) – four secondary schools in Wales
- Rutter et al. (1979) – 12 London secondary schools
- Mortimore et al. (1988) – 50 London junior schools
- Smith and Tomlinson (1989) – 18 urban multicultural secondary schools
- Brown et al. (1996) – four secondary schools in Scotland
- Sammons et al. (1997) – 94 London secondary schools
- MacBeath and Mortimore (2001) – 36 secondary schools in Scotland.

Despite the methodological criticisms mentioned earlier, the various studies in different countries have reached remarkably similar conclusions. We have

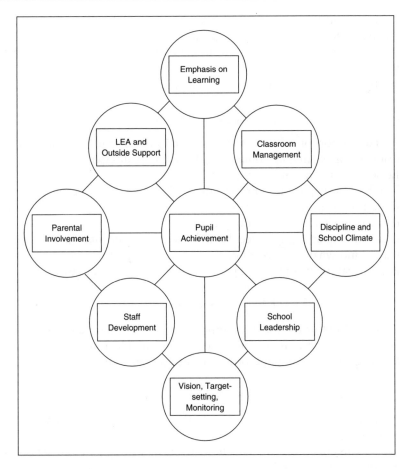

Figure 13.1   Factors characterising effective schools

Source: Weindling (1999)

synthesised the findings from the UK and US research under eight broad headings (see Figure 13.1). There is now consensus that more effective, or high-attaining, schools tend to be characterised by some or all of the following eight factors or correlates. It is probable that effective leadership spread throughout the school could affect all the other factors over time. Governance has not been seen as a separate factor but as part of school leadership.

1   An emphasis on learning

- A curriculum which has relevance for *all* students. Heads and teachers need to consider how the National Curriculum can be made relevant for all. The key term is, of course, differentiation, but this is very difficult to put into practice.
- Teachers have high expectations, a belief that all children can learn, given the right conditions. Related to this is another important factor, 'efficacy'.

Effective teachers have high efficacy – they really believe that they can make a difference to children's learning.

- Regular setting and marking of 'homework' – which in primary schools would include sending reading books home, etc.
- Visible rewards are given for academic excellence and improvement.

2   Classroom management

- A high proportion of time is spent on the subject matter of the lesson (as distinct from setting up equipment, dealing with disciplinary matters, etc.).
- Lessons begin and end on time.
- Teaching strategies are appropriate to the topic and type of lesson, e.g. some things are best taught whole-class, others in small groups. Skilled teachers have a range of strategies to draw on.
- Clear and unambiguous feedback is given to students on their performance and what is expected of them.
- Ample praise given for good performance – celebrate success.

3   Discipline and school climate

- Keeping good order and promoting a safe and orderly climate, which is not oppressive, and is conducive to teaching and learning.
- Buildings are kept in good order, repair and decoration.

4   School leadership

- Positive leadership by the head and other senior staff is necessary to both initiate and maintain school improvement.
- Leadership functions are widely distributed throughout the school and include the governing body.
- A management style which encourages collegial work and shared decision-making.
- The head and senior staff are skilled and knowledgeable about the management of change and the application of strategic planning.

5   Vision and monitoring

- A shared vision is needed by the governors and all the staff. Clear and achievable goals for school improvement must be established.
- Regular monitoring of students' progress is necessary to determine whether the goals are being realised. This information should be used as feedback to inform decision-making.

6   Staff development

- To influence the whole school, staff development has to be school-wide, rather than specific to individual teachers' needs, and closely related to the curriculum.

- An effective school development plan is needed which integrates staff development, institutional development and curriculum development.
- Staff development activities need to be phased throughout the improvement process, and not just used at the pre-implementation stage.

7   Parental involvement

- Parents are viewed and valued as full partners in the learning process.
- Staff work to achieve positive home–school relations in which parents actively support the school.
- The school reaches out to the community and encourages it to play an active role in the learning process.

8   LEA and outside support

- Fundamental changes require support from the LEA or other outside agencies and few of the variables listed are likely to be realised without this support.
- Consultants can provide valuable information and training, and facilitate the school improvement process.
- Research on the management of change shows powerful effects when a blend of inside and outside assistance is used. School improvement requires both pressure and support.

Reynolds (1992) reviewed and summarised the work on effective schools and pointed out that while home background and individual capability are still recognised as the major factors in children's achievement, there are variations between schools, and about 15 percent of the total variance can be attributed to the school. Also the classroom and school factors interact, and school performance varies over time – in other words, a school does not necessarily remain effective from year to year without sustained efforts from the head and staff (see Sammons et al., 2004). A meta-analysis by Scheerens and Bosker (1997) concluded that the net effects (after controlling for intake) are larger for mathematics than language, and largest for studies based on composite measures of achievement. Effect sizes are generally found to be greater in studies of developing countries. On average schools accounted for around eight percent of the achievement differences between students after control for initial differences. Classroom level or teacher effects tended to be substantially larger than school effects.

Different studies indicate that the proportion of schools identified as significantly more or less effective can vary between 15 to 33 percent of those included in an analysis. For example, a London study of 94 secondary schools showed that, on average, 30 percent of schools could be identified as statistically significant positive or significant negative outliers in a particular year, using value-added methods. However, only a small number of schools are likely to be consistent outliers over several years – probably less than five percent (Sammons et al., 1997; 2004).

A recent report from the National Audit Office (2003) examined the amount of difference schools made to the academic achievement of their pupils after taking account of a number of important external influences on performance. The analysis was based on the national value-added data set for more than one million pupils in 3,100 secondary schools who sat their GCSE examinations in 2002. (This is the largest study currently undertaken in England.)

The effect of taking these external factors into account is to change the performance ranking of many schools and LEAs, and to narrow the gap between the highest and lowest performing schools – though considerable differences remained. For example, of the 621 schools ranked in the bottom 20 percent by GCSE levels in 2002, just 272 remain in the bottom 20 percent when performance is adjusted for external factors, and 60 move into the top 20 percent. Conversely, some highly ranked schools fall. As examples of LEA changes, five inner London boroughs ranked substantially higher when the adjusted data were applied: Lambeth moved from 114th (out of 150) to 16th; Southwark from 139th to 31st; Hackney from 128th to 42nd; Islington from 114th to 51st; and Haringey from 137th to 105th.

Of the factors taken into account, prior academic achievement, as used in the DfES value-added tables for 2002, had the strongest association with current achievement, followed by eligibility for free school meals. There is some association between different types of school and academic achievement, and between ethnicity and achievement, though the latter is highly complex.

SCHOOL IMPROVEMENT

Although we now know about the factors associated with effective schools, we do not know how these particular schools became effective, or a simple way of how to help a school become more effective. In 1984, when many states in the US were rushing to apply the effective schools research, Cuban (1984, p. 131) gave the following warning:

> Unlike the way things happen in fairy tales, school reforms require more than a kiss to convert a frog into a shining prince. Furthermore, productive schooling entails more than raising test scores ... No one knows how to grow effective schools ... Road signs exist, but no maps are yet for sale.

Since the mid-1980s when this was written we have more information about the processes underpinning school improvement. We now have some sketch maps, but there is no single blueprint – no 'one best way', which will fit all schools. Each school has to tailor the factors to fit their particular situation. While it is helpful to consider each of the factors, in reality schools do not operate on the basis of a list. Barth (1992) is very critical of what he calls 'list logic'. The factors are not separate and must interact in some complex way. Schools in different contexts and circumstances may need to work on some factors before they look at others.

School improvement is the planned and deliberate attempt to help schools move forward. Hopkins defines it as: 'A strategy for educational change that focuses on the learning and achievement of students by enhancing classroom practice and adapting the management arrangements within the school to support the teaching and learning process' (Hopkins, 2001, p. x). To begin the process heads and staff should conduct an audit and review the school's strengths and weaknesses on each of the school effectiveness factors in order to establish priorities for the school development plan. However, it is important to remember that over time all the factors must be addressed.

It is essential to have an agreed and shared vision to guide the change process and release the potential for school improvement that exists within the school (Barth, 1992). You cannot achieve school improvement by simply trying to bolt on another initiative, because schools are suffering from innovation overload. School culture seems to be the critical factor. Changing schools means changing people's behaviours and attitudes as well as the school's organisation and norms. Hence, Fullan's (1991) emphasis on the importance of the meaning of educational change – people need to construct their own understanding of what the change means for them. There has to be a sustained effort which changes the school culture. It is important to remember that school improvement is steady work and cannot be achieved by means of a quick-fix solution. The research shows that improvement in student outcomes tends to show first in primary schools, and it takes longer to see the effects in secondary schools. Generally at least three to five years is needed, so the advice is to look for small improvements annually.

NFER HEADS' VIEWS

Education is constantly faced with a bewildering number of initiatives, all claimed by their advocates to dramatically improve the situation. But which of these initiatives is the 'good' medicine and which is just the 'quack juice'? In 1993 we put this question to the secondary heads who had started their headships in 1982–83, as part of the continuing NFER study. The heads were asked to indicate on a five-point scale how successful they thought each of 12 specified initiatives would be in improving the quality of education for pupils. Table 13.1 shows the results from the 100 heads who returned questionnaires.

The initiative regarded most positively was clearly *local management of schools* (LMS) which heads felt gave them a greater degree of control over their budgets. However, at least 19 of the 100 schools had been 'losers' under the formula funding and these schools tended to account for most of the lower ratings. One head also pointed out the pressure facing them when appointing staff: 'Since school budgets are not based on actual staff costs, there is an incentive to replace senior staff, in terms of length of experience, with newly qualified teachers.'

Both devolved *in-service training funding* and *staff appraisal* – provided it was not linked to performance-related pay – were seen positively by the majority of heads.

Although *open enrolment* was seen positively by some, most of the heads who commented expressed concern about the validity of the market concept

Table 13.1 Heads' views on recent initiatives in 1993 (percentages)

	Very successful	Successful	Partly successful	Not at all successful	Don't know/ missing data
LMS	50	22	23	2	3
Devolved INSET budgets	34	41	17	4	4
Staff appraisal	17	37	34	7	5
Investors in People	16	15	19	9	41
Total Quality Management	14	18	17	11	40
Grant maintained status	12	7	14	31	36
National Curriculum	11	32	46	8	3
Open enrolment	9	16	28	33	14
School-based initial teacher training	8	19	26	18	29
Ofsted inspections	7	20	29	11	33
Performance-related pay	3	2	12	69	14
BS5750	2	6	18	26	46

as applied to schools: 'Open enrolment gives freedom of choice for very few', 'Schools are not in the market place – education is a process not a product' or 'The market concept of open enrolment just does not work. Costs are prohibitive. For every oversubscribed school which wants to expand, an unpopular school will have surplus places. There is no guarantee that this leads to an improvement in the quality of education for the pupils'.

Unsurprisingly perhaps, *grant maintained status* (GMS) was an issue which polarised the heads. The 12 GM schools were very positive, with nine marking this item as 'very successful' and the other three saying 'successful'. However, only seven of the 85 LEA maintained school heads coded GM status in either of these categories. Indeed, a significant number of non-GM heads were opposed to the notion. As one head said: 'GMS has emasculated some LEAs and will continue to do so.'

Only one in 20 heads saw *performance-related pay* (PRP) as likely to be successful. It was condemned by the overwhelming majority of the heads and seen as divisive rather than motivating: 'PRP can be a total disaster and blow the staffroom apart' and 'I have yet to find any evidence that PRP is of any benefit whatsoever'.

Over 40 percent of the heads thought that the *National Curriculum* (NC) was likely to be either 'successful' or 'very successful' in improving the quality of education. But as many commented that they were concerned about the management of change here: 'Too many/complex changes bedevil the NC to allow successful growth.'

Views on *Ofsted inspections* were very mixed but, of course, very few of the heads had experienced an inspection when they completed the questionnaire in 1994, hence the large number of 'don't know' answers. The following comments were offered: 'The Ofsted inspection has generated more anxiety than it should have. It is unfortunate that it has appeared at a time when so many people appear willing to vilify teachers'; 'Ofsted needs to look more carefully at the added value a school gives'; and 'Having experienced Ofsted, I think it has great potential here'. One head commented that a recent Ofsted inspection had helped to move the school forward, but at the expense of considerably more teacher stress.

The main concern for heads about *school-based initial teacher training* (ITT) was insufficient funding for schools. Heads were also worried about the impact of ITT on the quality of pupils' education.

The response to quality initiatives derived largely from industry, such as *Total Quality Management, Investors in People* and *British Standard 5750* (now replaced by *ISO 2000)*, clearly varied. Each of these quality initiatives had high numbers of 'don't knows', some of which may be due to lack of knowledge. Some heads had begun to explore these areas, and a few had begun work towards *Investors in People* (IIP). Many others, however, were sceptical about attempting to borrow management ideas from industry and commerce, and their relevance and applicability to schools: 'I'm fairly sceptical about "quality assurance" ideas which are superimposed on top of existing structures: I think quality is improved by developing a school ethos in which *evaluation* followed by *action* is the norm for staff and pupils'; and 'IIP is a hyped version of what any good management should be doing anyway, while BS5750 is being publicised beyond its remit. Schools may use them to gain publicity in the hope of increasing enrolment'.

One head who disliked most of the initiatives and only rated a few as 'partly successful' raised the following points: 'Which of these admirable initiatives could have been advantageous? Which of the above have brought extra work for staff? Who protects staff from initiative fatigue? Which initiative is designed to help a school monitor the quality of pupil experience?' He went on to say:

> One refreshing 'tot' might do me some good, but 12 have the education service reeling about. Teachers teach – if they don't do it, who does? It is the head's job to protect them from intrusions, to keep them on course, to support them in their best efforts, and to say 'well done' to those who have done well. Surely your research will pay testimony to the unsinkable faith and enthusiasm of these 'old' heads.

All the 12 initiatives discussed so far have originated from outside the school although, of course, involvement in some was voluntary. We were especially interested in changes which had their origin inside the school. The heads were asked to outline how they thought the school had improved in the last five years.

Table 13.2 provides a content analysis of their responses under six broad headings. As this was an open-ended question and most of the heads made several comments, the number of responses in each category must be interpreted with caution and only used as broad indicators.

Table 13.2   School improvements from 1989 to 1993

Area of improvement	Percentages
Public examinations	
Improved examination results	29
Buildings & facilities	
Improvements to buildings & facilities	27
Curriculum	
A more relevant, broad-based curriculum	12
Improvements in vocational education	5
Improvements from TVEI	5
Improved IT	3
Extra-curricular initiatives	2
Improvements in SEN	1
Pupils	
Improved pastoral systems	8
Improved teaching and learning	7
Increased roll, oversubscribed	7
Improved discipline, behaviour	6
Increased pupil motivation, improved attitudes	3
Improved pupil–teacher ratio	2
Larger 6th form	2
Improved assessment, recording, reporting	2
Staff & management	
More effective senior management	9
Better trained staff, improved INSET	9
Higher staff morale	7
Improved communication	6
More effective use of finance and resources	6
Clearer sense of purpose	5
Better teamwork	5
Improved ethos	5
Improved planning and target-setting	4
Greater staff commitment	4
Greater participation in decision-making by staff	3
Improved middle management	2
New roles for non-teaching staff, better motivated	2
Parents, governors & the community	
School image improved	12
Improved school–community links	10
Greater parental involvement and support	4
Better links with industry	3
Improved relations with the governing body	1
Better links with higher education	1

School improvement, in all its forms, is obviously the major quest for all heads. From our longitudinal research, it seems that most of the groundwork is put in place during the first five years of a headship, and then further refinements are made. This involves setting up a number of working parties, curriculum and organisational restructuring, modelling appropriate behaviour and appointing key staff (particularly at senior and middle management level). Changing the culture of a school cannot be done easily or quickly, and the third survey showed that the 'class of '82' had successfully continued this difficult task.

'FAILING SCHOOLS'

In England the introduction in 1992 of a national external inspection by Ofsted brought the issue of school improvement to the centre of attention. (Readers interested in the origins and development of Ofsted should consult Ferguson et al., 2000.) By the summer of 1999 some 900 schools had been deemed as failing to provide an adequate education for their pupls and therefore requiring 'Special Measures'. The numbers of school in this category represented around three percent of all secondary schools, about three percent of primary schools, eight percent of special schools and six percent of pupil referral units (Gray, 2000), although the total number has gradually declined. In 1997–8, there were 515 schools in Special Measures compared with 282 schools in 2002–03 (Adams, 2004).

Special measures is a very tightly monitored process involving termly visits by HMI. The schools, with support from their LEAs, are given about two years in which to show substantial improvement or they will be closed.

Gray (2000) reviewed the findings on the special measures schools and concluded:

- Some nine out of ten schools can eventually be expected to emerge successfully from Special Measures.
- Between 20 and 22 months has been the average time needed for primary and special schools to get out of Special Measures, whilst in secondaries it has taken around 27 months. However, these figures mask considerable variations.
- The most obvious contextual characteristic shared by schools in Special Measures is that they tend to be located in areas experiencing very high levels of social deprivation.
- Small primary schools, small primary schools in rural areas, boys' secondary schools serving inner city communities and schools with falling rolls are more likely to be in Special Measures as are special schools for pupils with emotional and behavioural difficulties.

Schools removed from Special Measures appear to improve:

- quality of teaching
- attendance – more pronounced for secondary and special schools
- reduction in exclusion.

Gray suggests that more research is needed on the improvement in attainment following removal from Special Measures and that many schools still face sizeable agendas even after coming off the register of 'failing schools'.

Factors which facilitated rapid change include:

- creation/renewal of teachers' commitment to the school
- acceptance of need to change by staff (and pupils)
- involvement of concerned parents and governors
- use of external support to encourage developments
- recent changes in leadership at senior level
- 'fresh but experienced' blood in classrooms
- clarification of the school's future
- reductions in competition for pupils with other local schools
- the absence of extreme social deprivation
- a relatively short history of problems at the school.

It seems that in these 'worst case scenarios' simply trying to introduce the factors which have been associated with effective schools may not bring about the required improvements. Examples of work with schools in difficulty is reported in Earley (1996) and Stoll and Myers (1997), whilst case study examples of schools coming off Special Measures can be found in Mortimore (1997) *The Road to Success*. In the latter collection, one of the authors was involved in writing up the experiences of Northicote Secondary school in the West Midlands – the first school to be deemed failing and the first to come off Special Measures (Earley, 1997a). (The headteacher of this school has since written about the school's experiences – see Hampton and Jones, 2000.) The role governing bodies can play in the process is also discussed in detail in Earley (1997a).

While all schools can do much for themselves, support from outside is also needed. In the current UK school improvement projects this is provided by LEA personnel and a range of different consultants. School improvement is not achieved by either top-down or bottom-up programmes, but through a combination of these. A blend of pressure and support is required, but different amounts of each are needed at different points in the school improvement process. Outside assistance is obviously very useful in providing support in terms of professional development and general facilitation, but pressure to sustain the project is also required as schools struggle to cope with the myriad of issues that confront them every day.

School improvement can be approached in a number of different ways. Joyce (1991) uses the analogy of opening various doors to school improvement, and the following points are adapted from his work. In order to achieve maximum impact the approaches should be integrated to provide a comprehensive strategy.

- Use the research findings on effective schools and effective teaching.
- Gather school-specific information, e.g. conduct a needs assessment and analyse student performance data. Also use any relevant inspection information.

Table 13.3 Typology of strategies to raise achievement

Strategy	Examples
Target-setting	Using progress data to establish targets for: a) groups of students b) individual students
Increasing learning time	Homework Clubs e.g. lunchtime/after school/weekends Revision Centres e.g. at Easter and other holidays
Additional support for pupils	Tutoring/Mentoring by adults e.g. teachers, parents and other adults supporting individuals or small groups of students Tutoring by pupils e.g. older students giving 1-to-1 reading support with younger students (cross-age tutoring) or, 1-to-1 support by the same age students (peer tutoring) Intensive intervention programmes e.g. Reading Recovery
Changes to classroom organisation	Setting and subject specialist teaching in primary schools Seating and grouping e.g. single-sex teaching groups for some subjects; boy/girl seating
Changes to teaching and learning (pedagogy)	National literacy and numeracy projects Cognitive Acceleration in Science Thinking Skills programmes Teaching metacognitive strategies
Use of ICT	Integrated learning systems e.g. Success Maker Learning Resource Centres Effective use of laptops The internet
Improved use of homework	Faster and more specific feedback; planned coverage of a wider range of study skills
Greater parental involvement	Paired Reading at home or in school Parental workshops Parents working in school Home visits

- Foster staff development and collegiality, e.g. through team teaching, peer coaching and involvement in schemes such as Investors in People.
- Explore a variety of teaching methods, e.g. the study of teaching skills, thinking skills and strategies such as co-operative learning.
- Make effective use of a range of curricular initiatives – whole curricular (e.g. the National Curriculum), and subject-specific guidance.
- Improve relations with parents and employers, e.g. by introducing parental involvement programmes, and Education Business Partnerships.

Schools are now adopting a wide range of approaches to improve pupil achievement. In Table 13.3 we have developed a typology to categorise the types of strategies. In practice the categories overlap and schools are using a combination of strategies.

Schools need to use a range of available information, including external inspections, to determine the particular priorities for their school development and improvement plans and action plans. School self-evaluation, which we argue elsewhere has been one of the positive consequences of external inspections (see Ferguson et al., 2000) will play a key role.

The difficult part, of course, is providing the right conditions. We now know that 'if you keep doing what you have always done you will get the results you have always got'. To really improve children's learning and enhance outcomes you have to plan and implement powerful interventions and systematically monitor pupils' progress over time. Schools really can make a difference and, as our own research and others' has shown, leadership, management and governance have crucial roles to play in the processes of school improvement. Crucially, you have to believe passionately that *all* children can learn more than they currently do – given the right conditions.

14

Developing Leaders and Leadership Capacity

Problems experienced by heads
Training and development needs
Leadership development opportunities
Key features of leadership programmes
Creating a learning community
Final thoughts

Throughout the world the role of the headteacher and other school leaders is undergoing change, which in turn has affected leadership development programmes. Hallinger (2003b) identifies a number of trends between 1980 to 2002 and points out that global forces such as school-based management, integrated and centralised curriculum, high-stakes testing and accountability, have created major changes in the education systems. Challenges are being faced worldwide as education systems develop from predominantly bureaucratic, hierarchical models to those which give greater emphasis to school site management, where leadership is distributed and institutional level leaders take decision-making responsibilities, working collaboratively with colleagues. Ongoing training and development, especially leadership development, is therefore crucial and in this final chapter we examine how leaders can be developed and their schools become learning communities.

We begin by examining what research tells us are the main problems experienced by heads before considering their and other school leaders' training and development needs. The key factors known to be associated with successful leadership programmes and development are also documented. The importance of heads as 'lead learners' and creators of learning communities cannot be underestimated. A key part of a learning community is the professional and personal development of all staff and the focus on learning and pupil outcomes. A culture of continuing professional development is crucial to the success of schools and relies on shared vision, teamworking and the head being perceived as the 'lead learner'. Modern notions of leadership, including distributed leadership, rely heavily on leadership, alongside effective management, being successfully demonstrated at the apex of the organisation. We conclude with a brief review of the future role of headteachers against a context of recruitment and retention problems, and stress and burnout.

PROBLEMS EXPERIENCED BY HEADS

To begin with it is important to examine the perceptions of leaders concerning the range of problems they experience at the school level and then to consider how these are addressed in leadership development programmes.

The National College for School Leadership recently commissioned a systematic review of the research literature concerning the problems and support strategies for the early years of headship (Hobson et al., 2003). From the review the main problems identified were:

- feelings of professional isolation and loneliness
- dealing with the legacy, practice and style of the previous headteacher
- dealing with multiple tasks, managing time and priorities
- dealing with the school budget
- dealing with ineffective staff
- implementing new government initiatives, notably new curricula or school improvement projects
- dealing with school buildings and site management.

It is important to note that the problems were largely similar in different countries and to some extent, consistent over time, although contemporary government initiatives might bring with them particular problems. The fact that most new heads experience these problems can be explained by the processes of socialisation, which affects all new leaders (in school and in business), as they try to understand their new role and take charge of an organisation (see Chapter 2).

Relatively little research has been conducted to examine the problems of more experienced heads. However, our ten-year longitudinal study of heads (1983 to 1993) was able to compare the problems as they changed over time. Reassuringly perhaps, most problems were perceived by the heads to lessen over time, for example: getting staff to accept new ideas; creating a good public image of the school; dealing with poor staff morale; improving communication and consultation; managing staff development; establishing discipline; dealing with finance; and issues concerning support staff. However, a few problems seemed to have increased, such as managing time and working with the governors, while the challenges of dealing with incompetent staff appeared to have continued over time.

These findings are due to a combination of several factors. Over time the head and staff get to know each other better; the head makes several key appointments; a deeper understanding of the school is gained and many of their intended changes have been introduced. But the world outside has also changed. During this ten-year period a large number of external, government

Table 14.1 Perceptions of preparation for headship (percentages)

	Very prepared (1)	(2)	(3)	Not prepared at all (4)
Heads (pre-headship) (n = 608)	17	50	25	9
Heads (post-headship) (n = 597)	12	45	35	9

imposed changes such as LMS, National Curriculum, performance tables, and Ofsted inspection were mandated. The combination of these initiatives has had a profound impact on the heads and their schools.

TRAINING AND DEVELOPMENT NEEDS

What then do school leaders consider to be their main training and development needs? The DfES study of the state of school leadership (Earley et al., 2002) examined this in great detail and suggests that individuals' willingness to take on leadership and management responsibilities is likely to be affected by a number of factors, but a crucial one is the quality of the training and support that they have received over the course of their careers.

We asked headteachers how well they thought they were prepared for their role *prior* to taking up their first headship, and how well they thought they were prepared once they had *actually* taken up the role. As can be seen from Table 14.1, 17 percent of headteachers thought they were 'very prepared', with nearly one in ten (9%) stating that they were 'not prepared at all'. The percentage reporting lack of preparedness remained exactly the same (9%) once the heads had actually taken up the post, but those who saw themselves as 'very prepared' decreased from 17 to 12 percent. In other words only about one in eight headteachers were prepared to say that, on actually taking up their first headship, they regarded themselves as well equipped to take it on.

There were no significant differences between male and female respondents but there was, however, a significant difference for school phase with secondary heads reporting higher levels of preparedness both before *and* after headship than their primary school counterparts. Neither the age category of the headteacher, nor whether or not they had been an internal appointment to the post, were found to be related to perception of adequacy of preparation.

We asked heads, deputies and people doing NPQH about their development needs matched to the *National Standards for Headteachers*. Table 14.2 shows the findings for the three groups of respondents.

The standards where further or new training and development opportunities would be welcomed were to 'promote and secure good teaching, effective learning and high standards of achievement' and to 'manage time, finance, accommodation and resources and ensure value for money'. The latter standard was ranked highly by deputy heads, but not by headteachers. Heads perceived

Table 14.2   Training needs with reference to the National Standards

Element of the National Standards	Heads (n = 612) %	NPQH candidates (n = 151) %	Deputy heads (n = 226) %
Develop an educational vision and the strategic direction for your school	15	24	27
Secure the commitment of others to the vision	23	26	19
Implement the vision through strategic planning, operational planning and target-setting	25	33 (4)	31
Keep the work of the school under review and account for its improvement	44 (3)	28	32 (5)
Promote and secure good teaching, effective learning and high standards of achievement	58 (1)	28	49 (1)
Monitor, evaluate and review the quality of teaching and learning	41 (4=)	32 (5)	37 (4)
Agree, develop and implement positive equal opportunities strategies	10	10	10
Agree, develop and implement systems to meet the learning needs of all pupils	47 (2)	30	32
Develop and maintain the trust and support of all members of the school community	25	29	24
Plan, allocate, support and evaluate work undertaken by teams, groups and individuals	25	29	19
Lead, support and co-ordinate high quality professional development for all staff, including your own personal and professional development	41 (4=)	21	30
Determine, implement and sustain effective systems for managing performance of all staff	41 (4=)	26	24
Ensure that the curriculum, management, finance, organisation and administration of the school support its vision, aims and values	26	51 (2)	43 (3)
Work with governors to recruit, induct, develop and retain staff of the highest quality	11	17	19
Manage time, finance, accommodation and resources and ensure value for money	24	66 (1)	44 (2)
Lead and enable innovations and changes to take place appropriately and effectively, including ICT	27	35 (3)	27

Note: The numbers in brackets represent the top five priorities for further training.

the standard 'agree, develop and implement systems to meet the learning needs of all pupils' as a key developmental area. This was not the case for either NPQH candidates or deputies. On the other hand, 'ensure that the curriculum, management, finance, organisation and administration of the school support its vision, aims and values' was given a high priority by the deputies and NPQH candidates but not by the headteachers.

The only standard where there was considerable difference between secondary and primary heads was 'lead, support and co-ordinate high quality professional development for all staff, including your own personal and professional development'. Primary heads (49%) identified this as a priority area much more than their secondary colleagues (30%).

When asked about other training and development requirements, school leaders identified time management, personnel issues, conflict management and financial planning.

LEADERSHIP DEVELOPMENT OPPORTUNITIES

We asked heads and deputies what they perceived to be the single most powerful development experiences (both 'on the job' and 'off the job') of their career so far.

The most valuable 'on the job' activity was working with others, especially an effective headteacher. They also found everyday work experience, working in a good school and being an acting headteacher valuable. As for 'off the job' development opportunities, postgraduate study was the single most powerful. Some identified involvement in the NCSL's national programmes, such as NPQH and the Leadership Programme for Serving Headteachers (LPSH), whilst others referred to CPD courses in general. Others cited visiting other schools, networking (which involves a range of activities, both informal and formal) and working with other headteachers, working on specialist tasks (such as for the LEA or professional association) and meetings/contacts with non-educationists. Being a parent and 'general life experience' were also mentioned as useful.

A key concern was how best to deal with the professional development needs of experienced headteachers in a coherent and cohesive manner. There was support for developing the role of experienced heads as mentors/coaches for those new to the role, or as trainers and tutors on national programmes. Self-help groups, such as action learning sets, in which people in similar positions and experience work together, were also thought to be helpful. External advisers (to governing bodies regarding performance management) also had a role to play in identifying professional development objectives (Earley, 2004b).

About 80 percent of heads, NPQH candidates and deputy heads had undertaken professional development specific to their leadership role (other than participation in the national programmes). The main sources of professional development opportunities and activities experienced for these school leaders over the last three years are shown in Table 14.3 which also shows the three

Table 14.3   Professional development experienced over the last three years

Opportunities provided by:	Heads (% of sample) (n = 613)	NPQH (% of sample) (n = 151)	Deputy heads (% of sample) (n = 226)
Mentoring from other headteachers/colleagues	39 (3)	54 (1=)	48 (2)
Business and other mentors	22	8	13
Conversations with other educationists	70 (1)	58 (1=)	63 (3)
Higher education institutions	26	37	30
Local education authorities	61 (2)	66 (3)	67 (1)
Education consultants	48	38	48
Professional associations	36	17	22
Private sector organisations	17	9	16
Public sector organisations	12	10	12
Involvement in Investors in People	34	30	35
Any other opportunities	19	15	13

Note: The numbers in brackets represent views of the three most frequent activities.

activities or opportunities which they felt had been most effective in their own development as leaders. There was general agreement about the most effective activities: opportunities provided by LEAs, conversations with other education professionals, and mentoring from other headteachers and colleagues were ranked as most effective.

The important role played by LEAs in leadership development and training was further explored when we were commissioned by NCSL to produce a good practice guide (Earley and Evans, 2002b; available at www.ncsl.org.uk). Examples of LEA provision are given under each of the NCSL's five stages of leadership development. Some LEAs have begun to integrate their provision by providing programmes, which are planned to cover each of the career stages.

KEY FEATURES OF LEADERSHIP PROGRAMMES

There is a useful review of the key features and principles of leadership development programmes (see Weindling, 2003; available at www.ncsl.org.uk), which also gives examples of good practice from throughout the world. It lists components that aim to help heads and other school leaders deal with the problems and challenges they are likely to face. Areas covered include:

- learning theories
- mentoring and coaching
- reflection
- problem-based learning and case studies
- action learning

- storytelling and drama
- journals and portfolios
- e-learning and computer simulations
- cohorts, groups and learning communities.

Learning theories

Underlying leadership programmes are theories of learning, such as:

- Learning is an active rather than a passive process.
- Learning is by nature social and is most likely to occur when learners share ideas, inquire and problem solve together.
- Learners, to go beyond rote learning, must have opportunities to make sense of new knowledge and create meaning for themselves based on individual and shared experiences.
- Reflection and metacognition contribute to the construction of knowledge and the process of sense making.
- New learning is mediated by prior experience, values and beliefs (Szabo and Lambert, 2002).

There is a well-established body of knowledge regarding the theory of adult learning (Knowles, 1980; Merriam and Caffarella, 1999), which can support the design of leadership development activities. One of the best summaries of the findings from the study of adult learning is provided by Wood and Thompson (1980):

- Adults learn when the goals and objectives are considered realistic and important to the learner, that is, job related and perceived as being useful.
- Adult learners need to see the results of their efforts and have accurate feedback about progress towards their goals.
- Adults come to the learning situation with a wide range of previous experiences, knowledge, skills, interests and competence. Individualisation, therefore, is appropriate for adults as well as children.
- Adults want to be involved in the selection of objectives, content, activities and assessment of their in-service education.
- Learning a new skill, technique or concept may provoke anxiety and fear of external judgement.
- Adults will resist learning situations, which they believe are an attack on their competence. They also reject prescriptions by others for their learning.

Mentoring and coaching

Research has shown that mentoring is a particularly popular and useful form of support for school leaders. While different approaches are used, the most common is for an experienced head to work one-to-one with a new head for at least a year.

The largest study of mentoring was the national evaluation of the headteacher mentoring scheme in England and Wales (Bolam et al., 1995; Pocklington and Weindling, 1996), which studied 303 headteacher mentors and 238 new heads. The mentoring process moved through a series of phases from practical advice to a deeper consideration of their role as headteacher. Key features of successful mentoring programmes are the training of the mentors and to ensure that they meet face to face with their partners at least six times a year. The findings showed that new heads greatly welcomed the support they received through mentoring, which reduced their feelings of isolation and improved their confidence and competence. Benefits were two-way, with the mentors obtaining a new perspective on issues in their own school from their work with the new heads. The NCSL recently commissioned reviews of the research literature on mentoring and the problems and support strategies for early headship (see Hobson, 2003; Hobson et al., 2003).

Coaching overlaps with mentoring and the terms are often not used with great clarity. Coaching is best used to describe a process focused on specific skill building, while mentoring is longer term and covers a wider range of professional support. Coaching and/or mentoring underpin many of the NCSL's programmes and they encourage reflection.

Reflection

Probably the most prevalent concept that runs through today's leadership programmes is the use of reflection. This takes a variety of forms but can usually be traced back to Schon's (1983) notion of the 'reflective practitioner' and is often linked with experiential learning approaches such as Kolb's (1984) learning cycle. It is argued that these form fundamental ways of learning and various opportunities should be provided to allow school leaders to reflect on their experiences both of the training and their work situations.

Problem-based learning and case studies

Originating in medical education the use of problem-based learning (PBL) for school leadership development has grown in recent years. Problem-based learning in educational administration training was developed at Stanford University in 1987 by Bridges and Hallinger (1992), who outline the following key principles:

1 The starting point for learning is a problem (that is, a stimulus for which an individual lacks a ready response). The problem is usually presented in the form of a case study.
2 The problem is one that participants are likely to face as future professionals.
3 The knowledge that participants are expected to acquire during their training is organised around problems rather than disciplines.
4 Participants, individually and collectively, assume a major responsibility for their own instruction and learning (tutors act as facilitators, rather than dispensers of information).

5 Most of the learning occurs within the context of small groups rather than lectures.
6 The groups are provided with a set of resource materials such as references to books and articles, readings, video and audio clips.

Undertaking the process of PBL has been found to be highly motivating for participants because they learn by doing, interact with their peers and receive immediate feedback.

Action learning

Another common feature is the use of action learning techniques. This is a process of learning and reflection that takes place with the support of a group, or 'learning set' of colleagues working on real problems presented in turn by each member of the group. The aim is to help the individual with the understanding and solution of the problem. After discussion within the set the individual takes action in the work setting. There are three roles in the action learning set: the presenter, the supporters (the rest of the group) and the facilitator. Revans (1998) developed the initial idea in 1945 from work with the coal-mining industry. He believed, 'there can be no learning without action and no (sober and deliberate) action without learning' (ibid., p. xix).

There is sometimes confusion between action learning and action research. Action research is a research method originally developed by Kurt Lewin from his work with groups beginning in 1938. He believed that the feedback from research should inform action. Action learning and action research share the focus on learning from experience and both have action and reflection phases. They are both based on the learning cycle of: reflect – plan – act – observe – reflect again, etc. (which is similar to that of Kolb). But they have different origins and traditions. Action learning is a more general approach to learning and problem-solving using a set of colleagues. Research is not the primary aim, and the project may not involve any formal research at all.

Storytelling and drama

Interesting instructional techniques that have grown in use recently in the business world are those of storytelling and drama. Clandinin and Connelly (1991) use narrative material in a nine-year study of school leaders' practical knowledge.

In his educational administration courses Danzig (1999; 2001) asks participants to interview a school leader on two occasions. In the first session they ask about the leader's professional biography. In the second interview they focus on a specific problem when the person played a leadership role. Using Gardner's (1995) accounts of outstanding leaders as a model, the participants draw on the interview transcripts to write a leadership story in the first person. These are used to explore various aspects of leadership. Danzig believes that the stories require participants to use more reflective skills, and they provide deeper insights into the lives, hopes, successes and failures of the leaders.

Meyer (2001a; 2001b) makes use of drama based on real incidents with a technique that he calls 'Theatre as Representation' (TAR). A short scenario and a written script which participants read are acted out in the form of a drama. Examples include a scenario about the selection of a new principal; the principal dealing with parents, students and staff. Some people play the parts while others observe. After the presentation of the piece both the participants and observers reflect and discuss the issues. Meyer has used TAR since 1993 and finds that school leaders respond very positively. They find that it brings the reality of the situation to life and demonstrates the micro-political nature of school leadership.

Journals and portfolios

The learning journal is a well-tried means of helping the writer to record their developmental progress over time, and as a vehicle to encourage reflection and metacognition. A short summary on journal writing and adult learning is given in an ERIC digest by Kerka (1996).

A similar process to the use of journals is the learning portfolio. However, portfolios that are collections of writing, project reports or work samples, have been used for a wide variety of purposes, often as a means of providing more 'authentic' assessment. Wildy and Wallace (1998) examined the use of portfolios by Australian school leaders and found they were used for different purposes such as: evidence for improvement, a means of organising their thoughts about their work, to record their achievements, and as a collection of work samples (in a similar way to the original use of portfolios in art).

E-learning and computer simulations

These can be part of a qualification (e.g. NPQH and the Ontario Principals' Qualification Programme) and include the use of electronic leadership portfolios and on-line mentoring. In Ontario the mentors post weekly scenarios from their own experience as a principal and a group of 15–20 aspiring principal mentees discuss these on line. There are also on-line discussion groups that use commercial programmes such as 'Blackboard' or Firstclass to organise the forum.

In England, Jones (2001) describe the establishment of an on-line community for the NCSL pilot programme of 'Talking Heads'. Crawford (2002) evaluated the use of a virtual learning community, which was part of the LPSH programme. She found that the heads varied considerably in their usage. A recent evaluation was commissioned by the NCSL of all their on-line communities (talk2learn, available from www.ncsl.org.uk). The findings showed that informal on-line communities helped to reduce headteacher isolation, enabled them to generate and exchange insights into school practice, find and share expertise for school improvement, and improve their ICT skills.

Computer simulations are sometimes used for leadership development. Hallinger (2003b) has developed three computer simulations: the first, 'In the centre of things' (ITCOT), is based on school improvement research and asks participants to consider how to improve student learning in the case study school. Another programme is concerned with managing change in a school, while the third programme is about developing learning organisations. Each simulation uses problem-based learning and asks heads to work in small teams of three. This facilitates their reflection for both individual and group learning. The NCSL's 'Leading from the Middle' programme uses a 'Virtual School', developed with the BBC, which provides a simulation of school-based decisions and their consequences.

Cohorts, groups and learning communities

Many leadership programmes run with a group of participants who meet regularly over a period of time. There are numerous advantages to working as a group rather than as individuals and some NCSL programmes involve whole-school leadership teams (e.g. 'Working together for success').

Following Mohr (1998) there are a number of factors for successful work with groups of school leaders:

- The groups are small (from six to 15 members).
- They have a facilitator who is responsible for convening the group, setting the agenda with the group, and keeping members on task.
- Participants come together to build knowledge by looking at their own work, pupils' work and research.
- They use structured protocols which build-in time for presenting work, listening (without responding), for giving and getting feedback, and for debriefing the process.
- Participants focus on learning how to deepen their understanding by being more descriptive and less judgemental.

The ideas of Wenger (1998) have had a considerable influence on leadership development programmes as they attempt to establish favourable conditions to facilitate professional learning communities. Wenger stresses the social nature of learning and defines a community of practice as: 'a group of people who share a concern, a set of problems, or a passion about a topic, and who deepen their knowledge and expertise in this area by interacting on an ongoing basis'. Communities of practice are everywhere, and they are not new. But, as Wenger points out, not all communities are communities of practice and not all practice gives rise to a community. The terms *community* and *practice* refer to a very specific type of social structure with a very specific purpose. In a more recent book, he looks at the principles required to cultivate a community of practice, their stages of development, and the positive and negative aspects of communities of practice (Wenger et al., 2002). Schools as learning communities and heads as 'lead learners' is the subject of the next section.

CREATING A LEARNING COMMUNITY

Creating a culture of learning in schools is crucial and this is shaped by the attitude and approach of leaders towards CPD (Earley and Bubb, 2004). What messages are being given about the importance of professional development? Are they participating in training themselves, particularly in school-based events, are they 'leading the learning'? As Senge et al. (2000, p. 423) have noted: 'effective leadership depends not merely on how you set up the circumstances for people to learn together, but on how you learn with them'. Heads and other school leaders have to ensure that training and development programmes meet the needs of both individual staff and their schools, minimising any tensions that may exist between system needs and priorities (the school development plan) and those of individuals (the individual development plan).

An organisation wishing to become a learning community would therefore take its professional development responsibilities very seriously and strive to secure effective learning for both its pupils and staff. Leaders of such communities must engender an ethos that all in the school – pupils, teachers and support staff – are seen as learners in their own right. They must also seek everyone's views and involve all, in various ways, in decision-making processes, supporting, developing and empowering them to feel a sense of ownership in the future direction of their organisation. An active participation by all in a collaborative culture means that everyone takes responsibility for learning. Teachers and others working in such communities will discuss their work openly and seek to improve and develop their pedagogy through collaborative enquiry and the sharing of good practice. Can we ensure that what may be an effective learning environment in the classroom is mirrored in the staffroom or school as a whole?

Effective leaders more than anyone else help determine the culture of their organisation by their behaviour, for example, by constantly questioning the status quo to find better ways of achieving goals, creating environments where positive results and credits are widely dispersed; evaluating and affirming people; thinking positively and realising that every problem presents a learning opportunity; and seeking to integrate the best ideas in the task of building people and the organisation (Diggins, 1997, p. 422). Learning communities are 'deeply committed to maintaining, developing and promoting the human capital they have' believing that they 'will become a reality when leaders become passionate about making the careers of other people happen' (ibid., p. 424).

Leaders in learning communities promote a strong sense of shared vision for the future; they lead the learning, by being seen to be learning with everyone else; they share and distribute leadership and empower others; and continuous improvement is built into the fabric of the organisation. Collaboration and collegiality are seen as contributing significantly to both individual and

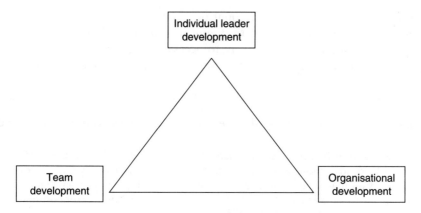

Figure 14.1   Three levels of development

organisational development. However, these terms are often ill defined, their meaning not clear and open to different interpretations.

Collegiality can help to develop an emotionally supportive work environment and one that truly engenders significant professional development. For colleagues truly to 'collaborate' and take ownership of the process of enquiry together, they need to have some shared values, goals and/or a common vision of teaching and learning. They must have a relationship that is characterised by trust, care, tolerance and mutual respect. Collaboration implies collegiality, acceptance, co-operation, teamwork, sharing of ideas and networking.

The culture of a learning community is therefore likely to be supportive and collaborative where staff are empowered to take a central role in their work; information is used to drive improvement; there is a commitment to working together as learners, and where staff and pupils have a sense of community and work together co-operatively. Groups of teachers who correspond outside school, either electronically or in face-to-face meetings or networks show great potential as sites for focused, ongoing and self-directed inquiry. These voluntary groups are now increasingly seen as a legitimate forum to promote development (Earley, 2004b; Jackson, 2003). Importantly, it is development that occurs at three levels – the individual, the team and the school (see Figure 14.1).

Kochan et al. (2002, p. 300) highlight the role of the head as the 'steward of learning' who 'strive[s] to keep the focus of the school on learning for students, teachers, and themselves'. Many leadership development programmes have now realigned their curriculum to focus on how leaders can help adults', and particularly, children's learning.

NCSL provision

Throughout this chapter reference has been made to the national programmes and other offerings of the National College for School Leadership. It is not appropriate to give a detailed account of NCSL provision here; it is growing rapidly and therefore subject to frequent change and amendment. The College's website is the easiest way to access current offerings but a useful overview of the main programmes is found in Earley and Bubb (2004).

FINAL THOUGHTS

London (2002, p. 251) in his study of leadership development concludes by saying:

> Leaders need to be continuous learners. Their jobs demand it, and their careers would be dead without it – at least their careers would probably have an early demise. Continuous learning is a frame of mind and a set of behaviours that contribute to ongoing professional renewal and the creation of opportunities. Continuous learners are self-directed and proactive about assessing the gaps in their knowledge and skills and finding and taking advantage of learning resources.

Schools leaders have a responsibility to develop themselves, their teams and their schools – one measure of success is how many leaders they have developed or how the leadership capacity of the school has improved. But they need support from other parties to be able successfully to do this. Support and resources, including time, are needed to ensure that the job of school leaders is achievable. Shared and distributed leadership is one way forward as the responsibilities are simply too great for the individual leader no matter how effective they might be. As we conclude this book, rarely do we read the educational press without there being some reference to recruitment and retention problems or the stress and burnout associated with school leadership. The government's remodelling agenda (DfES, 2002a) is an attempt to tackle this and it is crucial that the conditions under which school leaders work are such that others are not discouraged from putting themselves forward. The future of our schools depends on there being a constant flow of teachers willing to take on such responsibilities. But it also depends on schools and LEAs taking a proactive stance in leadership development – in building leadership capacity. A recent NCSL research report, entitled *Growing Tomorrow's School Leaders: The Challenge* (Hartle and Thomas, 2003), states that the changing trends in school leadership – e.g. towards a multiple model of distributive and learning-centred leadership and collaboration – intensifies the challenge because the number of potential school leaders is much higher. They state:

> Instead of having to develop sufficient numbers to fill the 25,000 headteacher posts, it could be as many as 250,000 leaders to be developed to cover all senior and middle manager posts in schools. Many will be young teachers with only a few years' experience; they will need substantial help and effective leadership to develop their own leadership potential and skills.

(ibid., p. 3)

Capacity-building, leadership succession and leadership development practices are therefore crucial and the authors argue that 'collective and integrated action at national, local and school levels is required to meet the future demands for school leaders' (ibid., p. 4). Their research report outlines what such action might look like but also notes that an effective development programme improves the quality of teaching and learning which, they remind us, is the core purpose of schools.

There are clearly some major challenges ahead but our overall conclusion remains a positive one. Distributed and shared leadership, whilst welcomed, still rely heavily on leadership, alongside effective management, being successfully demonstrated at the *apex* of the organisation. Our research over the years, including our unique longitudinal study of a cohort of heads appointed in the early 1980s, shows that headship remains an exciting prospect and that most heads continue to enjoy the work. Sergiovanni (2001, p. 1) notes that the job can be fun 'if one is at ease with complexity, likes challenges and is willing to work hard'. But without question the head's role 'has become dramatically more complex, overloaded and unclear over the last decade' (Fullan, 2001, p. 137). Despite the complexities and the many changes to the role and its numerous never-ending challenges, headship is still considered by many to be 'the best job in education'!

References

Adair, J. (1986) *Effective Team Building*, London: Gower.

Adams, F. (2004) Schools get no satisfaction from the new Ofsted, *Times Educational Supplement*, 16 January, p. 19.

Audit Commission (1995) *Lessons in Teamwork*, London: Audit Commission.

Baker, L., Earley, P. and Weindling, D. (1994a) Benefits and burdens, *Managing Schools Today*, Vol. 4, No. 1, pp. 28–9.

Baker, L., Earley, P. and Weindling, D. (1994b) Heading into the future, *Managing Schools Today*, Vol. 4, No. 2, pp. 30–1.

Baker, L., Earley, P. and Weindling, D. (1995) Pleasure and pain, *Managing Schools Today*, Vol. 4, No. 7, pp. 38–9.

Barth, R. (1992) *Improving Schools From Within*, San Francisco: Jossey-Bass.

Bass, B. (1999) Two decades of research and development in transformational leadership, *European Journal of Work and Organisational Psychology*, Vol. 8, No. 3, pp. 9–32.

Beck, L. and Murphy, J. (1993) *Understanding the Principalship: a metaphorical analysis from 1920–1990*, New York: Teachers College Press.

Belbin, M. (1993) *Team Roles at Work*, Oxford: Butterworth-Heinneman.

Bennett, N. (1995) *Managing Professional Teachers: Middle Management in Primary and Secondary Schools*, London: Paul Chapman Publishing.

Bennett, N., Wise, C., Woods, P. and Harvey, J. (2003) *Distributed Leadership – Full Report*, Nottingham: NCSL.

Bennis, W. (1999) The leadership advantage, *Leader to Leader* 12, Spring, pp. 1–7.

Bennis, W. and Nanus, B. (1985) *Leaders: The Strategies for Taking Charge*, New York: Harper and Row.

Bird, S. (2002) *Governance Matters*, London: The Education Network.

Bird, S. (2003) *Do the right thing!* London: The Education Network.

Blake, R. and Mouton, J. (1964) *The Managerial Grid*, Houston: Gulf.

Blandford, S. (1996) *Middle Management in Schools*, London: Pitman.

Bleach, K. (1999) *The Induction and Mentoring of Newly Qualified Teachers*, London: David Fulton.

Blumberg, A. and Greenfield, W. (1986) *The Effective Principal*, 2nd edn, Boston: Allyn and Bacon.

Bolam, R., McMahon, A., Pocklington, K. and Weindling, D. (1993) *Effective Management in Schools*, London: Department for Education.

Bolam, R., McMahon, A., Pocklington, K. and Weindling, D. (1995) Mentoring for new headteachers: recent British experience, *Journal of Educational Administration*, Vol. 33, No. 5, pp. 29–44.

Bolman, L. and Deal, T. (1991) *Reframing Organizations*, San Francisco: Jossey-Bass.

Bolman, L. and Deal, T. (1997) *Reframing Organizations*, 2nd edn, San Francisco: Jossey-Bass.

Bolman, L. and Heller, R. (1995) Research on school leadership: the state of the art, in Bacharach, S. and Mundell, B. (eds), *Images of Schools*, Thousand Oaks, CA: Corwin Press.

Bredeson, P. (1985) An analysis of metaphorical perspectives on school principals, *Educational Administration Quarterly*, Vol. 21, No. 1, pp. 29–59.

Bredeson, P. (1987) Languages of leadership: metaphor making in educational administration, *Administrators Notebook*, Vol. 32, No. 6, pp. 1–5.

Bredeson, P. (1988) Perspectives on schools: metaphors and management in education, *Journal of Educational Administration*, Vol. 26, No. 3, pp. 293–310.

Bridges, E. and Hallinger, P. (1992) *Problem-Based Learning for Administrators*, Eugene, OR: ERIC Clearing House on Educational Management.

Brown, M. and Rutherford, D. (1996) Leadership for school improvement: the changing role of the head of department. Paper presented to the BEMAS Research Conference, Cambridge, March.

Brown, M., Boyle, R. and Boyle, T. (1999) Commonalities between perception and practice in models of school decision-making in secondary schools, *School Leadership and Management*, Vol. 19, No. 3, pp. 319–30.

Brown, M., Rutherford, D. and Boyle, B. (2000) Leadership for school improvement: the role of the HoD in UK secondary schools, *School Effectiveness and School Improvement*, Vol. 19, No. 2, pp. 237–58.

Brown, S., Riddell, S. and Duffield, J. (1996) Possibilities and problems of small-scale studies to unpack the findings of large-scale studies of school effectiveness, in Gray, J., Reynolds, D., Fitz-Gibbon, C. and Jesson, D. (eds), *Merging Traditions: The Future of Research on School Effectiveness and School Improvement*, London: Cassell.

Bubb, S. (2002) 'New kids on the rack', *Times Educational Supplement*, 12 July, p. 19.

Bubb, S. (2003a) *The Insider's Guide for New Teachers: Succeeding in Training and Induction*, London: TES/Kogan Page.

Bubb, S. (2003b) *A Newly Qualified Teacher's Manual: How to Meet the Induction Standards*, London: David Fulton.

Bubb, S. (2004) *The Insider's Guide to Early Professional Development: Succeed in your First Five Years*, London: TES/RoutledgeFalmer.

Bubb, S. and Earley, P. (2003) 'Rogue' school leaders and newly qualified teachers, *Management in Education*, Vol. 17, Issue 4, pp. 25–9.

Bubb, S., Heibronn, R., Jones, C., Totterdell, M. and Bailey, M. (2002) *Improving Induction: Research Based Best Practice for Schools*, London: RoutledgeFalmer.

Bullock, A. and Thomas, H. (1997) *Schools at the Centre? A Study of Decentralisation*, London: Routledge.

Burns, J.M. (1966) *Leadership*, London: Harper and Row.

Bush, T. and Glover, D. (2003) *School Leadership: Concepts and Evidence*, Nottingham: NCSL.

Busher, H. and Harris, A. with Wise, C. (2000) *Subject Leadership and School Improvement*, London: Paul Chapman Publishing.

Campbell, C., Gold, A. and Lunt, I. (2003) Articulating leadership values in action: conversations with school leaders, *International Journal of Leadership in Education*, Vol. 6, No. 3, pp. 203–21.

Carver, J. (1990) *Boards that Make a Difference*, San Francisco: Jossey-Bass.

Clandinin, D. and Connelly, M. (1991) Narrative and story in practice and research, in Schon, D. (ed.) *The Reflective Turn: Case Studies In and On Educational Practice*, New York: Teachers College Press.

Clayton, J. (2001) Sabbaticals – expectations and rights, *Professional Development Today*, Vol. 5, No. 1, pp. 27–32.

Coleman, J., Campbell, E., Hobson, C., Mcpartland, J., Mood, A., Weinfeld, F. and York, R. (1966) *Equality of Educational Opportunity*, Washington, DC: US Government Printing Office.

Coleman, M. (2002) *Women as Headteachers: Striking the Balance*, Stoke-on-Trent: Trentham Books.

Crawford, M. (2002) Enhancing school leadership: evaluating the use of virtual learning communities, *Education Management and Administration*, Vol. 30, No. 4, pp. 431–46.

Creese, M. (2000) Enhancing the effectiveness of governing bodies, *Professional Development Today*, Vol. 3, No. 3, pp. 49–58.

Creese, M. and Bradley, H. (1997) Ways in which governing bodies contribute to school improvement: findings from a pilot project, *School Leadership and Management*, Vol. 17, No. 1, pp. 105–15.

Creese, M. and Earley, P. (1999) *Improving Schools and Governing Bodies: Making a Difference*, London: Routledge.

Cuban, L. (1984) Transforming the frog into a prince: effective schools research, policy and practice at the district level, *Harvard Education Review*, Vol. 54, No. 2, pp. 129–51.

Danzig, A. (1999) The contribution of stories to leadership development, *International Studies in Educational Administration*, Vol. 27, No. 1, pp. 11–19.

Danzig, A. (2001) Teaching educational leadership via Web courses, *Journal of Research for Educational Leadership*, Vol. 1 No. 1 pp. 19–48.

Davis, J. (1991) Professions, trades and the obligation to inform, *Journal of Applied Philosophy*, Vol. 8, No. 2.

Day, C. and Bakioglu, A. (1996) Development and disenchantment in the professional lives of headteachers, in Goodison, I. and Hargreaves, A. (eds), *Teachers' Professional Lives*, London: Falmer Press.

Day, C. Harris, A. Hadfield, M. Tolley, H. and Beresford, J. (2000) *Leading Schools in Times of Change*, Buckingham: Open University Press.

Deal, T. (1987) Effective school principals: counsellors, engineers, pawnbrokers, poets or instructional leaders? in Greenfield, W. (ed.), *Instructional Leadership*, Boston: Allyn and Bacon.

Deem, R., Brehony, K. and Heath, S. (1995) *Active Citizenship and the Governing of Schools*, Buckingham: Open University Press.

Department for Education and Employment (DfEE) (1999) *The Induction Period for Newly Qualified Teachers*, Circular 5/99, London: DfEE.

Department for Education and Employment (DfEE) (2000a) *A Guide to the Law for School Governors*, London: DfEE.

Department for Education and Employment (DfEE) (2000b) *Roles of Governing Bodies and Head Teachers*, London: DfEE.

Department for Education and Employment (DfEE) (2000d) *The Leadership Group*, London: DfEE.

Department for Education and Skills (DfES) (2001) *National Induction Programme for Governors: Toolkit for Trainers*, London: DfES.

Department for Education and Skills (DfES) (2002a) *Time for standards*, London: DfES.

Department for Education and Skills (DfES) (2002b) *Steering not Rowing*, Conference report, London: DfES.

Department of Education and Science (DES) (1990) *Developing School Management: The Way Forward*, School Management Task Force, London: DES.

DFE/BIS/Ofsted (1995) *Governing Bodies and Effective Schools*, London: DFE.

Diggins, P. (1997) Reflections on leadership characteristics necessary to develop and sustain learning school communities, *School Leadership and Management*, Vol. 17, No. 3, pp. 413–25.

Duke, D. (1987) *School Leadership and Instructional Improvement*, New York: Random House.

Earley, P. (1992) *The School Management Competences Project*, 3 vols, Crawley: School Management South.

Earley, P. (1993) Developing competence in schools: a critique of standards-based approaches to management development, *Education Management and Administration*, Vol. 21, No. 4, pp. 233–44.

Earley, P. (1994) *School Governing Bodies: Making Progress?* Slough: NFER.

Earley, P. (ed.) (1996) *School Improvement after Inspection? School and LEA Responses*, London: Paul Chapman Publishing.

Earley, P. (1997a) External inspections, 'failing schools' and the role of governing bodies, *School Leadership and Management*, Vol. 17, No. 3, pp. 387–400.

Earley, P. (1997b) Norhicote School, in Mortimore, P. (ed.), *The Road to Success: Case Studies of Successful Schools*, London: Institute of Education/DfEE.

Earley, P. (1998) Middle management: the key to organisational success? in Middlewood, D. and Lumby, J. (eds), *Strategic Management in Schools and Colleges*, London: Paul Chapman Publishing.

Earley, P. (2003) Leaders or followers? Governing bodies and their role in school leadership, *Educational Management and Administration*, Vol. 31, No. 4, pp. 353–68.

Earley, P. (2004a) Managing the performance of headteachers: the role of school governing bodies in English schools. Paper presented to Education Management Association of South African conference, March.

Earley, P. (2004b) Continuing professional development: the learning community, in Coleman, M. and Earley, P. (eds), *The Leadership and Management of Schools: Cultures, Change and Continuity*, Oxford: Oxford University Press.

Earley, P. and Baker, L. (1989) *The Recruitment and Retention of Headteachers*, Slough: NFER.

Earley, P. and Bubb, S. (2004) *Leading and Managing CPD: Developing People, Developing Schools*, London: Sage/Paul Chapman Publishing.

Earley, P. and Creese, M. (2003) Lay or professional? Re-examining the role of school governors, in Davies, B. and West-Burnham, J. (eds), *Handbook of Educational Leadership and Management*, London: Pearson.

Earley, P. and Evans, J. (2002a) *Establishing the Current State of Leadership in Independent Schools*, London: Institute of Education.

Earley, P. and Evans, J. (2002b) *LEAding Provision: School Leadership Development in LEAs: A Good Practice Guide*, Nottingham: NCSL.

Earley, P. and Fletcher-Campbell, F. (1992) *The Time to Manage? Department and Faculty Heads at Work*, London: Routledge. First published in 1989 by NFER-Nelson, Windsor.

Earley, P. and Kinder, K. (1994) *Initiation Rights – Effective Induction Practices for New Teachers*, Slough: NFER.

Earley, P., Evans, J., Gold, A., Collarbone, P. and Halpin, D. (2002) *Establishing the Current State of School Leadership in England*, London: DfES.

Earley, P., Weindling, D. and Baker, L. (1990) *Keeping the Raft Afloat: Secondary Headship Five Years On*, Slough: NFER.

Earley, P., Weindling, D. and Baker, L. (1994/95) Secondary headship ten years on. A series of ten articles in, *Managing Schools Today*, Vol. 4, Nos 1–10.

Edmonds, R. (1979) Effective schools for the urban poor, *Educational Leadership*, Vol. 37, No. 1, pp. 15–24.

Edwards, R. (1985) Departmental organisation and management, in Edwards, R. and Bennett, D., *Schools in Action*, Cardiff: Welsh Office.

Egan, G. (1993) *Adding Value: A Systematic Guide to Business-Driven Management and Leadership*, San Francisco: Jossey-Bass.

Evans, L. (1999) *Managing to Motivate: A Guide for School Leaders*, London: Cassell.

Evetts, J. (1994) *Becoming a Secondary Headteacher*, London: Cassell.

Ferguson, N., Earley, P., Ouston, J. and Fidler, B. (2000) *Improving Schools and Inspection: The Self-inspecting School*, London: Paul Chapman Publishing.

Fidler, B. (1997) School leadership: some key ideas, *School Leadership and Management*, Vol. 17, No. 1, pp. 23–37.

Fidler, B. and Atton, T. (2004) *The Headship Game: the challenges of contemporary school leadership*, London: RoutledgeFalmer.

Fidler, B., with Edwards, M., Evans, B., Mann, P. and Thomas, P. (1996) *Strategic Planning for School Improvement*, London: Pitman.

Fiedler, F. (1967) *A Theory of Leadership Effectiveness*, New York: McGraw-Hill.

Field, K. and Holden, P. (2004) National standards for subject leaders, in Green, H. (ed.), *Professional Standards for Teachers and Headteachers: A Key to School Improvement*, London: Kogan Page.

Field, K., Holden, P. and Lawlor, H. (2000) *Effective Subject Leadership*, London: Routledge.

Flintham, A. (2003) *When Reservoirs Run Dry: Why some Heads Leave Headship Early*, Nottingham: NCSL.

Floyd, S. and Wooldridge, B. (1996) *The Strategic Middle Manager*, New York: Jossey-Bass.

Fullan, M. (1991) *The New Meaning of Educational Change*, (3rd edn, 2001), London: Cassell.

Fullan, M. (2001), *Leading in a Culture of Change*, San Francisco: Jossey-Bass.

Fullan, M. (2003a) We need lots of leaders, *Times Educational Supplement*, 11 July p. 21.

Fullan, M. (2003b) *The Moral Imperative of School Leadership*, London: Corwin Sage.

Gabarro, J. (1987) *The Dynamics of Taking Charge*. Boston: Harvard Business School Press.

Gardner, H. (1995) *Leading Minds: An Anatomy of Leadership*, New York: Basic Books.

Gold, A. (1997) *Principles in Practice: Head of Department*, London: Cassell.

Gold, A. and Evans, J. (2002) Piggy in the middle. Middle managers, emergent leaders or prospective senior leaders? Paper presented at British Educational Leadership, Management and Administration Society, Annual Conference, Birmingham, 20–22 September.

Gold, A., Evans, J., Earley, P., Halpin, D. and Collarbone, P. (2003) Principled principals? Values-driven leadership: evidence from ten case studies of 'outstanding' school leaders, *Educational Management and Administration*, Vol. 31, No. 2, 125–36.

Goleman, D. (1996) *Emotional Intelligence: Why it can matter more than IQ*, London: Bloomsbury.

Goleman, D. (1998) *Working with Emotional Intelligence*, London: Bloomsbury.

Goleman, D., Boyatzis, R. and McKee, A. (2002) *Primal Leadership: Realising the Power of Emotional Intelligence*, Boston: Harvard Business School Press.

Grady, N. (1993) Examining teachers' images through metaphor, *Studies in Educational Administration*, Vol. 58, Winter, pp. 23–31.

Gray, H. (1986) Why heads should not teach, *Contributions*, Vol. 9, pp. 40–4, Winter.

Gray, J. (2000) *Causing Concern But Improving: A Review of Schools' Experiences*, Research Brief 118, London: DfES.

Gray, J., Hopkins, D., Reynolds, D., Wilcox, B., Farrell, S. and Jesson, D. (1999) *Improving Schools: Performance and Potential*, Buckingham: Open University Press.

Gray, J., Reynolds, D., Fitz-Gibbon, C. and Jesson, D. (eds) (1996) *Merging Traditions: The Future of Research on School Effectiveness and School Improvement*, London: Cassell.

Green, H. (ed.) (2004) *Professional Standards for Teachers and Headteachers: A Key to School Improvement*, London: Routledge.

Gronn, P. (1993) Psychobiography on the couch: character, biography and the comparative study of leaders, *Journal of Applied Behavioural Science*, Vol. 29 No. 3, pp. 343–58.

Gronn, P. (1999) *The Making of Educational Leaders*, London: Cassell.

Gross, S. and Shapiro, J. (2002) Towards ethically responsible leadership in an era of accountability. Paper presented at AERA conference, New Orleans.

Hall, V. (1996) *Dancing on the Ceiling*, London: Paul Chapman Publishing.

Hallinger, P. (2003a) Leading educational change: reflections on the practice of instructional and transformational leadership, *Cambridge Journal of Education*, Vol. 33, No. 3, pp. 329–51.

Hallinger, P. (ed.) (2003b) *Reshaping the Landscape of School Leadership Development: A Global Perspective*, Lisse: Swets and Zeitlinger.

Hallinger, P. and Heck, R. (1998) Exploring the principal's contribution to school effectiveness: 1980–1995, *School Effectiveness and School Improvement*, Vol. 9, No. 2, pp. 157–91.

Hallinger, P. and Heck, R. (1999) Can leadership enhance school effectiveness?, in Bush, T., Bell, L., Bolam, R., Glatter, R. and Ribbins, P. (eds), *Educational Management: Redefining Theory, Policy and Practice*, London: Paul Chapman Publishing.

Hallinger, P. and Heck, R. (2003) Understanding the contribution of leadership to school leadership, in Wallace, M. and Poulson, L. (eds), *Learning to Read Critically in Educational Leadership and Management*, London: Sage/Paul Chapman Publishing.

Hampton, G. and Jones, J. (2000) *Transforming Northicote School: The Reality of School Improvement*, London: RoutledgeFalmer.

Harris, A. (1998) Improving ineffective departments in secondary schools, *Educational Management and Administration*, Vol. 26, No. 3, pp. 269–78.

Harris, A. (2003) Teacher leaders, in Davies, B. and West-Burnham, J. (eds) *Handbook of Educational Leadership and Management*, London: Pearson.

Harris, A. and Lambert, L. (2003) *Building Leadership Capacity for School Improvement*, Maidenhead: Open University Press.

Harris, A., Jamieson, I. and Russ, J. (1995) A study of 'effective' departments in secondary schools, *School Organisation*, Vol. 15, No. 3, pp. 283–300.

Hart, A. (1993) *Principal Succession: Establishing Leadership in Schools*. New York: State University of New York Press.

Hartle, F. and Thomas, K. (2003) *Growing Tomorrow's School Leaders: The Challenge*, Nottingham: NCSL.

Hay-McBer (2000) *Effective Teachers*, http://dfee.gov.uk/teachingreforms/leadership/mcber/.

Her Majesty's Inspectorate (HMI) (1984) *Departmental Organisation in Secondary Schools*, HMI (Wales) Occasional Paper, Welsh Office.

Hersey, P. and Blanchard, K. (1977) *Managing Organizational Behaviour: Utilizing Human Resources*, Englewood Cliffs, NJ: Prentice-Hall.

Hobson, A. (2003) *Mentoring and Coaching for New Leaders: A Review of the Literature*, Nottingham: NCSL available from www.ncsl.org.uk.

Hobson, A., Brown, E., Ashby, P., Keys, W., Sharp, C. and Benefield, P. (2003) *Issues of Early Headship – Problems and Support Strategies*, NCSL available from www.ncsl.org.uk.

Hopkins, D. (2001) *School Improvement for Real*, London: Falmer.

Hopkins, D., West, M. and Ainscow, M. (1996) *Improving the Quality of Education for All: Progress and Challenge*, London: David Fulton.

House of Commons, Education and Employment Committee (5th Report) (1999) *The Role of the Governing Body*, London: The Stationery Office.

Jackson, D. (2003) Building schools' capacity as learning communities, *Professional Development Today*, Vol. 5, No. 3, pp. 17–24.

Jenks, C., Smith, M., Acland, H., Bane, M., Cohen, D., Gintis, H., Heyns, B. and Michelson, S. (1972) *Inequality: A Reassessment of the Basic Effect of Family and Schooling in America*, New York: Basic Books.

Johnson, G. and Scholes, K. (1993) *Exploring Corporate Strategy*, Hemel Hempstead: Prentice-Hall.

Jones, J. and O'Sullivan, F. (1997) Energising middle management, in Tomlinson, H. (ed.), *Managing Continuing Professional Development in Schools*, London: Paul Chapman Publishing.

Jones, S. (2001) Establishing on-line communities for school leaders: an interim report. Paper given at the BERA conference.

Joyce, B. (1991) The doors of school improvement, *Educational Leadership*, Vol. 48, No. 8, pp. 59–62.

Kerka, S. (1996) Journal writing and adult learning, *ERIC Digest*, No. 174.

Kitson, N. and O'Neill, J. (eds) (1996) *Effective Curriculum Management: Co-ordinating Learning in the Primary School*, London: Routledge.

Knowles, M. (1980) *The Modern Practice of Adult Education: From Pedagogy to Andragogy*, New York: Cambridge Books.

Kochan, F., Bredeson, P. and Riehl, C. (2002) Rethinking the professional development of school leaders, in Murphy, J. (ed.), *The Educational Leadership Challenge: Redefining Leadership for the 21st Century*, 101st Yearbook of the National Society for the Study of Education, Chicago: University of Chicago Press.

Kogan, M. (1988) *Education Accountability: An Analytical Overview*, 2nd edn, London: Hutchinson.

Kolb, D. (1984) *Experiential Learning: Experience as a Source of Learning and Development*, New York: Prentice-Hall.

Lakoff, G. and Johnson, M. (1980) *Metaphors We Live By*, Chicago: University of Chicago Press.

Lawlor, H. and Sills, P. (1999) Successful Leadership-Evidence from highly effective headteachers. *Improving Schools*, Vol. 2, No. 2, pp. 53–60.

Leithwood, K. (1992) The socialisation of school leaders, in Leithwood, K., Begley, P. and Cousins, B. (eds), *Developing Expert Leadership for Future Schools*, London: Falmer Press.

Leithwood, K., Begley, P. and Cousins, B. (eds) (1992) *Developing Expert Leadership for Future Schools*. London: Falmer Press.

Leithwood, K., Jantzi, D. and Steinbach, R. (1999) *Changing Leadership for Changing Times*, Buckingham: Open University Press.

Levačić, R. (1995) *Local Management of Schools*, Buckingham: Open University Press.

Levine, D. and Lezotte, L. (1990) *Unusually Effective Schools*, Madison: National Center for Effective Schools.

Lewin, K., Lippitt, R. and White, R. (1939) Patterns of aggressive behavior in experimentally created 'social climates', *Journal of Social Psychology*, Vol. 10, pp. 271–308.

Little, R. (2002) Accelerated learning, *Governors' Agenda*, No. 22, April, pp. 10–11.

Lofthouse, M., Bush, T., Coleman, M., O'Neil, J., West-Burnham, J. and Glover, D. (1995) *Managing the Curriculum*, London: Pitman.

London, M. (2002) *Leadership Development: Paths to Self-insight and Professional Growth*, Hillsdale, NJ: Lawrence Erlbaum Associates.

Louis, M. (1980) Surprise and sense making: what newcomers experience in entering unfamiliar organisational settings, *Administrative Science Quarterly*, Vol. 25, No. 2, pp. 226–51.

MacBeath, J. and Mortimore, P. (eds) (2001) *Improving School Effectiveness*, Buckingham: Open University Press.

Marks, H. and Printy, S. (2003) Principal leadership and school performance: an integration of transformational and instructional leadership, *Educational Administration Quarterly*, Vol. 39, No. 3, pp. 370–97.

Martin, J. and Holt, A. (2002) *Joined-up Governance: Making Sense of the Role of the School Governor*, Ely: Adamson Books.

McGregor, D. (1960) *The Human Side of Enterprise*, New York: McGraw Hill.

Merriam, S. and Cafferella, R. (1999) *Learning In Adulthood: A Comprehensive Guide*, 2nd edn, San Francisco: Jossey-Bass.

Merton, R. (1963) *Social Theory and Social Structure*, New York: Free Press.

Meyer, M. (2001a) Illustrating issues of power and control: the use of dramatic scenario in administrative training, *Educational Management and Administration*, Vol. 29, No. 4, pp. 441–57.

Meyer, M. (2001b) Reflective leadership training in practice using theatre as representation, *International Journal of Leadership in Education*, Vol. 4, No. 2, pp. 149–69.

Mohr, N. (1998) Creating effective study groups for principals, *Educational Leadership*, Vol. 55, No. 7, pp. 41–4.

Morgan, C., Hall, V. and Mackay, H. (1983) *The Selection of Secondary Headteachers*, Buckingham: Open University Press.

Morgan, G. (1986) *Images of Organisation*, Newbury Park, CA: Sage.

Morgan, G. (1993) *Imaginization*, Newbury Park, CA: Sage.

Mortimore, P. (ed.) (1997) *The Road to Success: Case Studies of Successful Schools*, London: Institute of Education.

Mortimore, P., Sammons, P., Stoll, L., Lewis, D. and Ecob, R. (1988) *School Matters: The Junior Years*, Wells: Open Books.

Mullen, C., Gordon, S., Greenlee, B. and Anderson, R. (2002) Capacities for school leadership: emerging trends in the Literature, *International Journal of Educational Reform*, Vol. 11, No. 2, pp. 158–98.

National Audit Office (2003) *Making a Difference*, London: The Stationery Office.

National College for School Leadership (NCSL) (2001) *Leadership Development Framework*, Nottingham: NCSL.

National College for School Leadership (NCSL) (2002) *Building Capacity: Developing your School*, Nottingham: NCSL.

National College for School Leadership (NCSL) (2003a) *The Heart of the Matter: A Practical Guide to What Middle Leaders can Do to Improve Learning in Secondary Schools*, Nottingham: NCSL.

National College for School Leadership (NCSL) (2003b) Leading from the middle, supplement to *LDR*, May.

National College for School Leadership (NCSL) (2003c) National standards for heads – consultation, Nottingham: NCSL.

Nias, J., Southworth, G., and Yeomans, R. (1989) *Staff Relationships in the Primary School: A Study of Organisational Cultures*, London: Cassell.

Nicholson, N. and West, M. (1988) *Managerial Job Change: Men and Women in Transition*, Cambridge: Cambridge University Press.

O'Neill, O. (2002) *A Question of Trust*, The BBC Reith Lectures 2002, Cambridge: Cambridge University Press.

Ofsted (1994) *Improving Schools*, London: HMSO.

Ofsted (1996) *Subjects and Standards: Issues for School Development Arising from Ofsted Inspection Findings 1994–5, Key Stages 1 and 2*, London: Ofsted.

Ofsted (1997) *Subject Leadership in Schools*, London: Ofsted.

Ofsted (1998) *Making Headway*, London: Ofsted.

Ofsted (1999a) *The Inspection Framework for Secondary Schools*, London: The Stationery Office.

Ofsted (1999b) *Additional Inspectors*, London: Ofsted.

Ofsted (2001) *Making It Better: Improving School Governance*, a report from HM Chief Inspector of Schools, London: Ofsted.

Ofsted (2002a) *The Inspection Framework for Schools*, London: The Stationery Office.

Ofsted (2002b) *The Work of School Governors* (HMI 707), report from HMCI, London: Ofsted; see Ofsted website, www.ofsted.gov.uk/publications.

Ofsted (2003a) *Framework 2003 – Inspecting Schools*, London: Stationery Office; see Ofsted website, www.ofsted.gov.uk/publications.

Ofsted (2003b) *Leadership and Management – What Inspection Tells Us*, London: Ofsted.

Parkay, F. and Hall, G. (eds) (1992) *Becoming a Principal*, Boston: Allyn and Bacon.

Parkin, J. (2003) Inspectors to call with a new agenda, *Times Educational Supplement*, Leadership supplement, 6 June, p. 7.

Pedlar, M., Burgoyne, J. and Boydell, T. (2003) *A Manager's Guide to Leadership*, Maidenhead: McGraw-Hill.

Peters, T. (1988) *Thriving on Chaos: A Handbook for Management Revolution*, London: Macmillan.

Pfeffer, J. (1992) *Managing with Power*, Boston: Harvard Business School Press.

Phillips, J. (2003) Governors as leaders (Part 2), *Governors News*, No. 2, April, p. 1.

Pocklington, K. and Weindling, D. (1996) Promoting reflection on headship through the mentoring mirror, *Educational Management and Administration*, Vol. 24, No. 2, pp. 175–91.

Pollock, L. (2003) Birth of the sharing leadership model, *Times Educational Supplement*, 6 June, p. 27.

PricewaterhouseCoopers (2001) *Teacher Workload Study: Interim report*, London: DfES.

Reeves, J., Moos, L. and Forrest, J. (1998) The school leader's view, in MacBeath, J. (ed.), *Effective School Leadership*, London: Paul Chapman Publishing.

Revans, R. (1998) *ABC of Action Learning*, 3rd edn, London: Lemos and Crane.

Revell, P. (2002) Buckling under an impossible burden, *Times Educational Supplement*, 22 November, p. 29.

Revell, P. (2003) A theft too far, *Education Guardian*, 16 September, p. 6.

Reynolds, D. (1992) School effectiveness and school improvement: an updated review of the British literature, in Reynolds, D. and Cuttance, P. (eds) *School Effectiveness*, London: Cassell.

Reynolds, D., Jones, D. and St Ledger, S. (1976) Schools do make a difference, *New Society*, Vol. 37, pp. 223–5.

Ribbins, P. (1997) Heads on deputy headship, *Educational Management and Administration*, Vol. 25, No. 3, pp. 295–308.

Ribbins, P. (1998) On ladders and greasy poles; developing school leaders careers. Paper presented at the Third ESRC Seminar, Milton Keynes, June.

Rowan, J. and Taylor, P. (2002) Leading the English primary school, *Management in Education*, Vol. 16, No. 3, pp. 17–23.

Rutter, M., Maugham, B., Mortimore, P. and Ouston, J. (1979) *Fifteen Thousand Hours*, London: Open Books.

Sallis, J. (2001) *Heads in Partnership: Working with your Governors for a Successful School*, London: Pitman.

Sammons, P., Khamis, A. and Coleman, M. (2004) Educational effectiveness, in Coleman, M. and Earley, P. (eds), *The Leadership and Management of Schools: Cultures, Change and Continuity*, Oxford: Oxford University Press.

Sammons, P., Thomas, S. and Mortimore, P. (1997) *Forging Links: Effective Schools: Effective Departments*, London: Paul Chapman Publishing.

Scanlon, M., Earley, P. and Evans, J. (1999) *Improving the Effectiveness of School Governing Bodies*, London: DfEE.

Scheerens, J. and Bosker, R. (1997) *The Foundations of Educational Effectiveness*, Netherlands: Elsevier.

Schein, E. (1968) Organisational socialisation and the profession of management, *Industrial Management Review*, Vol. 9, No. 1, pp. 1–15.

Schein, E. (1987) *Organisational Culture and Leadership*, San Francisco: Jossey-Bass.

Schon, D. (1983) *The Reflective Practitioner*, New York: Basic Books.

Secondary Heads Association (2003) *Towards Intelligent Accountability in Schools*, Policy Paper 5, Leicester: SHA.

Senge, P. (1990) *The Fifth Discipline: The Art and Practice of the Learning Organisation*, New York: Century Business Books.

Senge, P., Cambron-McCabe, N., Lucas, T., Smith, B., Dutton, J. and Kleiner, A. (2000) *Schools that Learn*, London: Nicholas Brearley.

Sergiovanni, T. (2001) *Leadership: What's in It for Schools?* London: Routledge-Falmer.

Shearn, D., Broadbent, J., Laughlin, R. and Willig-Atherton, H. (1995a) The changing face of school governor responsibilities: a mismatch between government intention and actuality? *School Organisation*, Vol. 15, No. 2, pp. 175–88.

Shearn, D., Broadbent, J., Laughlin, R. and Willig-Atherton, H. (1995b) Headteachers, governors and local management of schools, in Wallace, G. (ed.), *Schools, Markets and Management*, Bournemouth: Hyde Publications.

Smircich, L. (1983) Concepts of culture and organizational analysis, *Administrative Science Quarterly*, Vol. 28, pp. 339–58.

Smith, D. and Tomlinson, S. (1989) *The School Effect: A Study of Multi-racial Comprehensives*, Exeter: Policy Studies Institute.

Southworth, G. (2003) *Primary School Leadership in Context: Leading Small, Medium and Large Sized Primary Schools*, London: RoutledgeFalmer.

Southworth, G. and Weindling, D. (2002) *Leadership in Large Primary Schools*, available from the NCSL website at www.ncsl.org.uk

Steinhoff, C. and Owens, R. (1989) The organisation culture assessment inventory: a metaphorical analysis of organisational culture in educational settings, *Journal of Educational Administration*, Vol. 27, No. 3, pp. 17–23.

Stoll, L. and Myers, K. (eds) (1997) *No Quick Fixes*, London: Falmer Press.

Szabo, M. and Lambert, L. (2002) The preparation of new constructivist leaders, in Lambert, L. (ed.), *The Constructivist Leader*, 2nd edn, New York: Teachers College Press.

Tannenbaum, R. and Schmidt, W. (1973) How to choose a leadership pattern, *Harvard Business Review*, Vol. 36, No. 2, pp. 95–101.

Teacher Training Agency (TTA) (1998a) *National Standards for Headteachers*, London: TTA.

Teacher Training Agency (TTA) (1998b) *National Standards for Subject Leaders*, London: TTA.

Teacher Training Agency (TTA) (2001) *Supporting Induction*, London: TTA.

Teddlie, C. and Reynolds, D. (2000) *The International Handbook of School Effectiveness Research*, London: RoutledgeFalmer.

Thomas, H. and Martin, J. (1996) *Managing Resources for School Improvement: Creating a Cost-effective School*, London: Routledge.

Totterdell, M., Heilbronn, R., Bubb, S. and Jones, C. (2002) *Evaluation of the Effectiveness of the Statutory Arrangements for the Induction of Newly Qualified Teachers*, Research brief and report No. 338, London: DfES.

Turner, C. (1996) The roles and tasks of a subject head of department in secondary schools: a neglected area of research? *School Organisation*, Vol. 16, No. 2, pp. 203–17.

Turner, C. (2003) A critical review of research on subject leaders in secondary schools, *School Leadership and Management*, Vol. 23, No. 1, pp. 41–58.

Ulrich, D. (1996) Credibility x capability, in Hesselbein, F., Goldsmith, M. and Beckhard, R., (eds), *The Leader of the Future*, San Francisco: Jossey-Bass.

Wallace, M. and Hall, V. (1994) *Senior Management Teams in Secondary Schools*, London: Routledge.

Wallace, M. and Huckman, L. (1996) Senior management teams in large primary schools: a headteacher's solution to the complexities of post-reform management? *School Organisation*, Vol. 16, No. 3, pp. 309–24.

Wallace, M. and Huckman, L. (1999) *Senior Management Teams in Primary Schools: The Quest for Synergy*, London: Routledge.

Wallace, M. and Weindling, D. (1996) *Managing Schools in the Post-Reform Era: Messages of Recent Research*, Swindon: Economic and Social Research Council.

Walters, J. and Richardson, C. (1997) *Governing Schools through Policy*, London: Lemos and Crane.

Webb, R. and Vulliamy, G. (1996) A deluge of directives: conflict between collegiality and managerialism in the post-ERA primary school, *British Educational Research Journal*, Vol. 22, No. 4.

Weindling, D. (1995) Principals, parents, pivots, or pizzas? Metaphors, schools and leadership, paper presented at the UCEA conference, Salt Lake City.

Weindling, D. (1997) Strategic planning in schools: some practical techniques, in Preedy, M., Glatter, R. and Levačić, R. *Educational Management: Strategy, Quality and Resources*, Buckingham: Open University Press.

Weindling, D. (1998) Reform, restructuring, role and other 'R' words: the effects on headteachers in England and Wales, *International Journal of Educational Research*, Vol. 29, pp. 299–310.

Weindling, D. (1999) Kissing the frog: moving from school effectiveness to school improvement, *TOPIC*, Vol. 21, Spring, Slough: NFER.

Weindling, D. (2003) *Leadership Development in Practice: Trends and Innovations*, Nottingham: NCSL.

Weindling, D. and Earley, P. (1987) *Secondary Headship: The First Years*, Windsor: NFER-Nelson.

Weindling, D. and Pocklington, K. (2004) *Headteacher Selection: A Pilot Study*, Nottingham: NCSL.

Wenger, E. (1988) *Communities of Practice*, Cambridge: Cambridge University Press.

Wenger, E., McDermot, R. and Synder, W. (2002) *Cultivating Communities of Practice*, Boston: Harvard Business School Press.

West, N. (1995) *Middle Management in the Primary School*, London: David Fulton.

Whitty, G., Power, S. and Halpin, D. (1998) *Devolution and Choice in Education: The School, the State and the Market*, Buckingham: Open University Press.

Wildy, H. and Wallace, J. (1998) Professionalism, portfolios and the development of school leaders, *School Leadership and Management*, Vol. 18, No. 1, pp. 123–40.

Wise, C. (2000) The monitoring role of the academic middle manager in secondary schools. Paper presented at the BEMAS research conference, Cambridge, March.

Wise, C. and Bush, T. (1999) From teacher to manager: the role of the academic middle manager in secondary schools, *Educational Research*, Vol. 41, No. 2, pp. 183–95.

Wood, F. and Thompson, S. (1980) Guidelines for better staff development, *Educational Leadership*, Vol. 37, No. 5, pp. 374–8.

Woods, R. (2002) *Enchanted Headteachers: Sustainability in Primary School Headship*, Nottingham: NCSL.

Index